Maddi Shelton

Color Guide to American Gardening

By Arthur Hellyer

A lavishly illustrated
guide to all that is best
in decorative gardening,
with full instructions
for cultivation

American Consultant **George Kalmbacher**
Taxonomist and Curator of the Herbarium,
Brooklyn Botanic Garden

Bounty Books · New York

Acknowledgments

Most of the color transparencies reproduced in this book are by Harry Smith, to whom we are grateful. Other photographers who have contributed are: *Amateur Gardening*; Kenneth Burras; Robert Corbin; Ernest Crowson; *The Field*; Valerie Finnis; Iris Hardwick; Anthony Huxley; Elsa Megson; L. F. Oland; Sheila Orme; Robert Pearson.

The map of hardiness zones of the United States and Canada appears by courtesy of the Arnold Arboretum of Harvard University

Copyright © MCMLXXV by The Hamlyn Publishing Group Limited
Library of Congress Catalog Card Number: 75-780
ISBN: 0-517-51494X
All rights reserved.
This edition is published by Bounty Books,
a division of Crown Publishers, Inc.,
by arrangement with The Hamlyn Group Limited.
No part of this book may be reproduced or utilized in
any form or by any means, electronic or mechanical,
including photocopying, recording, or by any
information storage and retrieval system, without
permission in writing from the Publisher.
Inquiries should be addressed to
Crown Publishers, Inc.,
419 Park Avenue South, New York, N.Y. 10016
Printed in the United States of America
Published simultaneously in Canada by
General Publishing Company Limited

Contents

Hardiness Zones of the United States and Canada

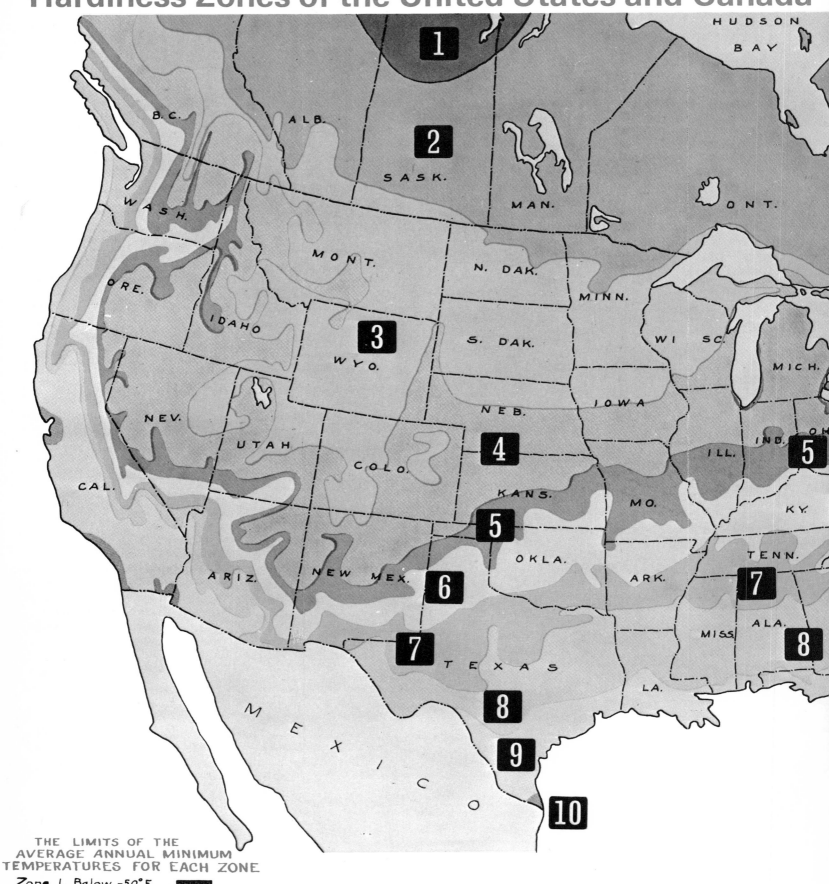

THE LIMITS OF THE
AVERAGE ANNUAL MINIMUM
TEMPERATURES FOR EACH ZONE

Zone 1. Below −50° F.
" 2. −50° to −35°
" 3. −35° to −20°
" 4. −20° to −10°
" 5. −10° to −5°
" 6. −5° to 5°
" 7. 5° to 10°
" 8. 10° to 20°
" 9. 20° to 30°
" 10. 30° to 40°

Compiled by
The Arnold Arboretum
Harvard University
Jamaica Plain, Mass.
May 1, 1967

Foreword

Gardening as a hobby has no superior for conditioning the health of the human body and mind. The benefits of fresh air, the good sun, of reasonable exercise, of fresh vegetables and herbs, berries and fruits, the happiness of floral gifts from one's own garden, the daily joy of viewing fondly the forms and colors provided by the Creator's own paintbrush, are the best medicines to be had for body, mind, and soul. The gardener is close to nature, the good earth, and spends his days following the thrilling mysteries of sprouting seed, the growing upward of the living organism and onward to the dormant new seed. The new seed—that little jewel package of wonder—is a compressed slumbering of a multitude of secrets yet to be expressed for another happy journey.

There are the satisfactions of cooperating and maneuvering, of solving problems, of accomplishment and mastery. There is also the joy of communicating useful information to others of the fellowship of gardeners, the joy of listening with admiration to another's accomplishments and views regarding your common wholesome bond, thus enlarging your grasp and understanding. Gardening is a very complex thing and does not stand still. The nearest thing to personal attention and instruction to help in the unfolding of its tenets is a book showing in color and by word "how to do," what are the tools to do with, what to choose and what to avoid, and what to plan.

In summation, the value of *Color Guide to American Gardening* is to give knowledge and confidence, and to help develop expertise to solve gardening problems as they arise.

Important: Unless otherwise specified as to zone, statements on the whole reflect cultivation in the New York Metropolitan area (Zone 6). For other zones account must be taken and adjustments made for the difference. Since each area of the United States is a "law unto itself," it is suggested that when questions arise gardeners contact their local County Agricultural Agent, located in practically all county seats. The officers of these agencies know their region, and can help, especially, with such problems as disease and insect damage.

Credit is hereby given to the following staff members of the Brooklyn Botanic Garden who gave help: Daphne Drury, Ed Moulin, Peter Malins, Diana Miller, Thomas Hofmann, George Gudekunst, Dr. Stephen Tim, Fred McGourty, Jr., Marie Giasi.

George Kalmbacher
Taxonomist and Custodian of the Herbarium
Brooklyn Botanic Garden

Introduction

This is a book about gardening for pleasure. It is concerned with plants grown for decoration in the garden or to provide cut flowers for the home, and there are many thousands of such plants.

In the 1960s a gradual change occurred from the traditional nursery practice of sending plants by mail or rail to a cash-and-carry trade based on container-grown plants. This is rapidly introducing gardeners to a great many plants they would not otherwise have known. Most plants that have to travel long distances can be moved safely from the open ground only when in a more or less dormant condition, usually from October to April. Plants must be ordered months ahead or purchased when there is little to indicate their true quality. By contrast, container-grown plants can be bought and established in the garden at almost any time of the year, even when in full bloom or leaf. Customers can see precisely what they are buying and actually pick out for themselves the individual plants they prefer. In this way they are being introduced to hundreds of varieties they would not otherwise have been likely to consider, and their gardens are benefiting.

In the early days of selling plants in containers fears were expressed that it would limit the variety of plants available, since nurseries and garden centers would stock only those plants for which there was a known popular demand. In fact, the opposite has proved to be true. Nurseries are finding it profitable to propagate many beautiful plants which were formerly known and ordered only by a few enthusiasts, but which now are readily purchased when customers see them.

Plants vary greatly in the amount of attention they require and much of the pleasure of gardening depends upon taking account of this when the garden is planned and planted. Some people enjoy looking after plants and do not in the least grudge the time and labor involved in caring for some of the more exacting kinds, such as the more difficult rock plants accustomed to alpine conditions or plants that have special requirements in soil or feeding or need some protection in cold weather.

Other gardeners—and they are the majority—want to have an attractive garden with the minimum of trouble; that is, they want low-maintenance gardening. To ensure this they must be careful not to cram too many plants into their garden and restrict their choice mainly to those plants that do not require frequent renewal. Above all they should learn to work with, rather than against, their local soil and climate. There are plants to suit every place if one takes the trouble to look for them.

A few well-chosen and well-placed plants can often produce a better effect than a far greater number planted with less forethought. Since all plants are likely to need attention at some time, the higher the number of plants in the garden the more work in maintenance there is likely to be. Nor are lawns as laborsaving as is often supposed. Mowing, watering, feeding, and aerating can all occupy a good deal of time, and if laborsaving is a prime consideration, paving may prove a better proposition than grass. In general, trees and shrubs require the least attention of all plants, particularly if selection is confined to really hardy varieties that are well suited to the often unimproved soil of the garden. Lime-hating plants, such as rhododendrons, azaleas, and many heathers, can be grown on limy soils but only with a great deal of care and attention and this kind of thing is best left to the enthusiasts who enjoy it. For every type of soil there are plants that have adapted themselves to it and a little observation in the locality and inquiries at local nurseries and public parks will soon disclose which these are.

Yet even the toughest and most adaptable of plants will require some care, especially in the early stages. Transplanting itself checks growth, though this can be minimized by careful work and by using well-established container-grown plants.

After planting, while roots are finding their way out into the soil, plants may require firm staking and fairly frequent watering. Feeding at this stage should not be too heavy, for only well-established plants can make full use of the chemicals in the soil and an excess of readily soluble fertilizer or even of animal manure can harm those recently transplanted.

Much of the subsequent care of plants is very largely a matter of common sense directed by observation of what is happening in the garden. Good gardeners acquire a feeling for their plants and quickly observe when something is going wrong. Again, it is much easier to acquire this sensibility if, at the outset, there are not too many plants to be observed.

Because this is a book about ornamental gardening out of doors no attempt has been made to include plants that can be satisfactorily grown only in a greenhouse or indoors. All the same, many seeds germinate more readily in an artificially maintained atmosphere than they do in the open, and similar conditions can also be an advantage when cuttings have to be rooted to increase or maintain the stock of plants. A greenhouse is ideal for these purposes, but a frame is almost as good, especially if it can be warmed when the weather is cold. Excellent soil or air-warming electrical cables can be purchased and are easy to install, though

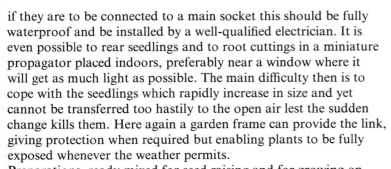

if they are to be connected to a main socket this should be fully waterproof and be installed by a well-qualified electrician. It is even possible to rear seedlings and to root cuttings in a miniature propagator placed indoors, preferably near a window where it will get as much light as possible. The main difficulty then is to cope with the seedlings which rapidly increase in size and yet cannot be transferred too hastily to the open air lest the sudden change kills them. Here again a garden frame can provide the link, giving protection when required but enabling plants to be fully exposed whenever the weather permits.

Preparations, ready-mixed for seed raising and for growing on seedlings, can be purchased at any garden center or garden supply store. The difference between seed and the growing-on mixes, the latter called potting mixes, is partly in the amount of chemical food they contain, the potting mixes being richer to cope with the increasing needs of the rapidly growing plants. Texture is also involved because of the aeration needs of the new rootlets and physical interrelation between rootlets and particles of the mix. Potting mixtures are of two kinds, soil and soilless, the latter usually with much more peat in proportion. Peat mixes are much lighter than soil mixes. To get seedlings established in peat products, it is necessary to make extra efforts to firm them. Success with plants in seed trays, pots, boxes, or other containers depends largely on proper watering. The aim is to keep the soil nicely moist from top to bottom without being waterlogged. Fortunately most modern seed and potting mixes are sufficiently porous to get rid of surplus water readily, so that overwatering is not now as common a cause of failure as it once was. It is dryness that is most troublesome, especially with peat mixes which, once they become really dry, turn water aside and are very difficult to moisten again. For this reason they are usually packed at the correct degree of moisture in sealed plastic bags.

Pests and diseases are not as troublesome in the ornamental garden as they are in the vegetable or fruit garden. Aphids are an almost universal nuisance, appearing suddenly, multiplying rapidly and often disappearing again just as quickly. Nowadays there are plenty of insecticides with which to destroy them. Some, such as Cygon and Isotox, are systemic; i.e., they enter the plant and become distributed right through it in its sap. Such insecticides usually remain effective for a month or more, and so two or three applications between May and August are sufficient to give immunity. Caterpillars are seldom troublesome but even a few capsid bugs can deform the leaves and flower buds of dahlias, fuchsias, and other plants. Kelthane will take care of both.

Slugs and snails are perhaps the most damaging flower garden pests since they can devour whole batches of seedlings in a night. Poison baits containing metaldehyde must be placed near plants liable to be attacked, or a solution of metaldehyde can be applied from a watering pot to any place where they may be hiding. Mice, too, can eat seedlings and various bulbs and corms, but they can be trapped, a positive and satisfactory way of destroying them. Birds are much more problematical since they strip winter buds, pull up seedlings, and damage flowers, yet are themselves so attractive that they cannot be killed. Protection with bird deterrent chemicals seems the most hopeful solution. Mildew can disfigure the leaves of roses, delphiniums, asters, lilacs, and some other plants, covering them with a flourlike outgrowth. Benomyl (Benlate) will prevent this happening provided it is applied before the mildew becomes established, but this may mean fairly frequent spraying to protect new growth as it appears. Much the same applies to black spot, one of the most troublesome diseases of roses, but for this it is Phaltan, wettable powder that will prove most effective.

Virus diseases are common in chrysanthemums, dahlias, and lilies and may affect other plants. They cause mottling of the leaves, leaf distortion, stunting, flower deformity, and other symptoms not easy to define and sometimes difficult to recognize. Sprays are useless against these diseases except insofar as they control the insects, mainly aphids, which carry them. As a rule it is best to burn infected plants as soon as they are recognized since viruses, once introduced, can spread rapidly.

Garden Planning

Surveying, Paper Plans

To draw a reasonably accurate plan of the plot it is necessary to take a few measurements from the boundaries, usually to the corners of the house. First make a very rough sketch on which to jot down the measurements. Then measure from each corner of the house to the boundary, keeping in line with the house wall. Now draw the house to scale on a sheet of graph paper, mark off the measurements from each corner of the plot to the nearest corner of the house and mark these on the plan.

On this outline plan the features required can now be filled in—paths, beds, borders, and trees. Draw them to scale but do it lightly in pencil at first so that alterations can be made.

If the ground is very irregular or sloping it may be necessary to take some sightings to see what the differences of level are. This can be done with a long plant stake or cane and a level. Fix the stake upright at a low point in the ground. Keeping the level perfectly horizontal, sight along it and at the same time move it up and down the stake until it is exactly aligned on the nearest high point of ground. Now measure the distance from the bottom of the stake to the level. This is the difference in height between the two points of high and low ground.

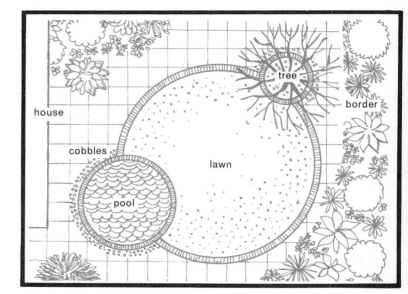

Successful garden planning involves a proper balance between taste and utility. If the garden is to be satisfactory and give lasting pleasure it must be well fitted for the purpose (or purposes, for there may well be several) for which it is required and also be pleasing to the eye. One garden maker may wish to devote most space to flowers, a second to fruit, a third to vegetables. It may be essential to have a place for the baby to crawl with safety, for children to romp, or for the washing to be aired. Some gardeners are interested in only a few types of plant, whereas others seek for maximum variety in the available space. It may even be that plants themselves are not a prime consideration, but rather design, which can be largely an architectural matter. Good gardens can be made to suit each of these needs or one garden may be divided into several sections, each with its own purpose or style. The really important point is to be quite clear at the outset what that purpose or style is and to plan accordingly.

In a garden intended for family use a lawn is usually highly desirable, though if space is very limited it may have to be replaced by paving, if only because small areas of grass simply will not withstand the wear of many feet. But where there are small children it may be wise to avoid gravel and cobbles, which can cause nasty cuts, and also bricks, which can be dangerously slippery in wet weather. Non-slip paving slabs laid quite level on a bed of concrete are usually the best substitute for a lawn.

Gardens, or garden features, planned exclusively for decoration, may be conceived as patterns or as pictures. The former are called formal gardens since they are usually more or less symmetrical and based on regular shapes such as rectangles, circles, and ovals. Picture gardens, by contrast, are nearly always informal, based on irregular curves and balanced, but not symmetrical, shapes.

One type of planning may lead to the other, perhaps a formal terrace or patio near to the house looking out on to an informal garden beyond. It is in some ways easier to design a formal rather than an informal garden since its pattern is revealed clearly on a paper plan, whereas the picture garden is very much more a three-dimensional affair, requiring a perspective drawing for clear depiction. Planting can be used to emphasize the pattern of a formal garden and to create the shapes, vistas, and focal points in a picture garden.

Water can be introduced into either style of garden, fountains in a formal garden or cascades in an informal setting, presenting no difficulty if the water is constantly recirculated by an electrically operated pump and proper provision is made for a central electric supply in the original planning.

Careful planning is essential to the success of any garden. Incorporated in this lovely town garden are many delightful features including a rectangular pool for fish. The grass border is for ornament only and the walking area is sensibly paved

Quantity Surveying

There are simple ways of estimating quantities of various materials and plants required.

Paving slabs are usually sold by the superficial area they will cover. Measure the length and breadth of each path, preferably in feet, and multiply the figures to get the area in square feet.

Bricks are sold by numbers; 35 laid flat or 53 laid on edge will cover an area of 10 sq. ft.

If paving slabs are sold by weight, approximately 1½ cwt. (hundredweight) of ¾- to 1½-in. thick paving will be required for each 10 sq. ft.; or 2½ cwt. of 1½- to 2½-in. thick paving. For 2-in. thick concrete 2½ cwt. of mixed cement and aggregate is required for each 10 sq. ft., and for 3-in. thickness 4 cwt. of the mixture will be needed.

Gravel for paths and drives is usually sold by the "yard," which means a cubic yard. If spread 2 in. thick a cubic yard will cover 18 sq. yd.

Seven cwt. of 6-in. wide walling stone will make a wall with a face area of 10 sq. ft.

Herbaceous plants are spaced on average 15 to 16 in. apart, so 6 are required for each 10 sq. ft. Shrubs are spaced on average 3 ft. apart so each takes 9 sq. ft.

Turfs are normally sold in 3 × 1-ft. strips. 4 turfs will cover 12 sq. ft.

Soil for filling is sold by the cubic yard or ton (about the same). One ton will raise a 10 sq. ft. bed between 2½ and 3 ft.

planting herbaceous plants

planting shrubs

Marking Out

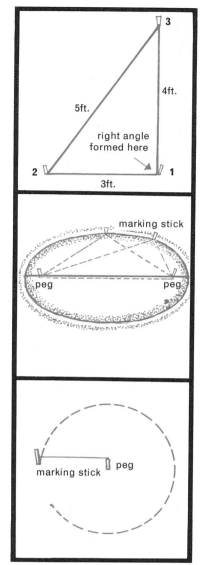

right angle formed here

marking stick

peg   peg

marking stick   peg

To mark out a right angle, drive in a peg at the corner and from this stretch a garden line to mark one side of the right angle. Drive in a peg against this line exactly 3 ft. from the first peg. Attach a string 4 ft. long to the corner and another exactly 5 ft. long to the second peg. Draw them together to form a triangle and where they touch drive in a third peg. A line stretched between pegs 1 and 3 will be at right angles to the line between pegs 1 and 2.

To mark out a circle drive a peg into the center. Loop over it a string exactly half the width of the circle required and draw it around at full stretch with a pointed stick inside the loop to scratch along the ground.

To mark an oval use a line to mark out the full length of the oval and midway, another at right angles to mark the width, and drive in a peg at one end of this line. Attach to this peg a piece of string exactly half the length of the oval and draw it tight so that it touches the long line first on one side of the center and then on the other side. Drive in a peg at each of these points. Measure the length from one of these pegs to the extreme end of the oval on the farther side. Make a loop of string exactly twice this length, throw it over the two pegs on the central line and pulling it taut, use a pointed stick to scratch out the oval on the ground.

After the garden has been planned the next step is to make an accurate assessment of the materials and plants needed—in this garden the number of plants for the herbaceous border and the weight of crazy paving slabs for the path

Straight edges, circles, ovals, and irregular curves should all be carefully marked out on the ground before paths are laid, lawns sown, and beds formed and planted. Simple geometrical methods can be used for the regular shapes

Paths and Terraces

All paths and terraces should be laid on a good layer of brickends, cinders, or other hard rubble for drainage. If the surface is to be of paving slabs or bricks, spread on top of this rubble a layer of either sand or mortar on which the paving can be laid absolutely flat. If mortar is used do not spread too much at a time as it soon starts to set. Use a square-edged plank to check the levels from time to time and make sure that each slab or brick is firmly bedded with no tendency to rock.

Paving slabs and bricks can be laid in patterns of many different kinds and some manufacturers supply slabs of different sizes to aid pattern making. For added interest colored slabs may be used or the materials may be mixed, for example by alternating panels of pebbles or cobblestones with paving slabs or bricks.

Concrete paths should be at least 2 in. thick and individual sections should not be more than 8 ft. long to allow for expansion and contraction. Sides should be formed by setting planks on edge as dividers between which the concrete is laid.

Screens, Arches, Pergolas

Screens can be used to give extra privacy or shelter to some part of the garden or to divide it into sections and are particularly useful as a partial surrounding screen for a terrace or patio. They can be made of wood either in the form of open-slat fencing or solid fencing, or they can be made of brick or concrete blocks. Particularly attractive are the precast pierced concrete blocks available in a large variety of patterns.

Arches give elevation to the garden design and in small areas may be preferable to trees since they do not grow. They can be of wood or of metal; timber of 3×2-in. section is suitable for their construction. All wood should be treated with a preservative harmless to plants, such as copper naphthenate, and the uprights should be embedded in soil or concrete.

Pergolas are covered walks like a continuous series of arches. Uprights may be of wood, brick, or concrete blocks, but the cross members are usually of timber which should be of 4×4-in. section and must also be treated with preservative.

The cross members could be of 4×2-in. timber on edge for widths up to 8 ft.

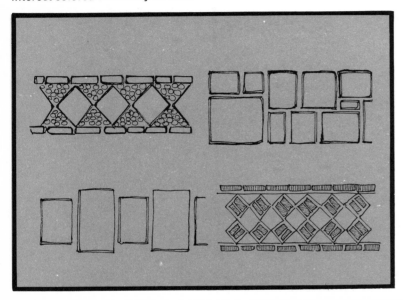

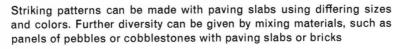
Striking patterns can be made with paving slabs using differing sizes and colors. Further diversity can be given by mixing materials, such as panels of pebbles or cobblestones with paving slabs or bricks

This little terrace has been well screened with precast perforated slabs. These break the wind and provide excellent support for climbing plants. Note the modern plant bowl

Statues and Ornaments

These can be used either as focal points to catch the eye and form the central feature in the garden picture, or be tucked away so that one comes upon them as delightful surprises. Light-colored statues and ornaments look well against a background of dark evergreen foliage or reflected in water.

Ornaments can be of many kinds. Large vases or jars of stone or terra-cotta make attractive plant containers, and so do old stone troughs. Excellent reproductions of these can be purchased, and some really imaginative garden ornaments are now cast in concrete. Natural rocks are often beautiful, or large rounded boulders gathered from the beach. Japanese gardeners make imagin-

ative use of natural objects of this kind. Large pieces of driftwood can also be attractive.

Ornaments and statues should be used sparingly and placed carefully. Too many give a cluttered appearance, dividing instead of concentrating attention.

Bird tables, birdbaths, and sundials are all popular ornaments. The first two need to be placed where they can be viewed from the house without disturbing the birds, but a sundial should obviously be put in the open.

It is also possible to purchase sundials for mounting on the side of south-facing walls. Always try to set the dial so that it really does indicate the time.

Garden Buildings

Arbors can be attractive features in themselves, or places from which the garden can be viewed to advantage. They can be built of timber or masonry as little pavilions, or fashioned out of shrubs or trees suitably clipped, or of climbing plants trained over structures such as a deep arch or small pergola. Similar details of material and construction apply.

Sheds and greenhouses are seldom ornamental and it is often a problem to know where to put them in a small garden. A shed may be screened by shrubs or covered with climbing plants, but a greenhouse must stand in an open position with plenty of light. It may have to stand quite close to the house if it is to be heated from the

house supply, in which case it may be best to treat it as a conservatory leading from the house to garden or to close in one side of a patio or terrace. It would then be wise to choose a greenhouse glazed to ground level for maximum display.

If a shed or greenhouse is at any distance from the house a path should be made leading as directly as possible to it, so that there is no temptation to take short cuts. It is also convenient to have a paved or graveled area close to a greenhouse on which pot plants can be stood in summer. If room permits, two or three frames may be added for hardening off.

This patio has been given an oriental touch by the careful choice and placing of ornaments combined with the use of dwarf evergreen shrubs. The flat rock bed is an interesting feature

Here an arbor in the form of a short pergola is placed against a wall on a terrace overlooking a sunken garden. The planting masks the formality of the design

Beds and Parterres

Parterre is the name given to any level area of ground occupied by a pattern of beds. In public parks and large gardens the parterres may be wonderfully elaborate but even in small gardens a simple parterre may be an effective feature, particularly near the house where such formal treatment is appropriate. Since it is the geometrical pattern of the beds that gives the parterre much of its charm this should stand out clearly, which means that plants used in the beds must not be so tall that they obscure the pattern. For the same reason it is an advantage if the parterre can be viewed from above, from windows of the house or from a raised terrace or patio. On flat ground it may be possible to obtain this difference of level by lowering the site of the parterre and using the excavated soil to build up a terrace or raised path, but care must be taken to retain the topsoil where plants are to be grown and to use the subsoil for building up paths and terraces.

Beds in parterres are usually designed symmetrically. They may be of any size and shape, arranged round some central focal point such as a pool, fountain, ornament, or sundial, or may be diversified with a few taller plants such as topiary specimens to give elevation without obscuring the plan.

Mixed Borders

A mixed border is one in which shrubs and herbaceous plants are used and possibly roses and bedding plants as well. In small gardens this has the obvious advantage that it overcomes the difficulty of finding separate places for different classes of plants, and even in big gardens, mixed borders may prove to be more interesting and to have a longer appeal than single-type borders. However, they do need careful planning to ensure that the shrubs do not in time occupy the greater part of the border, leaving little room for anything else.

Usually shrubs are used for the background, or to form bays within which herbaceous plants and roses are grouped in a pleasing way, with bedding plants added in season to fill in any gaps and to extend the flowering period. Bulbs can also be introduced, and with their aid it is possible to have a considerable display from spring to autumn, with something of interest even in the winter months.

Just as herbaceous borders can be replaced by herbaceous beds, so mixed borders can be replaced by mixed beds if these fit in with the site and plan better.

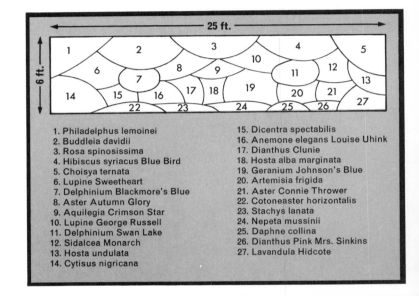

1. Philadelphus lemoinei
2. Buddleia davidii
3. Rosa spinosissima
4. Hibiscus syriacus Blue Bird
5. Choisya ternata
6. Lupine Sweetheart
7. Delphinium Blackmore's Blue
8. Aster Autumn Glory
9. Aquilegia Crimson Star
10. Lupine George Russell
11. Delphinium Swan Lake
12. Sidalcea Monarch
13. Hosta undulata
14. Cytisus nigricana
15. Dicentra spectabilis
16. Anemone elegans Louise Uhink
17. Dianthus Clunie
18. Hosta alba marginata
19. Geranium Johnson's Blue
20. Artemisia frigida
21. Aster Connie Thrower
22. Cotoneaster horizontalis
23. Stachys lanata
24. Nepeta mussinii
25. Daphne collina
26. Dianthus Pink Mrs. Sinkins
27. Lavandula Hidcote

The beds in this charming sunken garden have been planted with tulips and wallflowers. Parterres of this type are always best when viewed from above so that the geometrical pattern of the beds can be appreciated

A magnificent display of herbaceous and other plants in an attractive and well-planned border. Roses have been trained up the stone wall to create a colorful background

Vistas and Avenues

Avenues give a great sense of distance, delight the eye by their regularity, and invite exploration. They are only possible in gardens of some size, but even in comparatively small gardens a somewhat similar effect can be produced by contriving a vista—a long view enclosed on each side. It may be open-ended so that the eye is carried on to the distance, perhaps to rest on some prominent object such as a fine tree or building, or it may be closed.

A vista may be flanked by trees, shrubs, or any plants sufficiently tall to channel the view; it may be paved, grassed, or carpeted with low-growing flowers with perhaps a focal point of interest at its end.

When planning an avenue of trees consideration must be given to their ultimate growth. Where space is limited trees of erect, pyramidal, or columnar habit are to be preferred, such as Pyramida' Hornbeam and Fastigiate Oak. Erect-growing conifers may also be used, such as the narrow forms of Lawson's Cypress, Leyland Cypress, Irish Yew, and Irish Juniper. On a miniature scale the effect of an avenue can be obtained with standard roses or clipped yew or box, but for a higher enclosure, trees such as European lindens may be pleached, with branches trained and interwoven along the line of the avenue.

Specimen Plants

Some plants look their best when grown as isolated specimens. The most suitable are plants with a distinctive or symmetrical shape. Japanese maples have this quality and are an ideal size for small gardens. Columnar trees, such as the narrow varieties of Lawson's Cypress, also make good specimens and so do some regularly formed pyramidal trees, such as the Pyramidal Hornbeam, and weeping trees, such as Young's Weeping Birch and the Weeping Hemlock. All magnolias look best as single specimens.

Alternatively, evergreen trees or shrubs such as Portugal Laurel may be clipped as specimens.

Good flowering shrubs to plant as specimens include *Berberis stenophylla*, *Camellia* Donation or any variety of *C. japonica*, *Cornus alba spaethii*, *Viburnum tomentosum mariesii*, and *Weigela florida variegata*.

Some vigorous roses such as the hybrid musk Penelope make beautiful isolated specimens and some hardy perennials, including pampas grass, rheums, rodgersias, and hostas, are also good.

In very small gardens it is often more effective to grow one or two well-chosen plants as specimens with a groundwork of low-growing plants or mown grass or paving than to risk overcrowding. Since specimens occupy so conspicuous a place they should be specially well tended.

A vista planned to be seen from the French windows of the house. The path is made more interesting by varying the material and allowing plants to encroach on it

This weeping cedar, named *Cedrus deodara pendula*, makes a highly decorative and symmetrical specimen but will in time grow too wide for a small bed such as this

Lawn Making and Aftercare

Lawns may serve quite distinct purposes in a garden. They can provide the perfect color foil to beds of flowers as well as the open spaces. Finely proportioned trees and elegant shrubs can be effectively displayed as isolated specimens surrounded by grass. Lawns are for recreation and for relaxation, for games of skill or for children to play upon. A lawn may also serve a very utilitarian purpose as an airing ground for washing, and in its own right it can be one of the most decorative features in the garden. There are, in fact, many types of lawn and the grasses and methods of cultivation necessary for one may not be the best for another. For ball games requiring a very true playing surface fine grasses and close mowing are essential, but if the lawn is merely to provide a green carpet it may be quite satisfactory to use coarser grasses and to let them retain a great deal more of their growth. Where space is available there is much to be said for combining both types of lawn so that the smooth texture and lighter color of the close-mown grass contrasts with the rougher texture and darker color of the grass that is cut an inch or more above soil level. Some bulbs grow well in turf, provided it is not cut until their leaves are about to die down, usually some time in May or June. Daffodils, crocuses, and snowdrops are particularly suitable for this kind of planting which combines very satisfactorily with the rough cutting of certain areas of grass. Mown turf may also be considered as an alternative to paving in some parts of the garden, though it is unwise to use it where there will be heavy wear, since worn grass is unsightly and can be difficult to repair. All the same, the glade type of garden, in which curving beds for trees, shrubs, and other permanent plants are separated by grass paths of varying width as well as by wider areas of turf, has become very popular for gardens of medium to large size.

In very small gardens it may be better to dispense with turf altogether or to confine it to a purely decorative role, using it in small panels, only to be walked on when necessary for mowing and other care. There are even some difficult places in shade or in city gardens where grass used in this way may best be treated as an annual, to be reseeded each spring. Well cared for, a quick-growing rye or meadow grass can produce a fine effect in under a month. It is well to remember that the smaller the lawn the more difficult it will be to hide any imperfections.

In special places small lawns can be made of aromatic plants such as chamomile and thyme (*Thymus serpyllum*) but they are more troublesome to look after than grasses and also more costly to establish.

Choosing the Grass

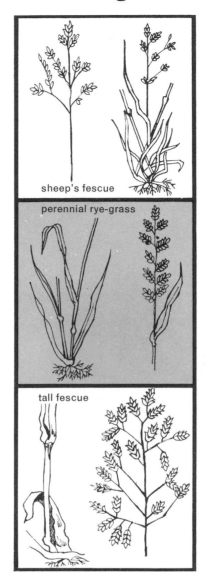

sheep's fescue

perennial rye-grass

tall fescue

There are many different kinds of grasses and by no means all are suited to lawn making. Even those that are suitable differ greatly in the kind of turf they produce. One of the advantages of growing a lawn from seed is that grasses can be selected to produce the kind of lawn one wants.

The finest lawns, such as those used for croquet and putting, are formed from slow-growing grasses with narrow leaves, such as the fescues (*Festuca* sp.) and the bents (*Agrostis* sp.). These lawns need the most care to maintain them in good condition.

Lawns likely to receive a lot of hard wear, such as children's playgrounds or grass paths, are usually made from coarser grasses, such as the perennial rye-grass (*Lolium perenne*), or smooth- or rough-stalked meadow grass (*Poa* sp.). The latter are also good for shady places and so is crested dog's-tail (*Cynosurus cristatus*).

Seedsmen seldom offer individual grasses, but prepare mixtures suitable for particular purposes. Mixtures of fine grasses cost more than coarse mixtures.

A well-tended lawn provides a perfect foil for border flowers. In this garden, the lawn is on two levels, joined by a simple flight of steps, which gives added interest

Digging and Leveling

Dig or fork the whole area thoroughly and be particularly careful to remove the roots of all perennial weeds, such as couch grass, bindweed, dandelions, docks, nettles, and thistles. If the site is very weed infested, kill these first by watering with a weed killer, such as diquat, which will not leave any harmful deposit in the soil.

Occasionally lawns are required to follow the natural contours of the ground however irregular these may be, but usually the aim is either for a level lawn or, at least, for a regular slope. If this involves much movement of soil, care must be taken to keep the topsoil at the surface.

Remove the topsoil to a depth of at least 8 in. and place it conveniently in heaps. Then drive in stakes every 10 ft. or so over the site, and level the tops with a line level and a long, straight-edged plank. Now remove subsoil from the highest to the lowest places until all are approximately the same distance below the tops of the pegs. Finally, return the top-soil, spreading it evenly all over and giving a final leveling with level and plank. Slopes can be engineered by sighting across the tops of the pegs, or by using two planks nailed together at the angle of the slope.

Final Preparation

For the final preparation, choose a day when the surface is reasonably dry and the clods of soil break up easily. Before breaking down the surface for seeding or turfing, give it a dressing of a good compound fertilizer at the rate recommended by the manufacturers, together with a dressing of peat at 6 to 8 lb. per sq. yd. Then break up the clods with the back of a fork and the smaller pieces with a rake, at the same time removing any large stones, pieces of stick, or any remaining weed roots.

Next, tread the whole site carefully, partly to assist in breaking any remaining lumps of soil but even more to ensure that there are no loose places which would settle later and cause hollows in the lawn. Work from side to side moving one way across the plot, and then repeat this at right angles, so that no piece of ground, however small, is missed.

Now rake the whole site again, this time working at right angles to the first raking. At this stage take great care to get the surface quite level with no humps or depressions which would render mowing difficult later on.

It is more necessary to get a very fine crumbly surface if seed is to be sown than it is if turfs are to be laid or tufts of creeping grass planted. It is an advantage if seeding, turfing, or planting can follow almost immediately after this final preparation is finished.

One of the first steps in producing a lawn is to dig or fork the plot thoroughly. The area above was watered a week earlier with diquat to kill weeds and native grasses and their roots are being pulled out

During the final raking it is important to ensure that the surface is level. A surprising degree of accuracy can be achieved with the eye alone but more precise leveling can be given with a level

Sowing

Spring and late summer (to early autumn) are the best periods for seed sowing, though grass can also be sown in summer if the seedbed can be kept well watered in dry weather.

Allow from 1 to 2 oz. of seed per sq. yd., the greater quantity when using fine grasses because of their slower germination and growth. Divide the site into yard-wide strips with string, measure out enough seed for each strip and sow each separately. By this means even distribution of seed should be obtained. A still more accurate way is to have two lots of strings, lengthwise and crosswise, so that the plot is marked out in square yards; find a measure that will just hold 2 oz. of seed (or 1 oz.

if the lower seeding rate is to be adopted) and scatter one measure of seed over each square. Alternatively, use a wheeled fertilizer distributor to spread the seed, but a little experimenting on a large sheet of paper may be necessary to get the correct adjustment for the required rate of sowing.

Cover the seed by raking it very lightly or by scattering sifted soil over it. Most grass seed is treated by the seedsman with a bird deterrent before it is sold, but if it has not been so treated, black string should be stretched between sticks over the site to keep birds away.

Turfing

Turfs are usually cut in rectangular strips 3 ft. by 1 ft. and about 1½ in. thick. They are rolled up for ease of delivery, but should be unrolled as soon as possible, for the grass soon turns yellow if deprived of light. Occasionally, turfs are cut in one-foot squares, and these are preferred by some green-keepers for very accurate work. Turfs can be laid at any time of the year but early autumn is the most favorable season.

If the lawn has straight edges, start laying the turfs along one of these, but if the edges are curved, stretch a line a little way in and start the first row of turfs against this. Lay the turfs lengthwise and see that each is quite level. Remove or add soil where

necessary to correct unevenness. Lay the next row of turfs so that the joins between them do not coincide with those in the first row and continue in this way so that only the lengthwise joins are continuous, the cross joins all being staggered, like bricks in a wall. Beat the turfs gently with the back of a spade to settle them firmly on the soil.

Do not lay small pieces of turf to finish off an edge, but use full turfs here and fill in with part turfs away from the edge where they are less likely to be dislodged.

When making a lawn from seed, the best results are obtained if the ground is marked out in yard-wide strips each to be sown separately with a measured quantity of seed

A plank is useful to kneel on while laying turfs in order to keep the surface of the soil level. A spade is used to beat the laid turfs gently to ensure close contact with the soil

Care of New Grass

Seedling grass should appear in anything from eight days to a month from the time of sowing, according to the weather and the type of seed used. If there is much seedling weed with the grass, water it with weed killer which can first be used approximately seven to ten days after the grass appears.

When the grass is about 1 in. high, roll it with a light roller. A few days later, when it is between 1½ and 2 in. high, give it its first cutting with the blades of the mower set 1 in. above soil level. The blades must be really sharp or there will be danger of dragging some of the seedlings out of the ground. Small lawns are best cut for the first time with sharp shears so that this danger is avoided.

Roll lawns from turf occasionally after the first two or three weeks, by which time the grass should be rooting down into the soil. Mowing can begin at about the same time if the turf is laid in spring or summer, but autumn-laid turf will grow very little before the following spring and one autumn cutting will probably be sufficient. Apply a light topdressing of fine peat or a mixture of peat and sand and brush this down into any crevices remaining between the turfs.

If new lawns are made in spring or summer, water freely in dry weather, but for seedling grass use a fine sprinkler so that the surface soil is not washed away.

Mowing

Mowing has a marked effect on the character of a lawn since the grasses and weeds that can survive constant close mowing are not the same as those that thrive with less severe cutting.

Northern lawns (except those of bent grass) should be mowed not lower than 1½ in., twice and even three times a week in the normally moist periods of spring and fall. In the summer during the hot weather, cut the lawn once a week at the 2 in. height. Bent grass may be cut at a 1 in. height, or even less, and must be cut more often.

Southern lawns of Bermuda, Centipede, and St. Augustine grasses do well mowed at a 1 in. height.

If the mower is driven by a roller fixed behind the blades it will give the lawn a striped appearance due to the grass being rolled in different directions. With a roller drive it is also possible to cut over the edge of the lawn.

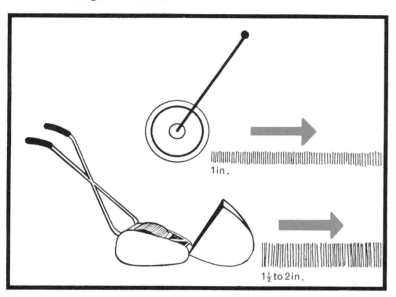

Newly laid turfs should be rolled occasionally once they have become established and have rooted into the soil below. This will help to consolidate the lawn and give a really professional finish

Mowing a well-established lawn with a motor mower. Lawn mowers of all types should be sharpened and oiled regularly and cutting height set to suit the purpose for which the lawn is required

Verges

Tidy edges to lawns can greatly improve their appearance. Clip the grass growing horizontally over the edge of the lawn with special long-handled shears or with a mechanical edge trimmer. Do this every time the lawn is mown.

Occasionally, cut the edge of the lawn with a sharp spade or a special edging tool, using a line stretched between pegs or a plank to get an absolutely straight edge. Do not overdo this cutting or the lawn will gradually get smaller and flanking beds or paths wider, but the natural tendency of wear and rolling is to spread the edges and it is right to correct this.

Where paths abut lawns, lay them ½ in. or so below the level of the lawn so that the lawn mower can be used right over the edge, and also leave a channel about 2 in. wide and 3 in. deep between the turf and the path so that the edges of the turf can be clipped easily. It is a good laborsaving idea to lay a line of flagstones between flower borders and lawns, keeping them just below the level of the turf and separated from it by a channel as just described. Plants growing at the edge of the border can then grow out over the flagstones without harming the grass or interfering with the edging.

Feeding

If the mowings are always picked up and removed from a lawn, it will require more feeding than if the lawn mowings are permitted to lie and rot, since by doing this they will return food to the soil. However, decaying grass cuttings will, in time, impart a spongy texture to the surface which is not desirable if the lawn is to be used for games requiring a firm surface. A reasonable compromise is to remove mowings in spring and autumn but leave them in hot summer weather, when they act as a useful mulch.

In either case, lawns must be fed to keep them in good condition. Apply a compound lawn fertilizer in March or April, usually at 4 oz. per sq. yd., but do not exceed the manufacturer's recommended rate. Give a second application at half this rate in June. In September apply a special autumn lawn dressing which will have a low percentage of nitrogen in relation to phosphoric acid and potash. At the same time topdress the lawn with fine peat at 4 oz. per sq. yd. and brush it into the turf.

Be careful to spread fertilizers evenly and at the correct rate. An overdose may scorch or kill the grass. A wheeled fertilizer distributor is particularly useful for even distribution.

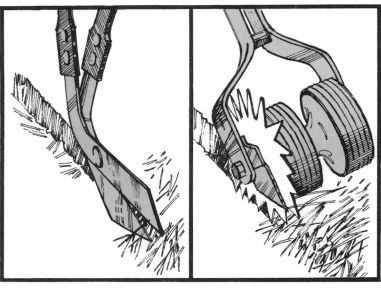

The edges of lawns spread with mowing and ordinary wear and should be cut back occasionally. Here, a special edging tool with a curved blade is being used, but a sharp spade is a good substitute

In September a dressing of finely milled peat will replenish the humus content of the soil, particularly important in a lawn which has been mown closely. This dressing can be brushed in with a broom of twigs

Watering

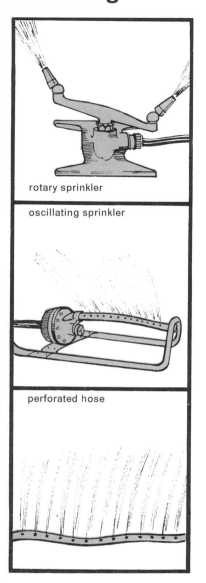

rotary sprinkler

oscillating sprinkler

perforated hose

If lawns are deprived of water, they quickly turn yellow and then brown. The fine grasses may be killed completely and only coarse grasses, clovers, and some deep-rooted weeds survive. So watering in dry weather is a very important item in the management of lawns. It is all the more vital if the lawn is closely mown and the mowings are removed, since the soil will be more exposed to the baking effect of the sun.

Water must be supplied in sufficient quantity to soak an inch or so into the soil, but not so fast that it cakes the surface and runs off it. For this reason, fine sprinklers are better than coarse jets. The oscillating type of sprinkler is particularly good since it waters a rectangle and can be moved from point to point in such a way that the whole area is watered to a similar degree.

Contrary to popular belief, it does not matter what time of day water is applied. Give it whenever it is most convenient, whether the sun is shining or not. Be particularly careful to water after fertilizer has been applied if it does not rain thoroughly in a few days, as it is only in solution that the fertilizer is of any use to the grass. If it is left lying on the grass for too long, or in too concentrated a solution, it may damage it.

Brushing and Raking

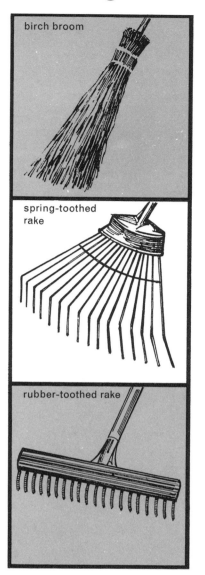

birch broom

spring-toothed rake

rubber-toothed rake

Brushing is necessary to scatter worm casts, which might otherwise be trodden down and smother small patches of grass, to work fertilizers and peat topdressings into the turf, and to get rid of debris, moss, etc., particularly after raking. The old-fashioned broom made of twigs is still an excellent lawn brush and is especially useful for collecting leaves and distributing worm casts, though many special lawn brushes are also made.

Raking is necessary to drag out the accumulations of dead but undecayed material which can collect under the surface of the grass, particularly when the soil is acid or the weather dry. It also drags out a lot of moss, though care must be taken to see that it does not actually spread the moss from one part of the lawn to another.

Use a spring-toothed lawn rake for this purpose, not a rigid steel garden rake, which would drag out the lawn grass. Rake about once every two weeks from spring to late summer and then, before applying the autumn fertilizer, give a much more thorough raking or use a slitter or spiker. Rake the lawn first in one direction and then at right angles so that nothing is missed.

Watering is generally necessary in the height of summer if a really green lawn is required. Oscillating sprinklers are particularly effective for this job as they cover a rectangle of turf

Brushing the lawn with an old-fashioned broom made of twigs to disperse worm casts and to sweep up debris. This is still a good tool, though there are now many excellent modern lawn brushes on the market

19

Aerating

Lawns that receive a lot of use, or are frequently rolled, become so hard that air can no longer penetrate to the grass roots and the quality of the turf declines. It is then necessary to loosen it again by slitting or spiking or by a combination of the two.

Slitting is done with a special tool which slices down into the turf and the soil beneath to a depth of an inch or so. Many different models are available, some for hand use, some power driven or for attachment to a power-driven lawn mower.

The simplest form of aeration is with a digging fork, usually called a spade fork. Thrust the tines about 3 in. into the turf, lever backwards on the handle suffi-ciently to raise the turf slightly and repeat every 6 in. or so all over the lawn. The work can be done more rapidly with special spiking tools, some of which are wheeled backwards and forwards across the lawn.

An alternative to spiking is hollow-tining, in which the solid spike is replaced by a hollow tine which punches out a core of turf and soil, leaving a little hole. This is most effective, especially if a dressing of sharp grit is given and brushed down into the holes. Small motorized aerators have become popular.

Aeration is usually done in early autumn, but may be carried out at any time if the condition of the turf necessitates it.

Weeds

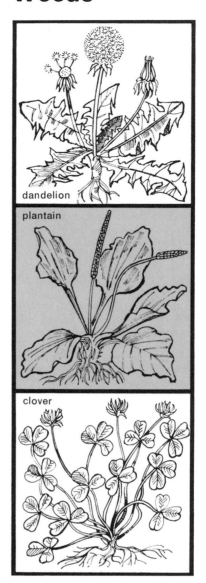
dandelion

plantain

clover

Many lawn weeds can be killed with special weed killers which may check the grass slightly but do it no permanent damage. They are known as selective lawn weed killers and the principal kinds are 2,4-D and Silvex, the last being particularly effective against clover and chickweed. These can be purchased separately or in various mixtures under trade names, ready for dilution with water according to the manufacturer's instructions.

Apply in spring and early summer, a few days after applying fertilizer. Some persistent weeds can only be eliminated by several applications at intervals of two or three weeks.

Some weeds are hosts to fungi, including rusts, and harmful insects. If not eradicated, these form a reservoir of harmful aggressors to gardens and garden crops.

A foot-operated spiker is very useful for aerating small areas of grass. A garden fork may also be used for this operation but for larger areas a wheel-mounted aerator will save much time

When making up solutions of weed killer great care must be taken to follow the manufacturer's instructions. Note the rubber gloves which are being worn to protect the hands from harmful chemicals

Pests

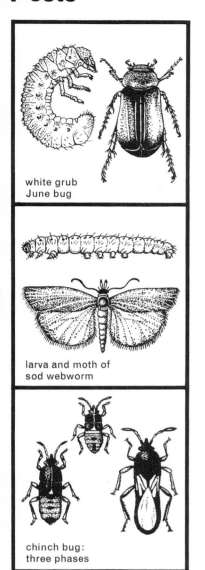

white grub
June bug

larva and moth of
sod webworm

chinch bug:
three phases

Common among the pests of lawns is the group of insect larvae called White Grubs. These worm-like bodies are the larval stages of certain beetles: Japanese beetle, May and June beetles, Oriental beetle, European chafer, among others. They are fat, sluggish, and white-bodied, with yellowish brown heads and legs. They get to be from ¾ to 1½ in. long. Control of these and the following lawn pests can be had by use of sevin or diazinon.

Cutworms are larvae of certain large moths, and are mostly nocturnal feeders chewing off leaves of grass.

Sod webworms are the larvae of certain small moths ("millers") attacking lawns. Young caterpillars skeletonize the grass leaves.

Another pest of lawns are the chinch bugs. The life cycle includes various stages, all of which damage lawns.

Moles and earthworms, though useful in some respects, can be a great nuisance on lawns; the moles by tunneling beneath the surface and throwing up heaps of excavated soil, the earthworms by covering the lawn with little heaps of soil or worm casts.

Moles can be caught with special spring traps set across their runs, and they can be kept out of a lawn by surrounding it with naphthalene moth balls dropped into holes 4 in. deep and 4 to 6 in. apart.

Diseases

Grass suffers from various diseases just as other plants do. These are likely to be most troublesome between autumn and spring, particularly if a fertilizer containing a high percentage of nitrogen has been applied late in the summer. The grass becomes yellow in patches which later turn brown, symptoms very similar to those produced by leatherjackets, which, however, usually appear in a hot, dry summer. Moreover, a close examination of diseased turf will often reveal white or pinkish threadlike growths of fungus on the dying grass.

Avoid the use of summer fertilizers after July; rake, brush, and aerate turf to keep it in good condition. Water the grass with a suspension of 4 percent calomel dust stirred into water at 2 oz. per gal., keeping the solution agitated while it is being applied. Commercial lawn fungicides can also be used as advised by the manufacturers.

Fairy rings are circles of lush, dark green grass surrounding areas of dead or dying grass. They are caused by a fungus in the soil which spreads outwards, first stimulating and then killing the grass. Soak the edge of the ring and just beyond it with sulfate of iron at the rate of 4 oz. per gal. of water, or make use of a lawn fungicide. In bad cases, dig out the whole ring to a depth of 1 ft., replace with fresh soil and reseed or turf.

Good cultivation is an important factor in promoting a healthy lawn, such as the one shown here. Mixed flower borders provide a gay contrast to the rich green lawn

A badly maintained lawn that has become infested with weeds and fungi. The fungi have formed a fairy ring, which, though interesting to look at, is very damaging to the grass

General Garden Cultivation

Plain Digging, Forking

Digging and forking, the simplest method of soil cultivation, consists of turning the soil over to the full depth of a spade blade or the tines of a fork (approximately 10 in.). A spade is better if the ground is covered with grass or weeds since it can be used to chop through their roots, and it is also preferable on sandy soils which tend to slip through the tines of a fork. But for heavy or wet soil or clay a fork is easier to use.

To dig soil properly, open up a trench about 8 in. wide and 10 in. deep across one end of the plot and wheel the soil taken out of the trench to the other end of the plot. Alternatively, divide the plot in half lengthwise, open up the trench across one half only and move the soil across to the other half, then work down one side of the plot and up the other to finish at the end where the work started.

In either case, lift the soil a spadeful (or a forkful) at a time, turning it over and throwing it forward into the trench already made. In this way another trench is formed, to be filled in turn with inverted soil. The last trench is filled with the soil that was displaced from the first trench.

Manure or decayed garden refuse can be spread on the surface and turned in as work proceeds or it can be spread along the bottom of each trench.

All plants with colored leaves obtain a great deal of their food from the air. From the soil they require water, often in considerable quantities, and various chemicals. They also need good anchorage for their roots, which means that the soil must be firm but not so hard that roots have difficulty in penetrating it. The purpose of soil cultivation is to improve the texture of the soil, enable it to store water without becoming waterlogged, and to stimulate those natural processes within the soil by which its food reserves are liberated. Feeding may be long term to build up those reserves, or short term to increase the immediately available supply of plant food.

The chemicals most likely to be in short supply are nitrogen, phosphorus, and potash, and sometimes also magnesium, manganese, and iron. All these can be added as chemical fertilizers or in animal manures and animal and vegetable waste in which they are present in varying quantity. The process of decay of these bulky organic materials liberates the chemicals and also produces humus; a brown, structureless, slimy substance which is extremely valuable in improving soil texture. Peat is rich in humus and for that reason is a valuable soil dressing despite the fact that it contributes little chemical food.

Deep cultivation of the soil is only possible when it is vacant. It is never wise to dig near established trees and shrubs, since this will destroy many of their roots which are quite near the surface. Even forking can do damage, though pricking the surface is a useful method of getting rid of weeds, letting in air, and stirring in topdressings of fertilizer or manure. Hoeing will produce similar results. Deep-rooted perennial weeds cannot be destroyed by such light cultivation.

When plants are moved from one place to another they inevitably suffer some check to growth, though the less the roots are injured or the soil around them disturbed the smaller this check is likely to be. That is the justification for growing young plants in containers from which they can be removed with a complete ball of soil and roots. Such plants can be moved at almost any time of the year, whereas plants dug up from the open ground can as a rule be moved safely only at certain periods of the year.

Most deciduous trees and shrubs (those that lose their leaves in winter) and roses are planted between late October and March. Evergreen shrubs and trees are most safely moved in April, May, or October, though with care they can also be moved during mild spells in winter. Most herbaceous plants are best planted after danger of frost is passed, though some transplant quite well in October.

Using a spade to chop out the turf when first digging a garden plot. Once cultivated a fork will dig just as well and be less laborious to use

Trenching and Ridging

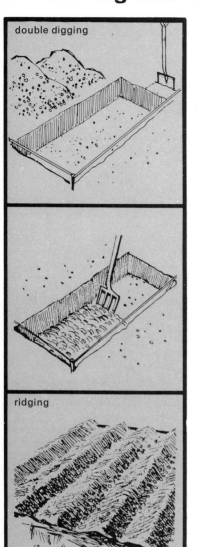

double digging

ridging

Trenching, or double digging, consists of breaking up soil to twice the depth of the blade of a spade or fork (approximately 20 in.). It is useful for very weedy or poorly drained ground and also in preparation for growing some special crops.

First open up a trench 2 ft. wide across one end of the plot and wheel the soil to the other end or divide lengthwise as for digging and transport the soil to one side. Then get into the open trench and, working from one end to the other, break up the soil in the bottom with a fork, using the full depth of the tines. Manure or garden refuse can be worked in at the same time.

Now mark out a second 2-ft. trench behind the first and dig the soil from it into the first trench, inverting each spadeful (or forkful) so that all grass or weed is buried. When the second trench is completed get into the bottom and break it up as before. Proceed in the same way, trench by trench, filling the last one with the soil taken from the first.

To ridge soil, divide the plot into 3-ft. wide strips and dig or fork each separately from end to end. Throw all the soil toward the center of each strip so leaving it in steep ridges, with a large surface exposed to wind and frost.

General Conditions

Planting should not be attempted when soil is frozen or is so wet that it sticks badly to tools and boots. When soil is very dry planting should be carried out only if it is possible to keep it well watered until rain falls or plants become established.

The ideal conditions for planting are moist soil and mild, showery weather.

If conditions are not quite ideal it will be helpful to prepare a special planting mixture beforehand and keep this covered with polyethylene sheeting. A good combination is equal parts of sifted soil, peat, and coarse sand, plus a handful of bonemeal to each bucketful of the mixture. A spadeful or so of this is worked around the roots and mixed with the ordinary garden soil as it is returned to the hole.

If soil and/or weather conditions are not right when plants arrive, open up the packages but leave the packing round the roots (or wrap them in damp moss or straw if there is no packing) and put the plants in a shed or garage for a few days, keeping the roots moist. If a longer waiting period seems likely, heel in the plants; that is, plant them temporarily close together in a trench in a sheltered place, making the soil firm around their roots. Lift and replant properly when conditions are right.

heeling in shrubs

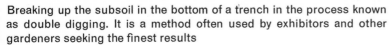
Breaking up the subsoil in the bottom of a trench in the process known as double digging. It is a method often used by exhibitors and other gardeners seeking the finest results

Planting under good soil conditions. Note that the spade is relatively clean, and firming is possible without puddling the soil which is crumbly without being dry

Special Tools

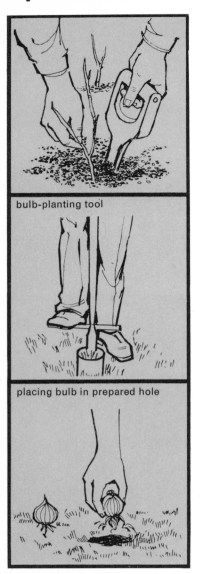

bulb-planting tool

placing bulb in prepared hole

Special planting tools include dibbers, bulb planters, and similar but smaller tools for pot plants.

A dibber is a short stick or shaft with a pointed or rounded end with which a hole can be bored in the soil. Large dibbers are often steel shod for easy use and long life. Dibbers are serviceable for planting seedlings and plants with fairly straight, downward-pointing roots, such as hollyhocks, wallflowers, cabbages, and cauliflowers. They are not suitable for plants with spreading roots since the hole made is too narrow, nor are they recommended for bulbs since there is a danger that the bulbs will be suspended in holes with a space beneath in which water will collect.

To plant with a dibber, press it well into the soil and withdraw it carefully, inserting the plant roots immediately. Then push the dibber in again an inch or so away and lever it toward the plant to close up the hole.

Bulb planters and similar larger tools cut out a plug of soil, leaving a clean, round hole into which a bulb or pot plant is placed. With bulbs the plug can then be replaced intact leaving practically no trace, even on well-kept lawns. With pot plants the plug is broken up and returned around and over the roots.

Using a Spade

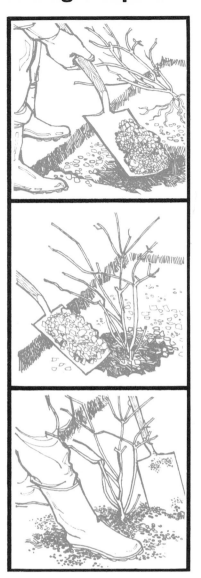

A spade is the most convenient tool with which to plant large plants such as shrubs and trees.

First measure the spread of the roots to be planted. Mark out an area of this size where the plant is to go and dig out a hole a little larger and of approximately the required depth. Place the plant carefully in position and check the depth. This can be done by placing a rod across the hole from side to side next to the stem of the plant. If the old soil mark can be seen—that is, the level on the stem to which the soil came in the place where the plant formerly grew—this should be about 1 in. below the rim of the hole. If the mark cannot be seen the depth of the hole should permit the uppermost roots to be covered with at least 2 in. of soil.

Remove the plant if it is necessary to adjust the depth, and then replace it in position and return the soil, breaking it up in the process and working it between the roots. When all are covered, firm by careful treading all round. Return the rest of the soil and leave the surface level and crumbly.

To support trees and large shrubs, drive a strong stake into the hole before filling in so that there is no danger of injuring roots when inserting the stake. Secure the plant to the stake at once to prevent wind rocking.

Daffodils and other bulbs look delightful when naturalized in irregular drifts in grass. A special tool, shown above, can be obtained for planting which removes a neat core of turf that can be replaced when the bulb has been dropped in

Planting conifers with a spade. The plants are placed close at hand so that the size of the root ball of each can be estimated and a hole of just the right size and depth prepared. Evergreens are a little more difficult to transplant than deciduous shrubs

Using a Trowel

planting bulbs with a trowel

putting in young plant

firming plant with a trowel

Nearly all small plants and bulbs are planted most conveniently with a trowel. A short-handled trowel is less tiring to wrist and arm than a long-handled trowel which saves little in stooping since the plant must in any case be held in position in the prepared hole.

Make the hole sufficiently large to accommodate all the roots spread out in a natural manner and not turned up at the tips. See that each hole is sufficiently deep to allow the collar of the plant (the point where leaves or stems join the roots) to be fractionally below the level of the soil.

Hold the plant in the center of the hole and return soil around its roots, breaking up any lumps in the process. Make the soil firm around the roots with the knuckles or the handle of the trowel and complete the job with a scattering of loose soil.

If frost occurs after planting make certain that the plants are still firmly in the soil, refirming them if necessary. When planting in spring or summer water freely after planting if the soil is dry.

Container-grown Plants

Many plants are grown and sold in containers so that they can be planted with a minimum check to growth. Such plants may be moved at almost any time of the year provided that the soil around the roots is retained undisturbed and the roots are not broken.

Containers may be conventional clay pots, plastic pots, treated paper pots, polyethylene bags, or tin cans. Whatever their nature, the plants must be removed from them without the soil balls being broken.

With a clay or plastic pot, place one hand over the soil and invert the pot, rapping the edge of it on something firm. Strip off paper pots and polyethylene bags, first slitting with a knife if necessary.

Slit tins vertically on two sides with a can opener so that the plant can be lifted out.

Plant immediately in a hole a little larger than the size of the ball of soil, working fine soil around the edges and making firm.

Water freely for several weeks after planting in spring or summer if the weather is at all hot and dry. Stake large plants securely.

"Balled" plants are lifted from the open ground after which burlap bags or polyethylene is wrapped around the roots to prevent soil falling off. Plant as for container-grown plants but do not remove the wrapping until the plant is actually in its hole.

planting container-grown shrub

removing burlap bag from shrub

Planting out stocks in the early summer using a short-handled trowel. The plants should be spaced sufficiently far apart to allow room for them to develop without becoming overcrowded and each hole must be of sufficient size to accommodate roots without cramping or doubling

When plants are container grown, they can be planted out at almost any time of the year as there is little root disturbance. This is particularly useful for a new garden when quick results are required. The container must be removed when planting

Aftercare

Cold and drying winds can do much damage to newly planted plants, especially to evergreens. Burlap bags or polyethylene screens can be used to protect them or cut branches of evergreens may be thrust firmly into the soil around them as a screen. Never cover plants right over but give protection only round their sides.

Rocking by wind disturbs roots, prevents reestablishment, and may cause the death of plants. To prevent this, stake securely all newly planted trees and large shrubs.

Frost may loosen the soil and allow roots to dry out or plants to be blown over. After frost examine new plantings and refirm the soil around plants where necessary.

Even under the most favorable conditions it takes weeks for roots to grow out into the surrounding soil and obtain food and moisture as freely as before being transplanted. In spring and summer keep all new plantings well watered, especially if the weather is hot and dry, until strong new growth indicates that plants are established.

Spread damp peat or grass clippings on the surface around plants to prevent evaporation and conserve moisture in the soil.

Do not feed new plantings with strong fertilizers until they are well established and growing.

protection from wind   spreading peat

Hoeing

Dutch hoe

draw hoe

The purpose of hoeing is to break up the surface soil—improving thereby the aeration of the soil—and at the same time to kill weeds. Hoeing is also used to thin overcrowded seedlings, a process known as singling. Some gardeners believe that hoeing helps to retain moisture in the soil by creating a loose layer on the surface through which water cannot rise readily. This layer also serves as a blanket to protect the lower soil from the sun's heat.

There are many different kinds of hoe but for the purpose of using them correctly they may be divided into two main groups—Dutch hoes and draw hoes.

A Dutch hoe has a blade set more or less in the same plane as the handle and it is pushed and pulled through the soil, the user usually moving backwards so that the freshly hoed soil is not walked on and flattened.

A draw hoe has the blade set roughly at right angles to the handle and is used with a chopping and pulling action, the user usually moving forwards, though possibly a little to one side of the ground actually hoed.

Dutch hoes are particularly serviceable for cutting off small weeds and keeping the surface tidy, draw hoes for cutting off large or tough weeds and breaking hard ground.

Protecting a newly planted shrub with a screen made of burlap bags and wooden stakes. This is particularly necessary in cold, exposed positions until the plants have become well established

Thinning out seedlings with an onion hoe. This tool, which is like a miniature draw hoe, was originally designed for work on onion crops but is now used for any job needing a small hoe

Mulching

Mulching means spreading some bulky material such as animal manure, decayed vegetable refuse, peat, spent hops, chopped straw, or grass mowings on the surface of the soil. It may serve one or all of three purposes: feeding plants, retaining soil moisture, and suppressing weeds.

Mulches are most useful if applied in spring and early summer and should be at least 1½ in. thick, preferably more. Feeding mulches may be thinner, according to the richness of the material used.

Mulches are best applied when the soil is reasonably moist. They then act as a blanket on the surface, protecting it from the sun's heat and reducing loss of water by evaporation. If mulches are applied in summer to soil that is already dry, they may have the opposite effect, absorbing light showers and preventing the water reaching the roots of plants. If mulches are applied too early, before the soil has warmed up, they will tend to keep the soil cold.

An alternative to mulches of organic material is a mulch of plastic, usually of thin black polyethylene, which may be perforated to allow rain to penetrate. Such mulches are very effective in suppressing weeds and in checking surface evaporation, but are not very sightly, and so are generally restricted to the fruit and vegetable gardens.

Lime

Lime can be obtained in various forms. Limestone, chalk, and seashells are different forms of the same chemical, calcium carbonate, while hydrated (slaked) lime is calcium carbonate that has been heated in a kiln to turn it into quicklime or calcium hydroxide. This is a fine white powder, dusty and choking if inhaled but fairly easily spread, and is best for the garden as it acts quickly on the soil. It is applied at rates varying from 2 to 8 oz. per sq. yd. of ground.

Calcium is an essential plant food but is usually present in sufficient quantity for the needs of plants. The principal reason for applying lime is to make the soil less acid, since this substance is alkaline (the opposite of acid).

Home kits are available for measuring the acid/alkaline reaction of soil which is expressed as the pH value. pH7 is neutral, being neither acid nor alkaline, while figures below 7 show increasing degrees of acidity and above 7 increasing degrees of alkalinity. Plants differ greatly in their preferences, some, such as rhododendrons, preferring acid soils and others, such as brassicas, preferring alkaline soils, but most will grow in soils within a range between pH6 and 7. Liming at two- to three-year intervals is most likely to be required on heavily manured and frequently cultivated ground

mulching

Well-rotted garden refuse is being spread around this bush as a mulch. This will act as a fertilizer, will help to suppress weeds and also to retain moisture in the soil by reducing surface evaporation

Using a soil testing kit to ascertain the pH of soil before applying lime. If the reading is pH7 or higher it is unlikely that lime will prove beneficial, but readings below this indicate increasing acidity

Animal Manures

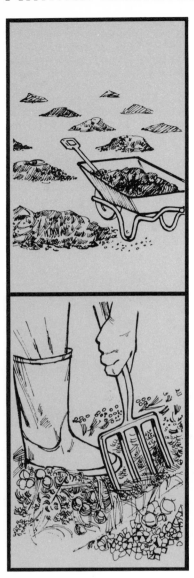

Manures of animal origin vary greatly in character, from the comparatively light texture of horse manure made with straw or peat bedding to the heavy, wet texture of pig manure containing little bedding, or the very rich but rather caustic fresh poultry manure.

The light, bulky manures are best for improving the texture of heavy soils and can be used at rates of 1 cwt. per 6 to 15 sq. yd. Heavy manures are better for light soils and can be used at similar rates. Concentrated manures such as poultry and pig droppings do not greatly improve soil texture and are best used dry, like chemical fertilizers, at rates of 8 to 12 oz. per sq. yd.

All animal manures contain a variety of chemicals which are used by plants as food, not only those most quickly exhausted but also many others, known as trace elements, deficiencies of which can cause some strange symptoms which are often mistaken for disease. The two most important advantages of using animal manures are that the bulky kinds improve the soil texture and all kinds supply some of the essential trace elements—that is, chemicals which are necessary to plants in very minute quantities.

The chemicals in animal manures are not immediately available to plants, but are liberated by decay, a process which starts in the manure heap before it is used.

Garden Compost

Garden compost is the name given to vegetable refuse which has been allowed to rot until it has become dark brown and of even texture throughout. It is a valuable substitute and fulfills the same functions as bulky animal manures, including returning trace elements to the soil. However, if the soil is lacking a particular chemical the plants growing in it will also be deficient and so will any compost made from them.

The best way to prepare compost is to build the garden refuse into heaps about 3 ft. wide, 3 ft. high and of any required length. Pile the heap up in layers 6 to 8 in. thick and spread animal manure over each layer or sprinkle them with one of the advertized compost "accelera-tors." If the materials are dry, wet them thoroughly as they are built into the heap. After four to six weeks turn the heap completely inside out. When the whole heap has decayed apply it to the beds in the same way and at the same rates as bulky animal manures.

Do not put badly diseased plants on the compost heap, or weeds that are full of seeds, as disease spores and weed seeds may not be killed in the process of decay. Burn such material, along with branches, twigs, and other hard plant matter which will not decay easily.

Animal manure being incorporated into the soil during digging. Such bulky manures will improve the texture of the soil and provide many of the chemical foods required by all plants

Leaves and all soft garden waste can be rotted down into an excellent manure substitute. Air must be able to penetrate the heap. A chemical compost accelerator will hasten decay and so will an adequate supply of water

Compound Fertilizers

Compound fertilizers are composed of several different chemicals to provide a more balanced feed than could be supplied with one chemical only. Most compound fertilizers contain nitrogen, phosphorus, and potash in varying proportions and some also supply other chemicals including iron, magnesium, and manganese. The percentage of nitrogen, phosphorus (shown as phosphoric acid equivalent), and potash must be shown on the bag or container. It usually appears simply as three figures: for instance, 6:8:4 would mean that the fertilizer contained 6% nitrogen, 8% phosphoric acid, and 4% potash. The manufacturer is not obliged to disclose what ingredients are used to obtain these percentages and rarely does so.

Compound fertilizers with roughly equal percentages of nitrogen, phosphoric acid, and potash are described as "well balanced" and are suitable for the general feeding of a wide variety of plants and crops.

Compound fertilizers with a preponderance of one chemical are described as "high nitrogen," "high phosphorus," or "high potash" according to which is in excess and are respectively useful for promoting rapid growth, good root production, and ripening.

All compound fertilizers should be used strictly according to manufacturers' instructions and never in larger quantities.

Organic Fertilizers

Organic fertilizers are those containing carbon but, since this is a characteristic of all soil dressings obtained from animal and vegetable waste, the term is often used as if it referred specifically to manure or compost. Plants do not feed directly on organic fertilizers but on the inorganic chemicals that are liberated from them by decay. In consequence, these fertilizers are often slower in action but longer lasting than inorganic fertilizers. The following are among the most useful:

Dried blood: supplies mainly nitrogen. Use at 2 to 4 oz. per sq. yd. in spring and summer.

Bone meal: supplies phosphorus and a little nitrogen. Use at 2 to 6 oz. per sq. yd. at any time.

Fish emulsion is cooked and ground fish, analyzing about 6:4:0. Use at 4 lb. to 100 sq. ft. of area.

Sludge is processed sewage manufactured at certain municipal sewage plants, a process of dehydration and pasteurization. Milorganite and Electra are names of such brands. Sludge that analyzes at about 5:3:0 is used at the rate of 5 lb. per 100 sq. ft.

Cottonseed and soybean meal are also of value as fertilizers.

Ureaform nitrogenous fertilizers supply nitrogen. Apply at 1 or 2 lb. per 100 sq. ft.

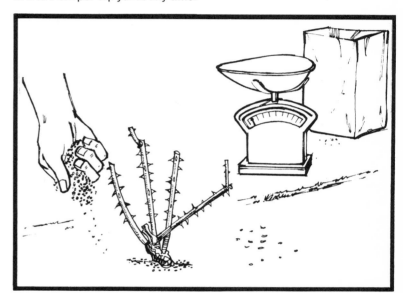

A compound fertilizer being applied to a lawn. Note the scales for accurate weighing of the fertilizer and the way in which the lawn has been marked out into strips to ensure even coverage

Bone meal will supply the plant with phosphorus and a little nitrogen. It can be applied at any time, at a rate of 2 to 6 oz. per sq. yd., is rather slow acting, and will last for many months

Simple Ways to Increase Plants

Sowing in Pots and Boxes

Pots, pans, and boxes in which seeds are germinated must be well provided with holes or slits through which surplus water can drain away. Cover these outlets with pieces of broken pot (crocks), small gravel, or coarse peat so that they cannot be blocked by fine soil and then fill up with seed mix. Press the mix in gently with the fingers and smooth it off level with a straight-edged piece of wood. Firm mixes based on loam with a smooth wooden block, but do not firm peat mixes. When ready for sowing, the surface of the mix should be about ½ in. below the rim of the receptacle.

Broadcast the seed thinly over the surface of the mix and cover by sifting soil, peat, or sand over it. Very small seeds need not be covered at all, but both types should be protected by a pane of glass laid over the container (but not touching the soil) with a sheet of paper on top. The paper must be removed as soon as the seedlings appear and the glass a day or so later.

Water the seeds thoroughly using a watering can fitted with a fine rose. For very small seeds, water by holding the pan for a few moments almost to its rim in a tub of water.

One of the most fascinating things about gardening is that it is possible to increase most plants very easily. Some plants actually need to be renewed from time to time; annuals and biennials each year, since they die once they have flowered and set seed; many fast-growing herbaceous perennials every two or three years since in that time they can spread too widely for convenience and starve themselves out by exhausting the soil. Some plants are also healthier and produce better quality flowers if renewed annually from cuttings, dahlias and chrysanthemums being notable examples.

There are two basic methods of increasing plants, one from seed; the other, known as vegetative reproduction, by division, cuttings layers, or grafts. Seedlings are genuinely new individuals, starting a fresh life of their own, whereas plants raised by vegetative means are really extensions of their parents, usually retaining every minute characteristic of their parents, sometimes even the pests and diseases which afflicted them. For this reason, it is important to use as parents only plants that are healthy, pest free and of really desirable quality. Seedlings often differ from their parents but vegetatively propagated plants exactly resemble them. All propagation should be done at the most favorable time of the year. Seeds need moisture, air, and warmth to germinate and seedlings require light. In a heated greenhouse the first three can be provided at any time, but light is often lacking in winter and so seed sowing is mostly done between March and July.

Out of doors, the soil is usually too cold to permit seeds to germinate before April and it is from then until early September that most seeds are sown, with particular emphasis on the spring, since this gives the seedlings plenty of time to grow into sturdy plants before the winter.

When seeds are sown in pots, pans, or trays, special seed mixes are generally used. A good formula is: one part by bulk of sterilized loam, one part shredded peat, and one part coarse sand, plus 1½ oz. of powdered superphosphate of lime to each bushel of mixture.

Or there are various commercial seed mixes, mostly based on peat; for instance, Jiffy Mix.

Out of doors it would not be practical to use relatively expensive mixes such as these, but the natural soil of the site can usually be made sufficiently crumbly and congenial by thorough digging followed by a generous topdressing of peat. The final preparation of outdoor seedbeds should be done when the soil is reasonably dry on top and clods break up easily.

A gay border of annuals. The hardy varieties can be sown where they are to flower but most half-hardy kinds are best sown in pots or boxes and germinated in a greenhouse or frame

Pricing Off

Pricking off is the equivalent of transplanting. Under glass it can be done earlier than outdoors, as the tiny seedlings are protected.

The first leaves produced by a seedling are of a different character, and often of simpler outline, than the leaves that follow. They are known as seed leaves, or cotyledons. Pricking off is best done when these are fully developed and the next pair have appeared.

As a rule, seedlings are pricked off into the same type of seed mix as that in which the seeds were germinated, but seedlings of vigorous, fast-growing plants, such as tomatoes, may go direct into potting mix.

Pricking off is usually into pans or boxes. Prepare the mix and fill the boxes or pots as for seed sowing, ensuring that the mix is moist throughout. Lift the seedlings, a few at a time, with a pointed stick or wooden plant label, carefully separating the plants. Use a small wooden dibber the size of a fountain pen to make a hole in the mix. Holding a seedling by a leaf or leaves (not by its growing tip or stem, neither of which must be bruised) lower the roots into the hole and press soil round them gently with the dibber. Continue until the pan or tray is full, spacing the seedlings at least 1½ in. apart— vigorous kinds 2 in. apart. Water thoroughly from a watering-can fitted with a fine rose to settle soil further around the roots, and allow to drain. In sunny weather, lightly shade for the first day.

Seedlings Under Glass

watering seedlings

hardening off seeds

Seedlings need a steady temperature, and adequate moisture and light. Too much heat or insufficient light will make them grow tall and thin. With too little heat they will be stunted and may change color to a bluish green. Strong sunlight may scorch them, especially if they are short of water. When the seedlings are checked by bad conditions it usually takes some time to get them growing again.

In spring, seedlings can usually take all the light that there is, and may benefit from being placed on shelves near the greenhouse glass. The boxes should be turned regularly. Summer seedlings are likely to need shading from strong, direct sunshine and may be better in an open frame, with glass protection at night only.

Water the seedlings thoroughly from a can fitted with a rose or by standing the containers for a moment or so up to the rims in water.

At least two weeks before seedlings raised under glass are to be planted out, place them in a frame and give free ventilation whenever the weather is favorable. For the last few days before being planted, remove all protection from the plants unless frost threatens. This hardening off is essential to accustom plants to cooler outdoor conditions. If a frame is not available, stand the seedlings in a sheltered place outdoors, covering with brown paper on cold nights.

Gazanias are readily raised from seed sown under glass, pricked out into boxes and later planted out of doors. They are low-growing plants ideal for rock gardens, banks, or the front of sunny borders but not completely winter hardy

Nemesias are highly colorful half-hardy annuals for summer bedding. Seeds are sown under glass in late March to provide plants for setting out in late May or early June. They do poorly in climates of high humidity or strong summer heat, or both

Sowing Broadcast

Broadcasting seed means scattering it as evenly as possible over the surface of the soil. It is the usual method of sowing lawns and also hardy annuals and other plants that are to grow and flower where sown.

To broadcast seed over a large area, such as a lawn, first mark it off in yard-wide strips, then divide the seed into a sufficient number of equal parts so that each strip can be sown separately. Place the measured quantity of seed in a bowl and scatter it from this by hand, taking care to spread it as evenly as possible. Cover the seed either by scattering fine soil over it or by careful raking so that it is stirred into the surface soil.

Smaller areas can be conveniently sown by slitting the seed packet cleanly with a sharp knife, opening it sufficiently to form a little scoop and sprinkling the seed from this. Thin and even sowing is desirable as crowded seedlings are likely to be weak and may suffer from disease. Cover the seed by sprinkling or sifting soil over it. Only lightly cover very small seeds, but large seeds can have a covering of soil equal to their own thickness.

The drawbacks to broadcasted seeds are that it may be difficult to distinguish weed seedlings from plant seedlings, and it is not possible to use a hoe to eliminate weeds.

Sowing in Drills

Drills are little furrows in which seeds are sown. They are then covered by drawing back the displaced soil. It is important that the drills should be of the correct depth to suit the seed to be sown and that they should be of an even depth throughout. If not, some seeds may be buried too deeply and fail to germinate, and some may be covered too thinly and be picked up by birds; in either case, germination will be uneven.

Make drills with the corner of a hoe or with a sharpened stick. Stretch a garden line to mark the exact position of the drill or use a rod for the same purpose. Hold the hoe or stick firmly and draw it through the soil close to the line with sharp but firm movements, so that minor obstructions are overcome. It is much easier to draw good drills in well-prepared seedbeds than in those that contain many large stones, and are uneven and lumpy.

For average seeds, drills should be $\frac{1}{2}$ to $\frac{3}{4}$ in. deep; for very small seeds, $\frac{1}{4}$ in., and for large seeds, such as peas and beans, about 2 in. deep.

Cover the seeds by drawing back displaced soil with a rake, using the flat of the rake to tamp the soil down gently over the seeds.

Mark the position of each drill before removing the line, so that the seedlings can be readily identified and a hoe run through the surface between rows to destroy weeds as they appear.

Limnanthes is a sweetly scented annual that is much sought after by bees. It is readily raised from seed scattered out of doors where the plants are to flower and lightly covered with soil

Sweet peas can either be raised in pots for planting out in spring or, for later flowering, can be sown in drills out of doors where they are to flower. This latter method has been used for these plants

Aids to Germination

stratifying seeds

chipping seed using a penknife

chipping seed using a nail file

Many seeds are conditioned by nature not to germinate until they have passed one winter outdoors. Stratification is a means of hastening this natural process or making it more effective. Seeds such as delphiniums may be artificially stratified by being stored for several months in a refrigerator at a temperature of 32 to 33°F.

Berries and fruits of various kinds, including rose hips, are conditioned by being put in sand-filled pots, covered with fine-mesh wire netting to keep out mice, and left for the winter in a sheltered but cold place out of doors, such as against a north-facing wall. In spring the seeds are rubbed out of the rotten flesh and sown in the ordinary way.

Some tough-coated seeds, such as peas, beans, and sweet corn, germinate more readily if soaked in water for 24 hours before sowing. A few seeds, including black-coated sweet peas, germinate better if a small chip is removed from the seed coat with a nail file or the point of a penknife. Be careful to make this chip at the opposite side of the seed to the "eye"—a small wrinkle indicating the position of the growing points—so that this is not damaged.

Thinning, Transplanting

Even when seeds are sown thinly it is probable that in places the seedlings will be overcrowded. They should then be either thinned or transplanted.

Thinning means pulling out surplus seedlings. Do this as soon as the seedlings can be conveniently handled, and take care not to dislodge the seedlings that are to be retained. Press two fingers on the soil on each side of the wanted seedling while others close to it are being pulled out. Thin when the soil is moist but not wet. Do not complete thinning in one operation, but leave about twice the required number of seedlings at first, in case some die or are eaten. About a week later, thin to the final spacing.

Thinnings may sometimes be replanted elsewhere, but generally for transplanting it is better to lift all the seedlings carefully with a hand fork so that their roots are damaged as little as possible. Do this when the seedlings are a few inches high (earlier for very small plants) and place the seedlings in a tray or basket. Replant them at once with a dibber or trowel, taking care to drop the roots well into the soil and to make them firm. Water thoroughly if the soil is at all dry. The most favorable period for transplanting is when the weather is showery and the soil moist.

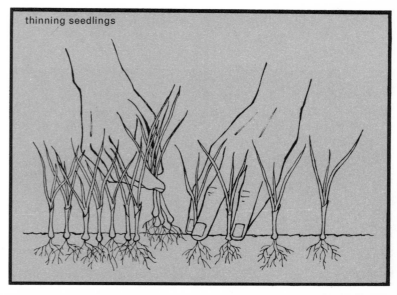

thinning seedlings

The handsome fruits, or hips, of *Rosa rugosa scabrosa*. The seeds they contain can be sown but will germinate better if not removed from the hips until these have spent a winter out of doors

Calendula Geisha Girl, a very easily grown hardy annual. Seed sown out of doors germinates freely and seedlings must be thinned. If removed carefully the thinnings can be replanted elsewhere

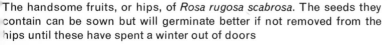

Softwood Cuttings

Softwood cuttings are made from the young shoots of plants before they have started to harden or ripen. They are used for many herbaceous plants and also for popular greenhouse and display plants, such as perpetual-flowering carnations, chrysanthemums, dahlias, fuchsias, and pelargoniums (including bedding geraniums). Occasionally softwood cuttings are used for trees and shrubs, but more usually half-ripe or hardwood cuttings are used for these.

Select firm, healthy shoots without flowers or flower buds and sever each cleanly below a joint, i.e., the point where a leaf or leaf stalk is attached to the stem. Carefully remove the lower leaves.

Take cuttings of perpetual-flowering carnations by breaking out short sideshoots from midway up the plants. Prepare chrysanthemum cuttings from young shoots growing directly from the roots. Take cuttings of pinks by pulling out the top 2 or 3 in. of each shoot at a joint; such pulled cuttings are known as "pipings." With all softwood cuttings, avoid shoots that are puffy or hollow. Cuttings of delphiniums and lupines are best severed close against the firm crown of the plant.

Half-ripe Cuttings

Half-ripe cuttings differ from softwood cuttings in being made from slightly older shoots which have started to become ripe and woody at the base though they are still soft at the tip. Such shoots are usually available in June, July, or August, so these cuttings are sometimes referred to as summer cuttings.

Half-ripe cuttings are mainly used as a means of propagating shrubs and shrubby rock plants. Success often depends on taking the cuttings at precisely the right stage of development, and since this can vary from one kind of plant to another, it is impossible to give exact timings. The state of growth is what matters and when in doubt it is wise to take several batches of cuttings at intervals of 7 to 10 days.

The length of the cuttings will also differ greatly according to the growth of the plant from which they are taken. Heather cuttings may be no more than 1 to 1½ in. long, whereas rose or hydrangea cuttings may be 4 to 5 in. long.

Half-ripe cuttings may be taken and prepared exactly as for softwood cuttings or, alternatively, they may be taken with a "heel." This means that the whole young shoot is pulled away from the older stem with a slip of this attached. This slip, or "heel," must be neatly trimmed with a sharp knife or razor blade before the cutting is inserted.

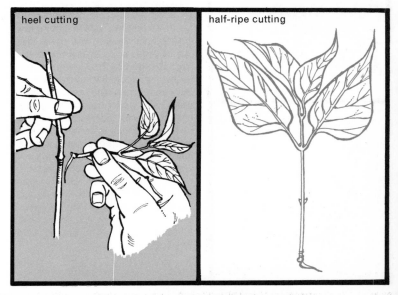

heel cutting

half-ripe cutting

Preparing cuttings of a herbaceous plant. Firm sturdy shoots should be selected, and should be trimmed below a leaf joint with a sharp knife before inserting in mix

Half-ripe wood cuttings of various shrubs rooting in an unheated frame. Note the neat way in which the cuttings have been grouped, and the clear labels which identify them

Success with Rooting

Softwood and half-ripe cuttings must be kept in a still, moist atmosphere to prevent flagging while they are forming roots. This can be provided in a small frame with a close-fitting light (i.e. a sheet of glass with a wooden frame) or in a box covered with a piece of glass or polyethylene, or within a polyethylene bag.

Cuttings can be rooted in sand, Vermiculite, peat, or special cutting mix. For most purposes a half-and-half mixture of gritty sand and shredded peat will do quite well.

Dip the base of each cutting in hormone rooting powder and then insert it to about one-third its length in the prepared mix, which may be in pots, pans, boxes, or a bed, whichever is most convenient. When all the cuttings have been inserted, water them well through a fine rose and cover them with glass or polyethylene sheeting and shade from strong sunshine. If polyethylene bags are used, slip one over each pot with an elastic band around to hold it lightly against the sides of the pot.

Water cuttings as frequently as is necessary to keep the mix moist right through. More frequent watering is usually required under glass than under polyethylene sheeting. When cuttings are well rooted, indicated by renewed growth, carefully separate them and pot singly in 3-in. pots in a soil or peat mix.

Hardwood Cuttings

Hardwood cuttings are made from young stems that have completed a season of growth and become hard and ripe. They are used to propagate trees and shrubs, including such fruit bushes as currants and gooseberries. Since they are usually taken in the autumn they are sometimes called autumn cuttings.

As a rule, hardwood cuttings are considerably longer than softwood or half-ripe cuttings—up to 12 in. for some plants. They may be severed below a joint or taken with a heel like half-ripe cuttings, but their treatment thereafter is quite different. Since they are usually taken at a time of year when growth is virtually at a standstill, they lose moisture very slowly and there is no need to keep them in a still, moist atmosphere. Many can be rooted out of doors, but evergreen shrubs should be protected in a frame. A hormone rooting powder specially for hardwood cuttings may be used.

Insert the cuttings in straight-backed trenches; evergreen cuttings should be covered to one-third of their length, deciduous cuttings to two-thirds their length. Scatter sharp sand in each trench, set the cuttings on this, return the soil, and make firm with the foot.

Hardwood cuttings usually take about 12 months to root.

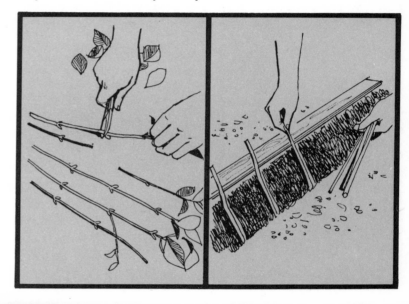

This propagating frame in a small greenhouse is being used for the rooting of dahlia cuttings inserted in pots to keep individual varieties separate. The polyethylene cover has been removed for watering

Placing hardwood cuttings in a narrow straight-sided trench. These will remain out of doors over winter so a sheltered position is desirable. They will root within 12 months

Division

Division is the simplest of all methods of propagation, but can be applied only to perennial plants with a more or less spreading habit of growth.

Lift plants carefully with a spade or fork and shake as much of the soil as possible from their roots so as to see where the plant can most readily be split. If it is the type of plant that will divide easily, break it up with the fingers, taking care that each piece has both shoots and roots. If this results in more pieces than are required for re-planting, retain the young outer portions and discard the woody center portions of the plants.

If the plant is too tough to be broken up with the fingers, thrust two hand forks (or for larger plants, two border forks) back to back through the center of the clump and lever apart. Repeat if necessary until the pieces are sufficiently small or can be broken by hand.

Some plants with fairly solid crowns, e.g. rhubarb and peonies, can be divided if the crown is carefully cut with a knife. It is usually best to wash off all soil before attempting this.

Spring and early autumn are favorable times for dividing plants.

Layering

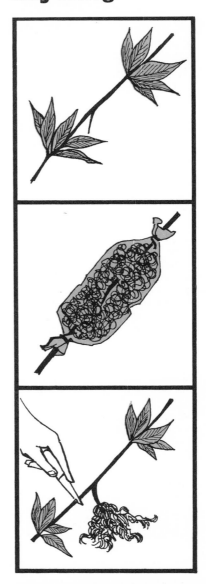

Layering is a method of propagating plants by inducing stems to form roots and then severing them from the parent plant. If the stems can be bent down to soil level they can be layered directly into the soil. Spring and early summer are favorable times for layering, but it can be done at any time.

Choose fairly young, pliable stems and either give each a sharp twist where it can be made to touch the ground most conveniently, or make an incision in it at this point. The incision may pass through a joint or may simply be a ring drawn round the stem with a knife to check the flow of sap. Dust the wound with hormone rooting powder, make a shallow hole in the soil, press the wounded part of the layer into this and secure with a forked stick or a piece of wire bent like a hairpin, and leave until rooted. Sever the layer from the parent plant, but leave for another week or so and then lift carefully and replant elsewhere. If a shrub has no branches sufficiently pliable or low growing to be bent down to soil level it may still be possible to layer them by bringing the growing medium up to the plant, and air layering it, as illustrated.

Strawberries and violets make runners naturally in summer. These can simply be pegged down to the soil and will form roots.

Shrub layers may take 12 months to form roots, but strawberries, violets, and carnations will root in 5 or 6 weeks.

Dividing a well-developed herbaceous plant with the aid of two garden forks which have been thrust into the middle and levered apart. When the clump is a little more manageable, it can be further divided by hand. It is the younger outside portions which make the best plants

Border carnation layering: An incision has been made through a joint in the stem and the wounded portion will be pushed into the soil. With shrubs it may be necessary to wrap damp sphagnum moss enclosed in a sealed polyethylene sleeve around the wound

What is Grafting?

Grafting is a means of joining two plants together. It is the usual method of propagating apples and pears, is also used for some ornamental trees and shrubs, including garden varieties of rhododendron, and even for a few herbaceous plants such as the double-flowered varieties of *Gypsophila paniculata* (baby's-breath).

In all these cases a shoot of the garden variety to be increased is grafted on to the root or stem of an allied species. This shoot is known as the "scion" and the plant to which it is united as the "stock." When the two are fully joined together, the stock is prevented from making any top growth and simply provides the roots which anchor the plant and supply it with water and chemicals from the soil. Sap rising from the roots is channeled through the scion from which all further top growth proceeds.

In a grafted plant the nature of the stock determines the character of the roots and to some extent the vigor and growth of the scion, but the scion determines the character of the leaves, flowers, and fruits which the plant produces. Grafting, therefore, is not only a means of increasing some plants which are difficult to raise from cuttings or layers, but is also a means of influencing their behavior to meet particular garden requirements.

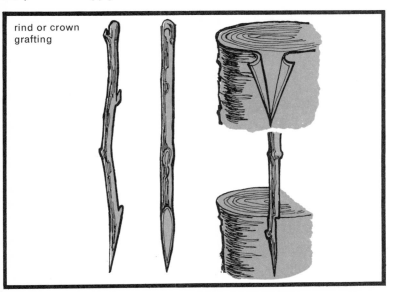

rind or crown grafting

Budding

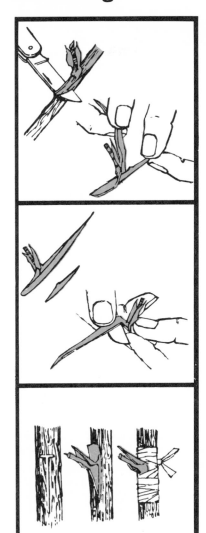

Budding is the name given to the special form of grafting used to propagate most garden roses. It is carried out in summer when roses are in full growth and sap is flowing freely.

To obtain suitable buds, cut strong young shoots from the rose to be propagated. Flowering shoots are suitable just as soon as the flowers have faded. Cut off the tops and remove all leaves but retain the leaf stalks.

In the angle between each leaf stalk and the stem there will be a little growth bud. Using a sharp knife (a special budding knife is best) cut this out with a shield-shaped portion of bark about $1\frac{1}{2}$ in. in length. Carefully remove the slip of wood which will be found on the inside of this "shield." Cut off the top of the shield $\frac{1}{2}$ in. above the bud. Make a T-shaped incision $1\frac{1}{4}$ in. long in the bark of the stock, and, using the thin scalpel-handle of the budding knife, raise the flaps of bark so formed.

Slip the shield and its bud beneath these flaps so that the exposed tissues lie snugly against those of the stock. Bind the whole in place with soft raffia or make use of the special ties which can be obtained for this purpose.

Examine about three weeks later, and if the bud has withered, repeat the operation elsewhere on the stock. Remove the top of the stock just above the bud the following March.

Making a whip, or tongue, graft. The sloping cut on both stock and scion should be as nearly identical in size as possible. The "tongues" made by the reverse cut serve to hold the two together while they are bound together and waxed

Budding is one of the chief methods of propagating roses and the stone fruits such as almonds and cherries. Specially designed budding knives are available with scalpel-shaped handles to draw back the bark so that the prepared bud can be slipped in easily

Shrubs for Year-round Interest

Shrubs of all kinds make a yearlong contribution to the garden scene. Even the deciduous kinds, which lose their leaves in the autumn and do not get any more until the following spring, have interesting branch patterns, sometimes given added attraction by distinctive bark color. Evergreen shrubs retain their leaves all winter and then stand out in sharp contrast to the deciduous kinds, a factor which needs to be taken into account when locating them. Evergreens with leaves variegated with white, cream, or yellow can be particularly valuable in winter.

Some shrubs are grown primarily for the conspicuous beauty of their flowers, some for their berries or other autumn fruits, some for the color of their foliage, and a few combine two or more of these attractions. There is also great variety in height and habit, from completely prostrate shrubs such as some species of cotoneaster, to almost tree-like specimens, such as the lilacs. Not all shrubs are equally hardy and this must be considered when selecting and placing them. A few, such as the hardier fuchsias, make a permanent framework of branches in the milder parts of the country, especially near the sea, but elsewhere tend to be killed to ground level each winter, sending up new shoots from the roots the following spring, almost like herbaceous plants.

Some shrubs dislike lime (including limestone) in the soil and must either be grown in moderately acid soil or be fed with specially prepared iron and manganese fertilizers to make up for the deficiencies of these chemicals that commonly occur in alkaline soils. Azaleas and rhododendrons are familiar lime haters and so are many varieties of heather, but not all, since *Erica carnea* together with its numerous varieties, and *E. darleyensis* and *E. terminalis* will all succeed even where there is a fair amount of limestone.

Shrubs are commonly grouped either with other shrubs or with herbaceous plants and annuals, but some kinds look their best planted as isolated specimens and some can be trained against walls. *Magnolia stellata* is an excellent example of the former type and pyracantha, Japanese quince, and ceanothus all do well against walls, where their stiff branches may provide support for genuine climbers, such as the less rampant varieties of clematis.

Most shrubs take several years to attain anything like their full size and this must be taken into account when spacing them. Temporary plants, such as dahlias, annuals, and herbaceous perennials, can be used to fill up the ground until such time as the shrubs require it all.

Cultivation

Thoroughly dig all ground intended for shrubs, work in some rotted manure or compost and remove all perennial weeds. Complete preparation several weeks before planting.

Plant deciduous shrubs lifted from the ground in the autumn or winter when the leaves are off the plants. Evergreen shrubs should be planted in early autumn or early spring. Shrubs grown in containers can be planted at any time as long as the roots are not disturbed. Always plant with a spade and make holes sufficiently large to accommodate all the roots spread out naturally. The old soil mark on the stem should lie just below the surface of the soil.

Space small shrubs 2 to 3 ft. apart, medium-sized shrubs 3 to 4 ft. apart and tall shrubs 4 to 6 ft. apart. Many shrubs look attractive when grown as isolated specimens so that they can be viewed from every side.

Feed shrubs each spring with well-rotted manure or compost spread liberally around them, or with a good compound fertilizer at 3 oz. per sq. yd. Never apply lime near lime-hating shrubs.

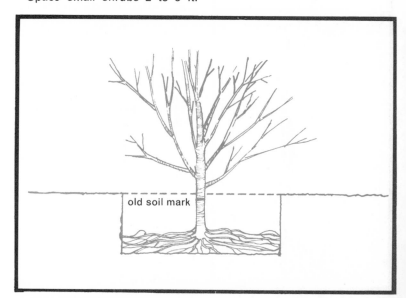

old soil mark

Viburnum opulus nanum, a dwarf variety of the Guelder Rose, has white flowers followed by scarlet berries. As an additional attraction the foliage colors brilliantly before it falls in the autumn

Pruning

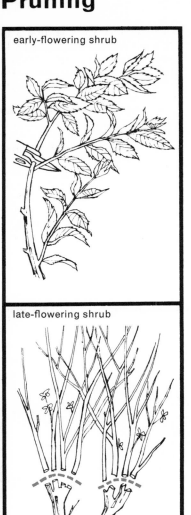

early-flowering shrub

late-flowering shrub

Most shrubs will grow and flower well without any pruning, but pruning is often useful to restrict the size of a shrub and can sometimes be used to improve the quality of the flowers.

Evergreen shrubs are best pruned in spring or early summer, but not while they are flowering. Generally, it is sufficient to cut back branches that are projecting too far and to thin out growth that is overcrowded.

For the purpose of pruning, deciduous shrubs can conveniently be divided into two groups: early-flowering shrubs, or those that flower before midsummer, and late-flowering shrubs, those that flower after midsummer.

Prune early-flowering shrubs as soon as they have finished flowering. Cut out most or all of the stems that have just flowered, if possible making each cut immediately above a young, non-flowering stem, a new shoot, or a growth bud from which a new shoot can grow.

Prune late-flowering shrubs in March or April, either by cutting out some of the older branches, or by shortening all branches so that strong, new flowering growth is made.

Bamboos

Most bamboos can impart an almost tropical look to a garden. They will grow in any reasonably good soil, can be planted at the waterside or in ordinary well-drained ground and will thrive in sun or shade, though in cold, windy places some of their leaves may become brown in winter. Some kinds spread rapidly by suckers and may have to be chopped back with a spade from time to time. Rooted pieces dug out in the process provide the best means of increase, for if they are replanted they will soon grow into good plants.

Bamboos are excellent for screening. They can be used as a background to other plants, or be planted beside streams and pools.

Pseudosasa japonica is the hardiest. It is light green and ranges to 12 ft. Among the best of the many different kinds are: *Arundinaria auricoma*, green and gold leaves, 4 ft. high; *Phyllostachys nigra* 'Henon,' deep green, 10 ft.; *Semiarundinaria (Arundinaria) fastuosa*, deep green, 15 ft.; *Shibatea kumasa*, bright green, 3 ft.; *Sinarundinaria murieliae*, slender, green, 8 ft.; *Sinarundinaria nitida*, small, elegant, bright green leaves, up to 20 ft.

Pseudosasa japonica

Sinarundinaria nitida

Many early-flowering shrubs, such as this forsythia, can be pruned as soon as the floral display has finished. The old flower stems are removed but all young growth is retained

Despite their almost tropical look, most bamboos are completely hardy and very accommodating for they thrive in all but the worst situations. *Pseudosasa japonica* is one of many excellent species

Deciduous Azaleas

Deciduous azaleas flower in May and June. They are immensely showy with good-sized flowers in fine clusters and a wonderful color range, including yellow, orange, pink, scarlet, crimson, and many intermediate shades. The flowers of some varieties are very fragrant. Bushes grow from 4 to 8 ft. high and as much in diameter. In some varieties, the leaves turn copper and crimson before falling in the autumn. Mollis varieties have larger and earlier flowers than Ghent varieties.

Azaleas are hardy, free flowering and easy to grow in soils that contain no lime. Where soil is limy, azaleas can be grown by building up special beds of peat and lime-free loam and by feeding the plants each spring with iron and manganese chelates.

They will grow in full sun or partial shade and can be planted in thin woodland. No regular pruning is required, but overgrown bushes can be thinned or reduced immediately after flowering.

Separate colors can be purchased as named varieties, e.g., Anthony Koster, yellow and orange; Dr. M. Oosthoek, orange red; (both mollis azaleas); Fanny, rose, (a Ghent azalea). Good mixtures are also available, usually at a cheaper price, e.g., Knap Hill Hybrids and Exbury Hybrids.

Evergreen Azaleas

The evergreen azaleas are low, densely branched spreading shrubs with neat leaves and small to medium-sized flowers, very freely produced in May and June. Their color range is from white to crimson, but with none of the yellow shades that characterize the taller, more open-branched deciduous azaleas and with greater emphasis on pinks, carmine, and scarlet. They are among the most showy of all shrubs when in flower, and being evergreen, give the garden a well-furnished appearance even in winter. Collectively they are often known as Japanese azaleas, one of the most useful types of which are the Kurume azaleas, so called since they were produced near the town of Kurume in Japan.

Because of their origin they are usually included in Japanese-style gardens.

All varieties dislike lime and prefer peaty or loamy soils in partial shade. They transplant well, even when quite old, need no regular pruning, though they can be thinned immediately after flowering, and are increased by summer cuttings.

Some good varieties are Benegiri, deep magenta; Christmas Cheer, crimson; Hinomayo, pink; Hinodegiri, carmine; Malvaticum, mauve; and Palestrina, white.

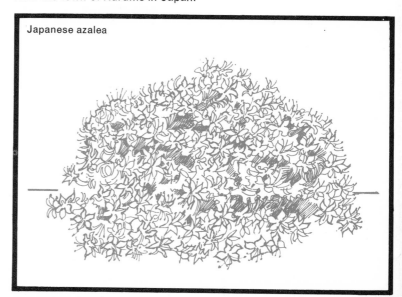

deciduous azalea

Japanese azalea

Deciduous azaleas are splendid shrubs for lime-free soils, making a spectacular display in May and June. This planting gives some idea of the lovely colors available

This delightful evergreen azalea belongs to the Kurume group and is named Hinomayo. It makes a low, spreading bush with small leaves, and it flowers freely in May or early June

Barberries

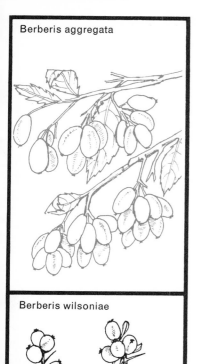

Berberis aggregata

Berberis wilsoniae

Barberry is the popular name for berberis. There are numerous different kinds, some of which are evergreen, some deciduous. All have yellow flowers followed by red or purple berries. In general, the deciduous barberries are grown principally for their flowers which make a fine display in spring.

All are hardy and easily grown in almost any soil. They will grow in shade, but flower and berry better in sun. No regular pruning is required, but overgrown bushes can be thinned; the evergreen kinds after flowering, the deciduous kinds in March.

The two most popular evergreen kinds are *Berberis darwinii* with small, hollylike leaves and clusters of orange flowers followed by little purple berries, and *B. stenophylla* with narrow leaves and yellow, sweetly scented flowers. Both make large bushes 8 to 10 ft. high and as much through.

The most popular deciduous barberries are *Berberis wilsoniae*, 3 ft. high with coral red berries, and *B. thunbergii atropurpurea*, 6 ft. high with reddish purple leaves. *B. aggregata* resembles *B. wilsoniae* but is twice the size. *B. darwinii* hardy to U.S. Zone 7.

Buddleias

Buddleia alternifolia

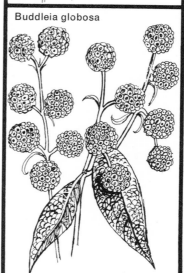

Buddleia globosa

The buddleias are large, branching shrubs which will grow practically anywhere, even on poor limy soils and in dry, rocky places.

The purple buddleia (*Buddleia davidii*) is the most popular. It produces its long, conical spikes of honey-scented flowers in late summer, and there are several varieties ranging in color from white through to lavender and intense purple. It will grow 12 ft. in height and width, but can be kept to half these dimensions by pruning each March. Do this either by cutting all stems to about 1 ft. from ground level or allow the plant to retain a framework of stout branches and shorten all other branches to within a few inches of these. Seed is freely produced but self-sown seedlings may vary in color from their parents.

Buddleia alternifolia makes a big, rounded bush with slender, arching branches wreathed in purple flowers in June. It can be thinned and shaped immediately after flowering, but should not be hard pruned. It can be trained on a main stem or trunk like a small tree.

Buddleia globosa is known as the Orange Ball Tree because its orange flowers are clustered in little balls, in May and June. It grows 10 to 12 ft. high and can be thinned or shortened after flowering is over.

Berberis darwinii, a splendid evergreen shrub, as valuable for hedge making as for a border or specimen planting. The leaves are small and shaped like those of holly

Royal Red is one of the deepest purple varieties of *Buddleia davidii*. This shrub flowers in late summer and its long, scented flowers attract butterflies. It is for this reason that it is often known by the common name of the Butterfly Bush

Brooms

Spartium junceum

Genista hispanica

Brooms have thin, whippy stems and small, pea-type flowers. They are sun lovers which will grow in any well-drained soil, even those that are rather poor and sandy. Brooms transplant badly so plant from pots or other containers, disturbing the roots as little as possible. Only prune when it is essential to keep the plants in check. Do this by shortening flowering stems as soon as the flowers fade, but never cut into mature wood.

Recommended types are: Common Broom (*Cytisus scoparius*) 6 to 8 ft. with yellow flowers in May and early June, and improved garden varieties such as Cornish Cream, cream; Donard Seedling, rose; Dorothy Walpole, crimson, and Lord Lambourne, yellow and red. Also, Early Broom (*Cytisus praecox*) 4 ft., cream, April to May; Portugal Broom (*Cytisus albus*) 6 to 8 ft., white, June; Spanish Broom (*Spartium junceum*) 6 to 8 ft., yellow fragrant flowers, July to August; Spanish Gorse (*Genista hispanica*) 2 ft., yellow, May to June; Mount Etna Broom (*Genista aethnensis*) 12 to 15 ft., yellow, July; and Madeira Broom (*Genista virgata*) 6 to 8 ft., yellow, June to July.

There are also dwarf brooms suitable for rock gardens, walls, and the fronts of borders such as *Cytisus beanii*, *C. kewensis*, *Genista lydia* and *G. tinctoria plena*.

Camellias

Contrary to popular belief many camellias are quite hardy, but they flower in late winter and spring and in exposed places the flowers may be damaged.

All camellias are evergreen, and the shining, dark green foliage is very handsome. All make quite big bushes in time but are rather slow growing and can be thinned immediately after flowering.

Camellias dislike lime but succeed in most other soils, preferring those of good loamy or peaty nature. They will grow in sun or shade, but do not like very hot, dry places. They can be trained against walls.

There are many different varieties which may be divided into four principal groups: Japonica, Williamsii, Reticulata, and Sasanqua.

Camellia japonica varieties are hardy and have showy flowers. Representative are: Adolph Audusson, semi-double, scarlet; *donckelarii*, semi-double, crimson and white; *elegans*, double, rose; Lady Clare, semi-double, pink; *magnoliaeflora*, semi-double, pink; White Swan, single, white.

The *C. williamsii* varieties are a little looser and more open in growth, and are fine garden shrubs. Representative are: J. C. Williams, single, shell pink and Donation, double, pink.

The *C. reticulata* varieties are tall and have very large flowers. *C. sasanqua* varieties have smaller flowers in winter and early spring. Both are more tender.

Camellia reticulata

Cytisus scoparius andreanus, Lord Lambourne, a broom which has for long been a favorite with those gardening on well-drained soils. All brooms are sun lovers and most tend to be rather short lived but some can be easily renewed from seed

The glossy dark green leaves of *Camellia japonica* make it a handsome evergreen shrub and they are a perfect foil for the shapely flowers. Camellias prefer sheltered places and lime-free soils. Suitable for U.S. Zone 7

Caryopteris, Ceratostigma

The chief similarities between caryopteris and ceratostigma are that they are both deciduous, flower in late summer and autumn, and have blue flowers and rather soft stems which are liable to be damaged by frost in winter. Caryopteris is sometimes given the common name of blue spiraea.

Caryopteris clandonensis, the most popular variety, has twiggy branches, small gray green leaves and little clusters of fluffy-looking lavender blue flowers in August and September. Kew Blue is a variety with deeper blue flowers. If pruned each April almost to soil level, caryopteris will remain reasonably compact, reach a height of about 3 ft., and produce finer flower clusters.

Ceratostigma willmottianum has green leaves, thin 2-ft. stems and bright blue, phlox-like flowers from July to October. It will also benefit from being cut back each April.

Both caryopteris and ceratostigma like good, well-drained soil and a sunny, fairly sheltered place. Ceratostigma makes an excellent edging plant or it may be used to fill a narrow border at the foot of a sunny wall.

Both shrubs can be increased by summer cuttings.

Cistus

Cistus are called rock roses because they will grow in hot, dry, rocky places and their flowers look like single roses. They are all evergreen and many are quite small shrubs, but most are a little tender and may be damaged or even killed in very exposed places or during unusually severe winters. They are very suitable for sunny banks, terraces, and rock gardens.

They will grow in most well-drained soils, including chalky and limy soils. No regular pruning is required but overgrown branches can be shortened moderately in spring. All can be increased readily from seed and also by summer cuttings.

The hardiest kinds are: *Cistus crispus*, also known as Sunset, 2 ft. high, magenta rose; *C. corbariensis*, 3 ft., white; *C. cyprius*, 5 ft., white and maroon; *C. laurifolius*, 5 ft., white; and *C. Silver Pink*, 2 to 3 ft., pale pink.

Other fine kinds, needing a little more shelter in winter, are: *Cistus ladaniferus*, known as the Gum Cistus, because its leaves are slightly sticky, 5 ft., white; *C. lusitanicus*, 5 ft., white and maroon; and *C. purpureus*, 4 ft., deep rose and maroon.

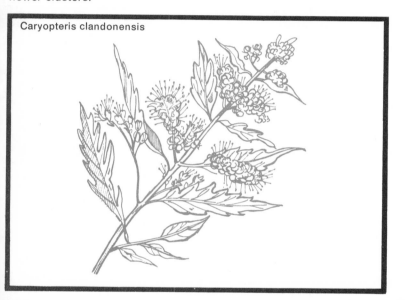

Caryopteris clandonensis

Cistus cyprius

Cistus purpureus

Among the shrubs still in flower during October is *Ceratostigma willmottianum*. It should be planted in a sheltered, sunny border and in a well-drained soil. It often dies down to ground level in winter. Suitable for U.S. Zone 8

Cistus purpureus is a charming evergreen shrub of moderate size. It will succeed well in hot, dry, rocky places and may be damaged by frost in an exposed place or during a severe winter. Suitable for U.S. Zone 7

Ceanothus

These fine shrubs are mainly of Californian origin. They like good, well-cultivated, well-drained soils and sunny, rather sheltered places. There are two main groups: the evergreen varieties mostly flowering in May and June, and the deciduous ones flowering in summer and early autumn.

The evergreen varieties make densely branched bushes about 6 ft. high with small, neat leaves and little tight clusters of blue flowers. They can be trained against sunny walls where they may reach a height of 10 to 15 ft. In such places forward-growing shoots should be shortened to a few inches annually after flowering.

The deciduous varieties make loosely branched bushes, about 8 ft. high, with sprays of blue or pink flowers. They can be cut hard back each March, which will reduce their height and improve the flower quality.

Good evergreen types are: *burkwoodii*, bright blue, July to October; Delight, rich blue, May; *impressus*, deep blue, May; *lobbianus*, bright blue, June; *thyrsiflorus*, bright blue, June; *veitchianus*, light blue, May.

Good deciduous types are: Gloire de Versailles, soft blue; Perle Rose, rose pink and Topaz, indigo blue.

Ceanothus burkwoodii

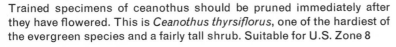
Trained specimens of ceanothus should be pruned immediately after they have flowered. This is *Ceanothus thyrsiflorus*, one of the hardiest of the evergreen species and a fairly tall shrub. Suitable for U.S. Zone 8

Cotoneasters

Cotoneaster dielsiana

Cotoneaster cornubia

Cotoneasters are grown primarily for their fine crops of berries in autumn, but many have good evergreen foliage and a decorative habit. They thrive in most soils and in sun or partial shade. They need no regular pruning, but when overgrown can be thinned in spring. All can be readily increased by seed and self-sown seedlings often appear in the garden.

Recommended kinds, all with red berries, are: *Cotoneaster conspicua*, 4 ft., evergreen, dome-shaped bush; *C. cornubia*, 12 ft. or more, deciduous, berries in large clusters; *C. dielsiana*, 8 ft., semi-evergreen; *C. frigida*, deciduous, 15 ft. or more (can be grown on a main stem or trunk like a small tree); *C. horizontalis*, 3 ft., deciduous, fan-like habit; *C. microphylla*, 3 ft., evergreen, stiffly branched; *C. simonsii*, 6 to 8 ft., deciduous, erect and *C. watereri*, 12 ft. or more, evergreen.

There are also prostrate kinds such as *C. adpressa* and *C. dammeri* which may be used as edging plants or to carpet the ground.

Cotoneaster horizontalis and *C. microphylla* may be planted against walls, over which they will spread themselves like a fan without any further support.

The evergreen *Cotoneaster conspicua decora* makes a compact dome-shaped bush with white flowers followed by deep red berries which usually persist all the winter when this is one of the most cheerful shrubs in the garden

Currants, Elders

Ribes sanguineum

Sambucus nigra laciniata

It is the American, or Flowering Currant, *Ribes sanguineum*, that is grown as an ornamental shrub. It is vigorous, easily grown and makes a fine show with its little clusters of rose pink or magenta red flowers in March and April, at about the same time as the yellow forsythia. It will grow in almost any soil, in sun or shade, and can be pruned annually each spring as soon as the flowers fade, by cutting the old flowering stems right out. *R. s. splendens* has extra-large clusters of flowers, rosy crimson in color.

The ordinary elder, *Sambucus nigra*, is a handsome European shrub, too large and common for most gardens, but it has a golden-leaved variety named *aurea*, which is well worth a place. There is also a variety named *laciniata* with finely cut green leaves. If pruned back to within about a foot of ground level each March or April, these varieties make bushes of about 5 ft. in height, with even finer leaves than normal. Like the Flowering Currant, they will grow practically anywhere.

Both Flowering Currants and elders can readily be increased by summer or autumn cuttings.

Daphnes

Daphnes are grown for their rich perfume as well as for the beauty of their flowers. Some are evergreen, some deciduous and most are quite small shrubs. All like reasonably good, well-cultivated soils and though a few will grow well in shade, the popular garden kinds enjoy open, sunny places. Most dislike root disturbance and should be purchased, if possible, in containers from which they can be planted with their roots intact. They are better left unpruned. All can be increased by summer cuttings or layers and some by seed.

Daphne mezereum is deciduous, erect, 3 ft. high and flowers on the bare stems in February and March. The flowers, purple or white and very fragrant, are followed by red berries which may produce seedlings. This daphne sometimes dies suddenly and for no obvious reason.

Daphne Somerset, also known as *D. burkwoodii*, is deciduous, 3 ft., freely branched with abundant pink, fragrant flowers in May.

Daphne odora is evergreen, 3 ft., with clusters of intensely fragrant, purple flowers in February and March. A variety named *aureo-marginata* has leaves bordered with yellow and is hardier. Suitable for U.S. Zone 7.

Daphne cneorum is evergreen, 1 ft., with fragrant, rose pink flowers in May. *D. blagayana* is quite prostrate with creamy white fragrant flowers in May. Both are suitable for rock gardens.

Daphne mezereum · Daphne burkwoodii

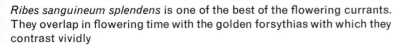
Ribes sanguineum splendens is one of the best of the flowering currants. They overlap in flowering time with the golden forsythias with which they contrast vividly

Daphne cneorum is a choice shrub for the rock garden or the front of a border. During May it is completely covered with fragrant flowers. It requires a lime-free soil

Deutzias

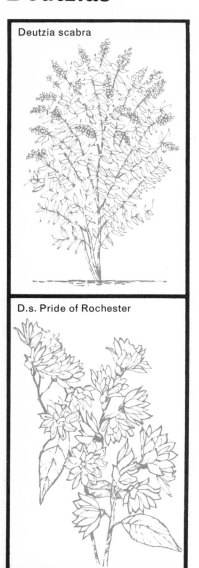

Deutzia scabra

D.s. Pride of Rochester

Deutzias are deciduous shrubs, flowering in spring and early summer. The white, pink, or purple flowers are small but numerous. Heights vary from 4 to 10 ft. All kinds are easily grown in most soils that are reasonably well drained. All prefer sunny positions though they will grow in shade. They may be pruned immediately after flowering, when flowering stems can be cut right out, and this practice is recommended as the older stems are inclined to die back in winter.

Deutzia scabra is 8 to 10 ft. high, but rather less through, with a shuttlecock habit of growth and white flowers in June. Pride of Rochester is a good variety with double flowers flushed with purple. There are also several garden varieties similar to *D. scabra* in habit, but shorter and with finer flowers. Recommended are: Mont Rose, rose pink; Perle Rose, soft rose; and Magician, purplish pink. All can readily be increased by summer or autumn cuttings.

Deutzia elegantissima is 4 to 5 ft. high, with slender, arching stems wreathed in rose pink flowers in May. Another hybrid of similar habit is *D. rosea*. It has several varieties of which *carminea* is one of the prettiest.

Dogwoods

There are many kinds of dogwood, or cornus, and they differ greatly in appearance and requirements. Most are deciduous.

The Westonbirt Dogwood, *Cornus alba sibirica*, and the Yellow-barked Dogwood, *C. stolonifera flaviramea*, are grown for the respectively red and yellow bark of the young stems, particularly attractive in winter and on plants that have been cut hard back the previous April. They will thrive in almost any soil and in sun or shade and have a particular liking for moist soils and the sides of streams. Exactly the same treatment suits *C. alba spaethii*, with golden variegated leaves, and *C. alba sibirica variegata*, with gray-green, silver-edged leaves.

Cornus kousa makes a large shrub or small tree 15 ft. or more, freely branched and spreading, with large white flowers along the stems in June. *C. florida* is similar but rather tender, and *C. florida rubra* has beautiful rose pink flowers. All need good, well-cultivated, well-drained soils and a sunny, sheltered position.

Cornus mas is also a tall shrub or small tree, with small, but very numerous, yellow flowers on the bare stems in March and April.

Cornus can be increased by summer cuttings or layers and all varieties of *Cornus alba*, *C. stolonifera*, and *C. mas* by rooted suckers dug up in the autumn.

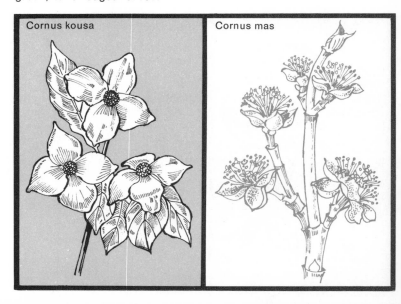

Cornus kousa

Cornus mas

The graceful *Deutzia rosea carminea*, a deciduous shrub some 4 ft. tall and twice as much through with prettily arching branches. It flowers in late May and early June and does best in a sunny position

The attractions of ornamental bark in winter should not be overlooked. The red-barked *Cornus stolonifera* and yellow-barked *C.s. flaviramea* shown in combination above are delightful if hard pruned each spring

Elaeagnus, Garrya

Elaeagnus pungens aureo-variegata is one of the best evergreen shrubs with golden variegated leaves. It makes a big, well-branched bush 10 ft. or more high but can easily be kept much smaller by annual thinning and cutting back in spring. It will grow in practically any soil and in sun or shade though the leaves will be larger and of brighter color in fairly rich, well-cultivated soil and a sunny place. The flowers are insignificant.

Garrya elliptica is an evergreen shrub of very unusual appearance since in winter it produces long, slender, gray green catkins, both male and female, borne on different bushes. The male catkins are longer and more decorative, but if a male bush is growing nearby, the female catkins are followed by trails of black fruits. Both types make shapely, well-branched bushes 6 to 8 ft. high or may be trained against walls where they can easily attain a height of 12 ft. They thrive in good, well-cultivated soils and sunny positions, and can be pruned to shape in spring when the catkins have fallen.

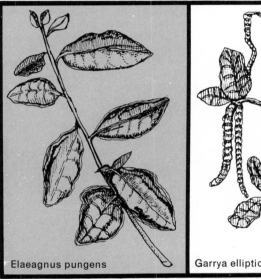 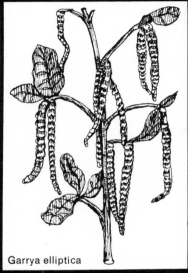

Elaeagnus pungens   Garrya elliptica

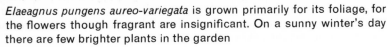
Elaeagnus pungens aureo-variegata is grown primarily for its foliage, for the flowers though fragrant are insignificant. On a sunny winter's day there are few brighter plants in the garden

Escallonias

The best varieties of escallonia are evergreen shrubs, freely branched, with numerous small pink or red flowers in summer. Some kinds make excellent hedges or screens and all can be planted in shrub borders or as isolated specimens. They will grow in any reasonably good, well-drained soil and sunny place. They are excellent seaside shrubs and will grow well in inland gardens, though a few are a little tender and not suitable for cold climates. All can be pruned in spring or immediately after flowering as much as is necessary to keep them in bounds, and they can all be increased readily by summer cuttings.

One of the loveliest and hardiest is *Escallonia langleyensis*, 6 to 8 ft., with arching stems wreathed in soft carmine flowers in July. Apple Blossom is similar in habit with pink and white flowers, Donard Seedling has pale pink flowers, and both Donard Brilliance and C. F. Ball are crimson.

Escallonia macrantha has large leaves and deep red flowers and is very popular in seaside areas as a hedge, but is rather tender elsewhere.

Escallonia langleyensis

Escallonias are splendid seaside shrubs and they will also grow well inland, thriving in good, well-drained soils and sunny positions. There are many lovely forms; this is Apple Blossom. Suitable for U.S. Zone 8

Euonymus

There are both evergreen and deciduous kinds of euonymus which look very different and serve quite different purposes.

The two best evergreen kinds are the Japanese Euonymus (*Euonymus japonicus*) and the Creeping Euonymus (*E. fortunei*). The Japanese Euonymus will grow to 20 ft., but can be pruned hard in spring or summer and is suitable for hedges. It has shining leaves which may be green or variegated with silver or gold. It will withstand sea gales.

The Creeping Euonymus has several varieties, some completely prostrate and useful as ground cover, some with silver or gold variegated leaves which form neat bushes.

The deciduous kinds, known as Spindle Trees, are grown for their clusters of little carmine and orange fruits in autumn. The two best are *Euonymus europaeus* and *E. latifolius*, both 6 to 8 ft. high.

All kinds will grow in almost any soil and in sun or shade. The spindle trees fruit best if more than one bush is planted for cross-fertilization. All suffer from attacks of blackfly which may be controlled by occasional spraying with the advised type of spray in late spring and early summer. Evergreen kinds are readily increased by summer or autumn cuttings, deciduous kinds by seed.

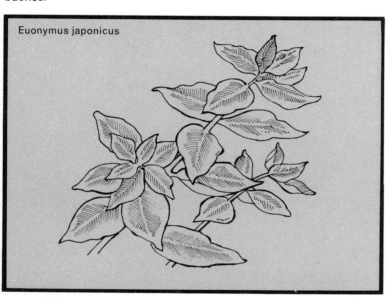

Euonymus japonicus

Forsythias

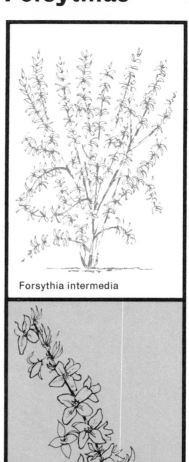

Forsythia intermedia

Forsythia suspensa

Forsythia is one of the first shrubs to make a big display in spring. Its yellow flowers open in March and in country gardens the flower buds are sometimes stripped by birds, but this seldom happens in towns. *Forsythia intermedia* Lynwood, with particularly large, deep yellow flowers, is one of the best varieties. It grows 8 ft. high and as much through but can be kept smaller by cutting out all old flowering stems just as soon as the flowers fade.

Forsythia suspensa has paler yellow flowers and longer, more slender stems. It can be trained against walls or fences, even those facing north. All forsythias are deciduous.

Forsythia will grow in almost any soil, though for best results it should be planted in moderately rich, well-cultivated soil and be fed with manure or fertilizer each spring. It will succeed in full sun or in shade. The best flowers are produced on strong, one-year-old stems and pruning, as described above, improves the quality of the flowers. Underplanting with blue-flowered chionodoxa makes a wonderful color contrast.

Forsythias are readily increased by summer or autumn cuttings.

The highly decorative fruits of the Spindle Tree (*Euonymus europaeus*). It will grow well in almost any soil, in sun or shade, but should be planted in small groups as isolated bushes sometimes fail to fruit for lack of effective pollination

The popularity of the forsythias is a tribute to their qualities as garden shrubs as well as to their ease of cultivation. This variety, Arnold Giant, has especially large flowers of fine quality

Fuchsias

Many fuchsias are rather too tender to be grown out of doors except in very mild climates but some are excellent garden plants, flowering all summer and well into the autumn. They like good, well-cultivated soil and will grow in shady places, but flower more freely where it is sunny.

They should be planted rather deep as the stems are often killed in winter, but new growth comes up from the roots which are protected by the soil. Stems damaged by frost should be cut out each March, even to ground level if necessary. Pruned in this way most varieties will grow to between 2 and 3 ft.

Fuchsias are easily raised from summer cuttings and it is as well to keep a few rooted cuttings if possible in a frame or greenhouse during the winter in case of losses out of doors.

Among the most reliable varieties are: Alice Hoffman, pink and white; Brilliant, red and purple; Brutus, red and violet; Chillerton Beauty, pink and violet; Lena, flesh pink and violet, double; *magellanica gracilis*, small red and purple flowers; Margaret, scarlet and violet; Mrs. W. P. Wood, small pale pink flowers; Tom Thumb, small cerise flowers on a 1-ft. plant; *riccartonii*, small scarlet flowers; Snowcap, red and white; Swingtime, double flowered, red and white; and Uncle Charley, pink and lavender.

Hebes

Hebe is the new name for evergreen shrubs formerly known as veronica, and it serves to distinguish them from herbaceous veronicas.

Hebes flower in summer and some varieties go on flowering spasmodically well on into the autumn and even the winter. They make well-branched, rounded bushes with good foliage and small flowers crowded in spikes which may be short or long according to the variety.

All will grow in almost any reasonably well-drained soil. They like warm, sunny places, and some kinds are rather tender and liable to be damaged or even killed in cold climates or severe winters, but all succeed well by the sea.

Regular pruning is unnecessary, but overgrown bushes can be thinned or cut back in spring. All hebes grow readily from summer cuttings.

One of the hardiest kinds is *Hebe brachysiphon* (also known as *H. traversii*), 5 ft., with white flowers in July. Other recommended varieties are: Autumn Glory, violet purple, 18 in., June to August; Great Orme, 3 ft., July to September, pink; Marjorie, light violet, 3 ft., July to September; and Midsummer Beauty, lavender, 5 ft., July to November. Alicia Amhurst, deep purple, and Simon Delaux, crimson, are 3 ft., and flower from July to November. They are more tender, but excellent for seaside gardens.

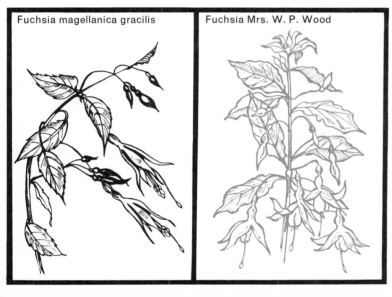

Fuchsia magellanica gracilis   Fuchsia Mrs. W. P. Wood

Hebe traversii   Hebe Great Orme

Tom Thumb, a dwarf and hardy fuchsia which will produce its small flowers freely throughout the summer and even later if there are no early autumn frosts. Suitable for U.S. Zone 7

Many forms of hebe, including Midsummer Beauty, provide a striking display of flowers throughout the summer and autumn months. All are evergreen but few are fully hardy. Suitable for U.S. Zone 10

Heathers

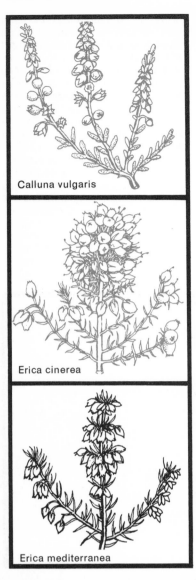

Calluna vulgaris

Erica cinerea

Erica mediterranea

There are a great many kinds of heather, of which the following are representative:

Calluna vulgaris, the Scotch Heather or Ling, flowers from August to October. Good varieties are: Gold Haze, with golden foliage, 18 in.; J. H. Hamilton, double, deep pink, 12 in.; Peter Sparkes, double, pink, 2 ft.; *flore albo pleno*, double white, 18 in.

Erica arborea alpina, the Tree Heath, 6 ft. or more, has white flowers in March and April.

Erica carnea flowers from January to March. Good varieties are: Springwood White, white, 18 in.; Springwood Pink, heather pink, 18 in. and *vivellii*, carmine, 6 in.

Erica ciliaris, the Dorset Heath, rosy red, 1 ft., June to October. There is also a white variety.

Erica cinerea, Bell Heather, June to August. Good varieties are: C. D. Eason, deep pink, 18 in.; *coccinea*, red, 1 ft.

Erica darleyensis, heather purple, 2 ft., November to April.

Erica mediterranea, rosy red, 4 ft., March to May. W. T. Rackliff is white flowered.

Erica terminalis, the Corsican Heath, rosy pink, 4 ft., June to September.

Erica vagans, the Cornish Heath, July to October. Good varieties are: Lyonesse, white, 1 ft., Mrs. D. F. Maxwell, cerise, 1 ft.

Daboecia cantabrica, the Irish Heath, 2 ft., has purple and white varieties and flowers from June to October.

Choisya, Hibiscus

The Mexican Orange Blossom, *Choisya ternata*, is an evergreen shrub 4 to 6 ft. high, with shining, light green leaves and clusters of white, scented flowers rather like those of the orange. It flowers most freely in May, but more flowers are usually produced on and off right through the summer and even into autumn. It enjoys good, well-cultivated soil and a sunny, rather sheltered position and is easily increased by summer cuttings. Suitable for U.S. Zone 7.

The Syrian Mallow, *Hibiscus syriacus*, is an erect-growing, deciduous shrub, 6 to 8 ft. high, flowering in August and September. The double or single flowers of various colors resemble those of the hollyhock on a much smaller scale. There are numerous varieties, such as: Bluebird, single, deep blue; Duc de Brabant, double, red; Hamabo, single, blush and crimson; Souvenir de Charles Breton, double, lilac; and Woodbridge, single, rose madder.

All like good, well-cultivated, well-drained soils and sunny places. They transplant rather badly so container-grown plants are to be preferred to those lifted from the open ground. Overgrown plants can be thinned or shortened in April. Propagation is by summer cuttings or layers.

Choisya ternata

Hibiscus syriacus Woodbridge

A group of Scotch Heathers, *Calluna vulgaris*, with the very showy double-flowered variety H. E. Beale in the foreground. This is one of the heathers which must have lime-free soil

Hibiscus syriacus Woodbridge has flowers like small single hollyhocks during August and September. It makes a stiffly branched shrub and likes a good, well-drained soil and a sunny position

Hydrangeas

Hydrangeas give the same kind of massive flower display from midsummer until autumn that rhododendrons give in May and June, though they are not so colorful. All will grow in any reasonably good soil and do not mind lime, but where this is present, flowers of colored varieties tend to be pink or red, rather than blue or purple. White varieties are unaffected by the soil. Hydrangeas will succeed in sun or shade.

Hydrangea paniculata is the hardiest kind. Its flowers are creamy white in conical heads and it will grow 6 ft. tall. By shortening the stems to at least half their length each March the height will be reduced, the size of the flowers increased.

The common garden hydrangeas are varieties of *Hydrangea macrophylla*. They grow 4 to 6 ft. high and more through and should not be pruned hard as this checks flowering. Faded flower heads should be removed in March and overcrowded bushes can be thinned then.

Recommended varieties are: *mariesii*, rosy pink or blue; Blue Wave, a "lace-cap;" Domotoi, double flowered, hardy; Blue Giant, massive globe-shaped trusses.

Hydrangea paniculata

The handsome *Hydrangea macrophylla mariesii*. Varieties of this type are often called lace-caps because the large outer flowers and beadlike inner ones suggest an old-fashioned lace cap

Hypericums

All hypericums have yellow flowers freely produced in summer but some are evergreen and some are deciduous and they can vary greatly in height from creeping plants such as *Hypericum calycinum*, the Rose of Sharon, to erect, freely branched shrubs 5 or 6 ft. high, such as *Hypericum* Hidcote. All are easily grown in any reasonably good soil, and in sun or shade. The Rose of Sharon, which is evergreen, has a particular liking for limy soils and can be used both to cover hot, sunny banks and as a carpet beneath other shrubs and trees.

Hypericum Hidcote retains many of its leaves in winter. *H. patulum*, which is 3 to 4 ft. high and has slightly smaller, more cup-shaped flowers, is deciduous. *H. moserianum* is only 18 in. high, but is spreading and useful for the front of a border.

Hypericums do not require any pruning, but can be thinned or reduced in size if desired in March or April. The Rose of Sharon can be clipped with shears at the same period to keep it neat and within bounds.

All can be increased by summer cuttings, and the Rose of Sharon can also be very easily increased by separating off rooted pieces at any time between October and March.

hypericum

The Rose of Sharon, *Hypericum calycinum*, is a splendid ground-cover plant for sun or shade, even under trees and other shrubs. An evergreen, it does not grow more than 18 in. tall

Kalmia, Pieris

Both kalmia and pieris are evergreen shrubs which dislike lime and grow best in loamy or peaty soils in partial shade.

Kalmia latifolia, sometimes known as the Calico Bush, makes a well-branched, rounded bush eventually 6 ft. or more high, but it is very slow growing. It has bright pink flowers, shaped like little Chinese lanterns, which appear in June. It needs no regular pruning, enjoys a topdressing of peat each spring, and does not like being dried out in summer.

There are several different kinds of pieris, all known as the lily of the valley bush, because the little sprays of white, urn-shaped flowers in spring look rather like those of lily of the valley. *Pieris japonica*, 6 to 8 ft. high, is one of the easiest to grow and best in flower, but *P. forrestii* Wakehurst Variety has magnificent rose and scarlet young growth.

Both kalmia and pieris are better unpruned, but if overgrown they can be cut back in spring, though this means sacrificing the flowers for one year. They can both be increased by layering in spring.

Kalmia latifolia

Pieris forrestii

Lavender, Rosemary

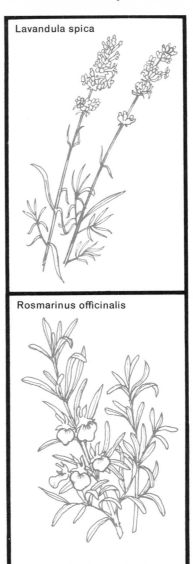
Lavandula spica

Rosmarinus officinalis

Both lavender and rosemary are very popular for their fragrance, as well as for their distinctive evergreen foliage and blue flowers.

Lavender delights in warm, sunny places and limy soils, though it can be grown in almost any reasonably well-drained soil. The flowers appear in July and can be picked and dried for filling sachets and making potpourri if desired. In any case, bushes should be clipped over in August or September to keep them neat. *Lavandula spica*, 3 ft. high with lavender blue flowers, is the Old English Lavender. Good varieties include Hidcote, 1 ft. high, deep purple, and Twickle Purple, 3 ft. high, purple. All have gray leaves.

Rosemary (*Rosmarinus officinalis*) has narrow, shining, dark leaves, and makes a bush about 4 ft. tall. The lavender-blue flowers start to open in winter and are at their best in May. *R.o.* Tuscan Blue has deeper blue flowers; *R. o. humilis*, also known as *R.o. prostratus*, is sprawling and will hang down over a wall, but needs a sunny, sheltered place as it is rather easily damaged by frost.

Bushes may be trimmed to shape after flowering. Both lavender and rosemary are readily increased by summer cuttings.

The individual flowers of *Kalmia latifolia*, the Calico Bush, resemble small Chinese lanterns. This is one of the most beautiful of the early summer-flowering evergreens but it requires lime-free soil

Especially strong coloring is a characteristic of Hidcote, a dwarf lavender which seldom exceeds 1 ft. in height. It makes a splendid edging and can be trimmed after flowering

Leycesteria, Rubus

Leycesteria formosa is popularly known as Himalayan Honeysuckle, though it does not come from the Himalayas or even look like a honeysuckle. It makes a thicket of long, rather soft green stems, hanging out short trails of claret purple and white flowers in summer, succeeded by dark purple berries. It will grow almost anywhere, in sun or shade, and in rich soil may reach a height of 7 or 8 ft. The older stems should be cut right out each March, leaving only the best young stems for flowering.

Rubus is the general name for the brambles, including the blackberry and loganberry. For decorative purposes there are several fine kinds, such as *Rubus* Tridel, a loose bush with long, canelike stems bearing large white flowers in May and June; *R. odoratus*, making a 7-ft. thicket of tangled stems bearing light magenta flowers from June to August; and *R. ulmifolius bellidiflorus*, like a blackberry with fully double pink flowers resembling little pompons in July and August. The Whitewash Bramble, *R. cockburnianus*, is so called because its long stems are white.

All will grow in any reasonably good soil and open or partially shaded position. Flowering stems should be cut out as soon as the last flowers fade.

Lilacs

Everyone loves the Common Lilac (*Syringa vulgaris*), which blooms in May and fills the air with its pleasant fragrance. It is a deciduous shrub or small tree, eventually growing 12 to 15 ft. high, though it can be kept smaller by thinning out older branches in autumn or winter. It will grow practically anywhere, but enjoys good, well-cultivated soil, which encourages the production of fine flower trusses. So does the regular removal of the faded flowers, though this may be difficult on large bushes.

Syringa persica, the Persian Lilac, is another species with particularly fragrant flowers. It forms a smaller bush than the Common Lilac, reaching 6 ft., and bears small sprays of lavender flowers in May.

There are a number of improved garden varieties with larger flowers, double in some, and in a range of colors from white to deep purple. Recommended varieties are: Charles Joly, double purple; Charles X, single purple; Katherine Havemayer, double mauve; Maud Notcutt, single white; Michael Buchner, double rosy lilac; Madame Lemoine, double white; and Primrose, single primrose yellow.

These garden varieties are often grafted on Common Lilac and then all suckers (shoots growing direct from the roots) should be removed.

Lilacs can also be increased by layering, in which case suckers will be of the same variety as the bush and can be retained or dug up with roots and planted elsewhere.

Leycesteria formosa

Rubus ulmifolius bellidiflorus

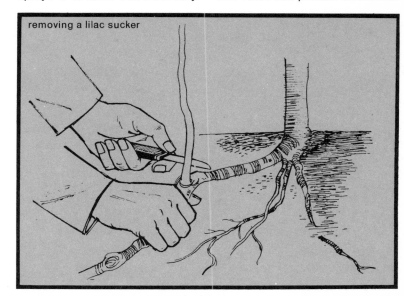

removing a lilac sucker

Leycesteria formosa can be killed to ground level during a hard winter, but in the spring it will shoot up again from the base like a herbaceous plant. The flowers are followed by dark purple berries. Suitable for U.S. Zone 7

There are a great many varieties of the fragrant Common Lilac, *Syringa vulgaris*, some single, some double flowered. This one is Clark's Giant, which has extra-large single flowers

53

Mahonia, Magnolia

Mahonias are evergreen shrubs with shining prickly leaves and clusters or sprays of yellow flowers in late winter and spring. They will grow almost anywhere in sun or shade, but for best results they should be grown in good, well-cultivated soil.

Mahonia aquifolium (the second name means "holly leaved") is 3 ft. high, flowers from February to April and often carries a good crop of purple berries afterwards. *M. japonica* is 5 ft. or more high and has long trails of lemon yellow, scented flowers in February and March. *M. repens*, the Creeping Barberry, is 1 ft. high, spreading and excellent for covering and binding a bank. Regular pruning is not necessary but all can be thinned or trimmed after flowering.

The only truly shrubby magnolia is *M. stellata*, an open, well-branched bush 8 to 10 ft. high. The white flowers, produced very freely in March and April, have narrower petals than the flowers of the tree magnolias. It likes a loamy or peaty soil, without lime, and a sunny sheltered position, for though quite hardy, the flowers may be damaged by frost. No pruning is required. Increase by layering after flowering.

Magnolia stellata

Handsome evergreen leaves and bold flower spikes make the choice *Mahonia lomariifolia* a splendid shrub for a prominent but sheltered position. The flowers appear in winter and early spring. Suitable for U.S. Zone 10

Olearia, Osmanthus

Olearias are evergreens, sometimes known as daisy bushes, because they have small, daisylike flowers usually very freely produced. The most generally useful is *Olearia haastii*, a shapely bush 6 ft. or more high with neat, rounded leaves and white flowers in July and August. It will grow practically anywhere and is a first-rate town shrub.

Olearia stellulata, 4 ft. high, with grayish leaves and white flowers in May, is even more decorative but less hardy. It succeeds well near the sea and inland in well-drained soil and sunny, sheltered places. *Olearia macrodonta* has large, hollylike leaves, grows 10 ft. or more high, and has large clusters of flowers in June and July, but is suitable only for milder areas.

Osmanthus delavayi (also known as *Siphonosmanthus delavayi*) is a densely branched evergreen, 8 ft. or more high, with small, dark green leaves and, in April, little white tubular flowers which are extremely fragrant. It will grow in any reasonably good, well-cultivated soil and sunny or partially shaded position.

Both olearias and osmanthus can be thinned or lightly cut back after flowering. They are increased by summer cuttings.

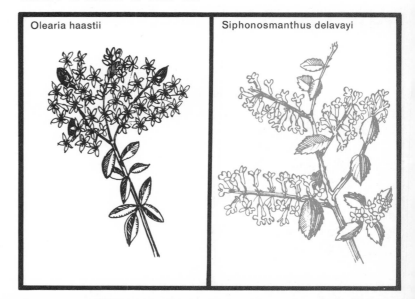

Olearia haastii

Siphonosmanthus delavayi

The small tube-shaped flowers of *Osmanthus delavayi* are produced in clusters in April and are intensely fragrant. It is a very bushy shrub with shining, neat evergreen leaves

Pernettya, Skimmia

Pernettya mucronata is an ever-green shrub making a dense 3-ft. thicket of growth slowly spreading by suckers. It has neat, dark green leaves, little bell-shaped white flowers mostly in May and June, followed by showy berries in a wide range of colors from white to plum purple with some remark-able shades of lilac and rose.

It likes a loamy or peaty soil without lime, and will grow in sunny or shady places. It needs no pruning and can be increased by digging out rooted suckers in autumn. Davis's Hybrids give all the colors and are self-fertilizing, though some other varieties need a male bush as a pollinator since male and female flowers are borne on separate bushes.

Skimmias are also evergreen and berry bearing, but the berries are always scarlet. They also dis-like lime, grow well in loamy or peaty soils in sun or shade. *Skimmia japonica*, 2 to 3 ft. high, with little spikes of white, fragrant flowers in May and June, bears male and female flowers on separate bushes. One male bush is sufficient to pollinate several females, if planted within a few yards. Only the female bushes produce berries, but the males have the best flowers. *Skimmia foremanii* is self-fertile, with flowers of both sexes growing on the same bush. Neither variety needs pruning and both can be increased by summer cuttings.

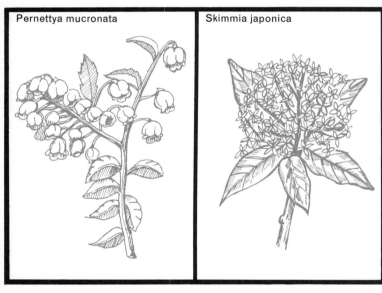

Pernettya mucronata   Skimmia japonica

Philadelphus

Philadelphus Sybille

Philadelphus Virginal

Philadelphuses are the shrubs which many people wrongly call syringas, a name that really be-longs to the lilacs. All kinds of philadelphus are deciduous and have mainly white flowers which are often very sweetly scented. They look and smell like orange blossom, and for this reason are known as Mock Oranges.

All are deciduous, flowering in June and July. They will grow almost anywhere, but flower more freely in open, sunny places than in shade. Some make very large shrubs but all can be reduced in size by pruning just as soon as the flowers fade, when the old flowering branches can be cut right out and only the best shoots or stems retained to flower the following year.

Two of the most heavily scented Mock Oranges are *Philadelphus coronarius*, with small, creamy-white flowers, and *P. delavayi*, white and purple, tall. *P. micro-phyllus* is also richly scented, with dainty flowers and small leaves. The most showy are the garden varieties, such as Beauclerk with large, single, white flowers each with a flush of purple in the center; Belle Etoile, with a more pro-nounced purple flush; Sybille, similar to Belle Etoile in flower but a smaller bush; and Virginal with large, double, white flowers. *P. microphyllus* and Sybille are 3 ft. high—the rest 6 to 8 ft.

All can be readily increased by summer or autumn cuttings.

Pernettya mucronata is a handsome evergreen shrub with small white flowers in May. These are followed by showy berries in a variety of colors including pink, puce, crimson, purple, and white

Belle Etoile, one of the many varieties of philadelphus, or Mock Orange. All have white or cream flowers, sometimes, as in this variety, with a purple blotch and many are very fragrant

Phlomis, Senecio

Phlomis fruticosa, called Jerusalem Sage, grows wild in eastern Mediterranean countries and has gray, sagelike leaves. Its whorls of hooded, bright yellow flowers are very decorative in June and July. It grows about 3 ft. high, and has rather soft stems which are sometimes damaged by winter frost. Bushes should be trimmed back a little each April to keep them tidy and get rid of damaged growth.

Senecio laxifolius also has rather soft stems and gray, rounded leaves, more leathery than those of the Jerusalem Sage. It grows 3 to 4 ft. high and produces sprays of bright yellow, daisy-type flowers in June and July. Like the Jerusalem Sage, it can be damaged by winter frost, but may be pruned in the same way.

Both shrubs like well-drained soils and warm, sunny places, and are a good choice for hot, dry borders and banks. Their soft, gray leaves contrast well with the various shades of green that tend to dominate shrub borders, and, being evergreen, they will continue to furnish the garden during the winter.

They can both be increased by summer cuttings.

Potentillas

Potentillas, also known as shrubby cinquefoils, are especially valuable because they are relatively small, compact shrubs which flower all through the summer. They will grow in any reasonably well-drained soil and prefer open, sunny places. All can be pruned each March when either some of the older stems can be removed to thin the bushes, or all stems can be cut to within a few inches of the ground, which will result in a smaller bush and larger flowers. All can be increased by summer cuttings.

There are a number of good varieties all derived from *Potentilla fruticosa*, which is deciduous, has small, deeply divided leaves and strawberry-type flowers. The variety Maanley's (Moonlight) have light yellow flowers; Katherine Dykes is deep yellow, 3 to 4 ft. high and similar in diameter; Tangerine has coppery orange flowers, is 1 ft. high, but may spread over several feet; *vilminiana* has silvery leaves and white flowers; and *beesii* has silvery leaves and yellow flowers. There are several other varieties, all in the same color range.

Phlomis fruticosa | Senecio laxifolius

shrubby cinquefoil

Senecio laxifolius is a wide-spreading evergreen shrub and it has abundant daisylike flowers in midsummer. Care should be taken not to let the soil get waterlogged in winter. Suitable for U.S. Zone 10

Potentilla fruticosa, the Shrubby Cinquefoil. These deciduous shrubs are valuable for their compact habit and long flowering season from early summer to autumn

Pyracanthas

The pyracanthas are known as fire thorns, because of their abundant crop of flaming red berries in autumn and winter. All are strong-growing shrubs with dark green, shiny, evergreen leaves and clusters of white flowers in June. They are often trained against walls, but will grow equally well in the open where they will make fine bushes 6 to 8 ft. high and through, though they can be kept smaller by pruning after flowering. When they are trained on walls, some pruning is usually required to keep them tidy. Overgrown or badly placed stems are cut out as far as possible without removing the clusters of young berries which will then be just forming.

Fire thorns will grow practically anywhere, in sun or shade, and in any reasonably good soil. They can be increased by seed or from summer cuttings, but seedlings may take several years to attain flowering and berry-bearing size.

Recommended kinds are: *Pyracantha coccinea lalandii*, with quite large, orange red berries; *P. atalantioides* (also known as *P. gibbsii*) with smaller, deeper red berries and *P.* Waterer's Orange with orange yellow berries. Birds may strip the berries in winter, but often leave those of *P. atalantioides*.

Japanese Quince

The Japanese Quince may appear in nurserymen's catalogues either as chaenomeles or cydonia, and is often known by gardeners simply as japonica. Typically it is a freely branched, suckering, deciduous shrub, 3 to 5 ft. high, and of almost any width, with scarlet flowers in spring, followed by large fruits (quinces) in late summer. It is commonly trained against walls where it may be in flower by March where climate permits, but it can equally well be grown as a bush in the open.

In addition to the common scarlet-flowered chaenomeles there are others with white, pink, orange, or crimson flowers. Recommended varieties are: Knap Hill Scarlet, scarlet; Nivalis, white; Apple Blossom (also known as *moerloesii*) blush pink; and *simonii*, crimson.

All may be grown in any reasonably good soil and in sun or shade. Cut out some of the older stems after flowering each year to prevent overcrowding, and, when grown against a wall, shorten side growths in June and main stems in August as necessary to fill the available space. Wires or trellis-work should be used to tie shoots to as they do not climb naturally.

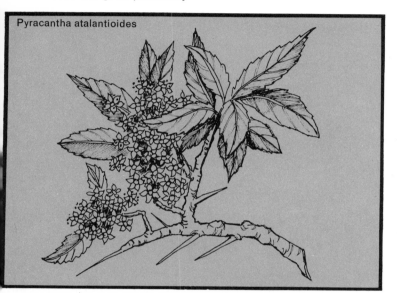

Pyracantha atalantioides

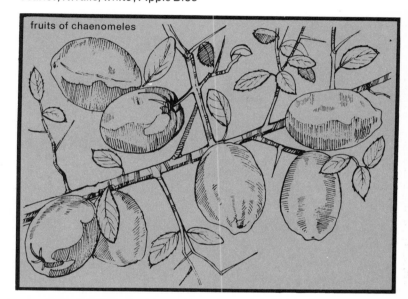

fruits of chaenomeles

Pyracanthas are popularly known as fire thorns and they make very attractive wall shrubs. They will also grow equally well as bushes in the open in sun or shade

Chaenomeles superba Knap Hill Scarlet will flower very early in the year when it is trained against a wall. It can also be grown as a bush but it is not evergreen

Rhododendrons

At the height of their flowering season in May and early June, rhododendrons are the most spectacular of all flowering shrubs, and for sheer display none surpass the group of varieties known as Hardy Hybrids. These are also the easiest to grow, for, as their name implies, they are quite hardy, and will thrive in sun or shade and in almost any soil that is not limy. If lime is present, they can be grown in specially prepared beds of lime-free loam and peat and will benefit from annual spring feeding with iron and manganese chelates.

All hardy hybrid rhododendrons are evergreen and make dome-shaped shrubs eventually 6 to 10 ft. high and as much through. Pruning is not necessary, but over-grown bushes can be cut back in spring, one year's flowers being sacrificed.

Rhododendrons transplant easily and even quite large bushes can be moved in autumn. All benefit from an annual spring topdressing of peat or leaf mold.

Recommended varieties are: Gomer Waterer, blush white and gold; Loder's White; Mother of Pearl, blush turning white; Mrs. Furnival, rose and maroon; Pink Pearl, rose pink; Sappho, white and maroon; Windbeam, prolific flowering, white suffused with pink, semi-dwarf; Mrs. Charles S. Sargent, rich carmine rose spotted yellow, and excellent for cold areas; Boule de Neige, flowers white, foliage handsome; Roseum Elegans, lavender pink, strong and hardy; Nova Zembla, red flowers; Ramapo, low and spreading, flowers violet blue, small, very hardy.

In addition to the hardy hybrid rhododendrons there are a great many other kinds which are excellent garden shrubs, all evergreen and all disliking lime. They succeed best in loamy or peaty soils and though some will grow in full sun most prefer a partially shaded place. Many are first-class shrubs for planting in thin woodland.

There are a great many varieties, of which the following are representative: *R. augustinii*, light blue, 6 to 8 ft.; Blue Diamond, lavender blue, 4 ft.; *R. impeditum*, deep blue, 1 ft., suitable for a rock garden; Loderi, white to pale pink, very large, fragrant flowers, 8 ft. or more; Naomi, various shades of lilac pink and greenish yellow, 8 ft. or more; *R. racemosum*, small rose pink flowers, 3 ft.; *R. williamsianum*, bell-shaped, pale pink flowers, 1½ ft.

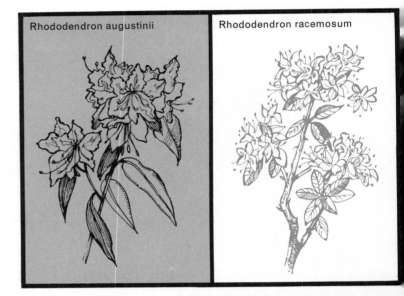

Rhododendron augustinii

Rhododendron racemosum

The hardy hybrid rhododendrons are a natural choice for rather more spacious lime-free gardens. Shown above is *Rhododendron fastuosum flore pleno*, one of the few double-flowered varieties

Rhododendron Blue Diamond is one of many good small varieties. It is slow-growing, compact shrub, and is seen here in front of *Berberis darwinii* and one of the taller red rhododendrons

Rhus, Tamarix

There are several kinds of rhus, all deciduous. *Rhus typhina*, the Staghorn Sumac, is a very open-branched shrub or small tree, 10 or 12 ft. high, with long, divided, fernlike leaves and curious erect spikes of crimson flowers in late summer. The leaves color brilliantly before they fall in autumn. *Cotinus coggygria (Rhus cotinus)* is a big bush with rounded leaves and tangled masses of silky filaments around the tiny flowers, which gives it the popular names Smoke Tree and Wig Tree. A variety named *atropurpureus* has purple leaves. Rhus enjoy good, well-drained soil and sunny places. They can be increased by digging out rooted suckers in autumn.

There are also several different kinds of tamarix, or tamarisk, which is the popular version of the name, but all are deciduous shrubs with thin, whippy branches set with tiny leaves and with very small but numerous pink or white flowers, the whole effect being very light and feathery. They grow well in light, sandy soils and open places and are first-rate seaside shrubs able to withstand the worst gales. The most beautiful kind is *Tamarix pentandra*, 6 ft. or more high, with rosy pink flowers in July and August. It can be cut hard back each March if desired, and increased by summer or autumn cuttings.

Cotinus coggygria

Tamarix pentandra

Rhus typhina laciniata, a cut-leaved variety of the Staghorn Sumac, is an extremely attractive small tree for the garden. The rich autumn coloring of the leaves makes it especially beautiful

Spiraeas

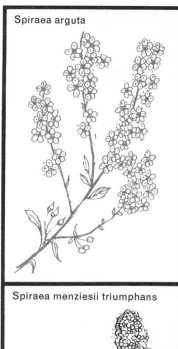

Spiraea arguta

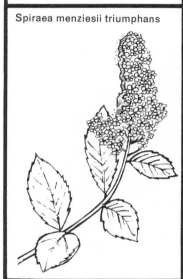

Spiraea menziesii triumphans

Most spiraeas are elegant, deciduous shrubs with slender, often arching branches and numerous small flowers either in clusters or scattered over the stems. All will grow in practically any soil and in sun or shade. Pruning is not essential but overgrown bushes can be thinned in March, and the late-flowering kinds, such as Anthony Waterer, can be cut almost to ground level at this time, thus reducing their size and improving the quality of the flowers.

Some kinds sucker freely and suckers may have to be dug out if they extend too far. They can be replanted elsewhere if desired. Spiraeas can also be increased by summer or autumn cuttings.

Spiraea thunbergii and *S. arguta* flower in spring and are 4 ft. high. *S. prunifolia plena* flowers in May and has double flowers, *S. vanhouttei* flowers at the same time and has single flowers. Both are about 6 ft. high. So is *S. cantoniensis flore pleno* with double flowers in June. *S. veitchii* is also June flowering and 9 to 12 ft. high. All the foregoing have white flowers.

S. menziesii triumphans has fluffy spikes of rose flowers in July and August and makes a 6-ft. thicket. Far better for small gardens is *S. bumalda* Anthony Waterer, only 3 ft. high, with cream-splashed leaves and flat heads of deep carmine flowers. This is an outstandingly good shrub.

Anthony Waterer is the best variety of *Spiraea bumalda*, a low-growing but rather spreading shrub with variegated young leaves to complement the carmine flowers

Viburnums

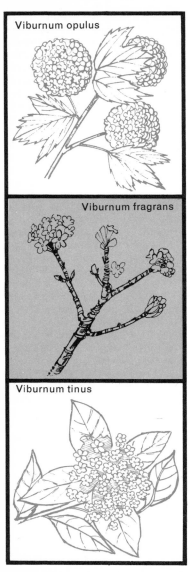

Viburnum opulus

Viburnum fragrans

Viburnum tinus

There are a lot of viburnums and they are nearly all good, easily grown garden shrubs. One, *Viburnum opulus*, grows wild in Western Europe and is known as the Guelder Rose. It is very beautiful, especially when covered with shining, scarlet berries in the autumn, and there is a shorter variety of it called *compactum* which is a better garden plant. Another variety, *V. o. sterile*, has large round clusters of white flowers in late May and early June and is known as the Snowball Tree.

The Japanese Snowball Tree, *Viburnum tomentosum plicatum*, has smaller but more numerous flower clusters, and *V. t. mariesii* has flat clusters of white flowers all along its branches in May. *V. fragrans* has very fragrant clusters of pinkish white flowers in winter and is 7 or 8 ft. high. *V. carlesii* is even more fragrant, only 4 ft. high, and flowers in April and May. All the foregoing are deciduous.

The Laurustinus, *Viburnum tinus*, is evergreen and carries its white and pink flowers from November to April. It makes a big, dense bush 6 to 8 ft. tall. All these viburnums can be grown in any reasonably good soil and in sun or shade. They need no pruning, but if they get too large, can be thinned or cut back in March.

Weigelas

Weigelas were formerly called diervillas. They are all fairly large, deciduous bushes with long arching stems wreathed in little trumpet-shaped pink or crimson flowers in early summer. They will grow practically anywhere, but flower best in open, sunny places. They can be pruned immediately after flowering when all stems that have just carried flowers are cut out, but young, nonflowering stems are kept to flower the following year. This reduces the size of the bushes and improves the quality of the flowers. All can be increased by summer or autumn cuttings.

Weigela florida, 6 to 8 ft. high, with rose-pink flowers is the common kind. It has an excellent variety named *variegata*, with paler pink flowers and leaves broadly edged with cream.

There are also a number of good garden varieties. Abel Carrière has large pink flowers; Bristol Ruby is ruby red; Eva Rathke is crimson and more compact than most; Newport Red is deep carmine and Styriaca has small, deep rose flowers, very freely produced. There is also a variety called *looymansii aurea* with rosy pink flowers and light golden leaves.

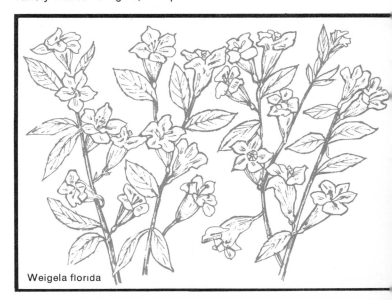

Weigela florida

Spectacular layers of flowers, raised tier on tier, are the glory of *Viburnum tomentosum mariesii*. These appear in May and have their perfect foil in the fresh green foliage

Abel Carrière is one of numerous attractive varieties of weigela. All are easily grown shrubs flowering in early summer. They can be pruned immediately after flowering

Winter Sweet, Witch Hazel

The Winter Sweet, *Chimonanthus praecox*, flowers in midwinter. The pale primrose and purple flowers are not at all showy, but they are very fragrant and scent the air for a considerable distance. The Winter Sweet is a deciduous, open-branched shrub about 8 ft. high. It likes a good, well-cultivated and well-drained soil, and sheltered position as it is not very hardy. It can be trained against a wall, in which case surplus growth can be cut out immediately after flowering.

There are several kinds of witch hazel, or hamamelis, and they too are all deciduous and flower in winter. The most popular is *Hamamelis mollis* with spidery, deep yellow, sweetly scented flowers. It makes a big, loosely branched bush 8 ft. or more in height, but it can be pruned moderately each March to keep it within bounds. A variety named *pallida* has larger primrose yellow flowers. *Hamamelis japonica* makes an even bigger bush or small tree, with smaller, yellow flowers. It has several varieties: *arborea* with yellow and purple flowers; *rubra* with orange and purple flowers; and *zuccariniana* with lemon yellow flowers. *H. intermedia* is an attractive hybrid of *H. mollis* and *H. japonica*.

Both Winter Sweet and witch hazels are best increased by layering in spring or early summer.

Chimonanthus praecox

Hamamelis mollis

Yuccas

Yucca filamentosa

There are no better shrubs than yuccas to impart a subtropical look to a garden, for, though several kinds are reasonably hardy, their large rosettes of stiff, sword-shaped evergreen leaves have a highly exotic appearance.

Yuccas enjoy light, well-drained soils and warm, sunny positions, but may often be seen growing in most unlikely places, even in grimy industrial areas. The creamy white cup-shaped flowers are borne in summer in long, erect spikes and add to the unusual appearance of the plant. It is widely believed that the flowers are only produced at intervals of many years, but this is untrue as plants in good health will flower annually. No pruning is required, but the faded flower spikes should be cut out.

Yucca filamentosa has rosettes 2 or 3 ft. high with 3- to 4-ft. flower spikes in August. *Y. flaccida* is very similar, but the leaves are less stiff. *Y. gloriosa*, also known as Adam's Needle, is the largest, and will, after a few years, make a distinct main trunk several feet high surmounted by large rosettes of leaves and with rather broad 4-ft. flower spikes in August.

Yuccas are increased by offsets and by root cuttings.

Hamamelis intermedia is an attractive hybrid witch hazel. The hazellike foliage takes on fine autumnal tints, and the yellow flowers follow on bare stems. *Gentiana sino-ornata* can be seen below

Stiff, sword-shaped leaves and stout spikes of cupped flowers make *Yucca flaccida* an interesting evergreen shrub. It is especially happy in seaside gardens because of the milder conditions there

Climbing and Screening Plants

Preparing and Planting

Since most climbers will remain undisturbed in the same place for many years the soil should be well cultivated before they are planted. Dig or fork it thoroughly, remove all perennial weeds, and work in some well-rotted manure or decayed garden refuse. Complete this preparation with a good dusting of bonemeal, or meat or fish meal, or a combination of these before planting.

The general principles of planting climbers are the same as those for any other plants, but there are a few points which apply particularly to climbers, especially when planted against walls or fences. Because the soil near a screen is sheltered from rain it is usually dry and so climbers should be planted a foot or so away from the wall, not hard up against it. If during planting it is inclined slightly toward the wall, it will be easy to tie the plant to the supports provided and this should be done immediately.

Many climbers are supplied in pots or other containers. When planting out remove the container completely, but do not attempt to unravel or otherwise disturb the roots. Work a little moist peat around the ball of soil, make firm, and keep well watered for the first few weeks if the weather should be dry.

If lawns and the shorter annuals and bedding plants may be likened to the carpet, rugs, and other floor coverings of rooms, climbers may be equated with wallpaper, curtains, and pictures. They fulfill an essential part in the furnishing of a well-organized garden and can even play a dominant role in determining its character. It is quite possible, even in the very limited space of a town garden, to create an air of junglelike profusion by the lavish use of vigorous climbers.

Climbers are of many different kinds. They may be shrubby, with more or less permanent woody stems, as in honeysuckle, roses, and wisteria; herbaceous perennial with soft stems dying to ground level each winter, as in Everlasting Pea and Golden-leaved Hop, or annual, completing their growth in one season and then dying, as in nasturtium and sweet pea.

Like other plants, climbers may be evergreen or deciduous and they may be grown primarily for their flowers, for their fruits, or for their foliage. Some kinds are tender but it may be possible to grow these against sheltered walls.

Methods of climbing also vary greatly. Some kinds, such as honeysuckle and Russian Vine, twine themselves around anything available, even quite large objects such as trunks of trees. Others, such as clematis and sweet pea, climb by tendrils which cling most readily to string, wire, or trelliswork. Yet others, such as ivy and ampelopsis, will attach themselves securely to walls and other smooth surfaces by means of aerial roots or adhesive discs.

Roses and various brambles sprawl through other plants and gain some support from their thorns. There are also shrubs, such as pyracantha (fire thorn), ceanothus, Japanese quince, and Fishbone Cotoneaster (*Cotoneaster horizontalis*), which can readily be trained against walls and, by reason of their stiff stems, are almost self-supporting. All the same, trellis or wires can greatly facilitate the training of such plants, since young growths have a natural tendency to grow forward away from the wall or fence and they can then be drawn back toward it. All such supports should be fixed an inch or so away from the wall so that the growth, tendrils, and ties can easily go round them.

When climbers are being selected for planting against houses or high walls, the direction which they will face must be considered since climbers on north-facing walls will get little direct sunshine, those on some south-facing walls may get too much, and those on east-facing walls may be exposed to cold winds. The problem hardly arises with fences since plants quickly rise above them. The soil close to house walls can be dry, and until climbers become established they may need regular watering.

Humulus lupulus aureus, the Golden-leaved Hop. This is a herbaceous perennial climber which grows very rapidly and is valued for its attractive foliage in summer

Arches and Pergolas

Many climbers grow well on arches and pergolas, which are a continuous linked string of arches covering the path or terrace in a cloister-like manner. Climbing roses, in particular, benefit from the free circulation of air they get when growing in this manner instead of against a wall or fence, but since arches and pergolas afford little or no protection from cold they are not so suitable for the more tender climbers such as solanums and passionflowers (passifloras).

Be sure that all such structures are sufficiently strong and durable to take the very considerable weight of growth they may eventually have to bear. Timber 4 in. square is the minimum size for uprights, and for large structures brick or block supports may be preferred. Cross members should be a minimum of 4 × 2-in. timber, more for structures over 6 ft. wide.

If uprights are bedded in concrete, bring the level of the concrete base above the ground and finish it off with a bevel to run off water. Treat all wood, whether in or out of the ground, with a good preservative which is harmless to plants. Creosote is not suitable because of the scorching fumes it can give off.

Ampelopsis and Others

Ampelopsis, vines, and Virginia Creeper are closely related plants and at different times they have been given different names so that it is sometimes hard to distinguish them in nursery catalogues. What most people call ampelopsis has leaves with three lobes, whereas the Virginia Creeper has leaves which are composed of five separate leaflets. Both cling to walls, fences, and trees by little suckers on their tendrils and both turn crimson before their leaves fall in autumn. The correct names of these two fine plants are *Parthenocissus tricuspidata* and *P. quinquefolia* respectively, but they may be listed as *Ampelopsis* (or *Vitis*) *inconstans* and *A.* (or *V.*) *quinquefolia*.

The Grape Vine, or *Vitis vinifera*, also has several good ornamental varieties, such as *purpurea* with reddish purple leaves and Brandt with leaves which turn crimson in the autumn. Like other vines, they climb by tendrils, not by suckers. So does *Vitis coignetiae* with large, rounded leaves that turn scarlet and crimson in the autumn. It is very vigorous.

All these climbers will grow in any reasonably good soil in sun or shade, but will color best in the sun. If they grow too vigorously they can be thinned or cut back after the leaves fall in the autumn.

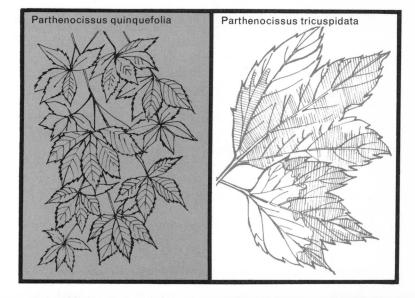

Parthenocissus quinquefolia

Parthenocissus tricuspidata

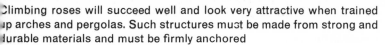
Climbing roses will succeed well and look very attractive when trained up arches and pergolas. Such structures must be made from strong and durable materials and must be firmly anchored

The self-clinging ampelopsis (Boston Ivy, in U.S.), *Parthenocissus tricuspidata*, will quickly cover a wall with a dense network of slender growths bearing handsome green leaves. These change to shades of scarlet and crimson before they fall in autumn

Akebia and Others

Akebia, celastrus, and polygonum are all very vigorous, hardy climbers that may be used to clothe unsightly objects quickly. Akebia makes many slender stems clothed in leaves composed of three or five separate leaflets, giving it an attractive appearance. The little, deep maroon flowers are curious rather than beautiful, but in sunny, sheltered places they may be followed by cylindrical, violet-colored fruits.

Celastrus is less attractive in leaf, but it can produce big crops of small yellow and scarlet fruits in autumn. It is important to buy the hermaphrodite form of this plant as other forms may be male or female and will bear no fruits unless two of different sexes are planted. The hermaphrodite has male and female flowers on the same plant.

The climbing polygonum (*P. baldschuanicum*) is often known as Russian Vine. Few climbers grow so fast and it will soon cover a large outdoor building or go to the top of a tall tree. From July to October it produces cascades of small, creamy white or pinkish white flowers.

All these climbers will grow in any reasonably good soil, the celastrus and polygonum in any location, but the akebias in a sunny place. If they grow too far they can be thinned or shortened in March or April.

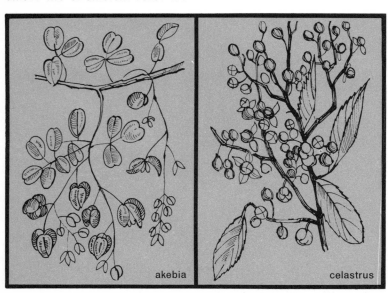
akebia   celastrus

Polygonum baldschuanicum, the Russian Vine, grows very quickly and from July to October is covered with cascades of small cream flowers. It will thrive in any reasonably good soil and in sun or shade

Clematis

Clematis alpina

Clematis montana

Clematis tangutica

Clematis are among the most valuable of garden climbers because there are a great many varieties differing in vigor of growth, time of flowering, and the size and color of their blooms. In consequence something can be selected for almost every purpose.

Clematis may be broadly divided into small-flowered kinds, many of which are wild plants introduced to gardens, and large-flowered kinds, most of which are hybrids produced in gardens.

Of the small-flowered species, *Clematis armandii* is one of the first to flower, opening its clusters of small white flowers in late March and continuing throughout April. The leaves are evergreen.

Clematis alpina and *C. macropetala* both have little nodding bell-shaped blue or soft mauve-pink flowers in April and May.

Clematis montana has masses of small white or pink flowers in May. It is one of the most vigorous of all clematis, but can be kept in check by shortening side growths in early August.

Clematis viticella has medium-size purple or red flowers in July and August. There are several varieties of it, all very showy.

Clematis tangutica and *C. orientalis* have small yellow flowers from August to October.

There are many varieties of clematis, differing in vigor of growth, time of flowering, size, and color. *Clematis montana rubens* has a mass of pale pink blooms in May

The large-flowered clematis are divided into several groups according to their parentage. These groups are *florida*, flowering mainly in May and June; *jackmanii*, flowering mainly in July and August; *lanuginosa*, flowering at different times between June and August; *patens*, flowering mainly in May and June; *taxensis*, flowering mainly from July to September and *viticella*, also flowering mainly from July to September.

There are numerous varieties in each group and the following are representative:

C. florida: Belle of Woking, double-flowered, mauve; Duchess of Edinburgh, double-flowered, white.

C. jackmanii: Comtesse de Bou-chaud, soft pink; Gipsy Queen, violet purple; *superba*, deep violet-purple; Perle d'Azur, pale blue; Star of India, violet and red.

C. lanuginosa: Beauty of Worcester, violet blue with some double flowers; *henryi*, white; Lady Northcliffe, lavender; Mrs. Cholmondeley, light blue; William Kennett, deep lavender.

C. patens: Barbara Jackman, petunia purple; Lasurstern, purple blue; Nellie Moser, mauve and carmine.

C. texensis: Gravetye Beauty, red.

C. viticella: Ernest Markham, petunia red; Huldine, pearly white and mauve pink; Lady Betty Balfour, violet blue; Ville de Lyon, carmine.

Clematis like good, well-cultivated and well-manured soil. They grow best with their roots shaded but their stems in the sun, which can often be done by planting them behind a low-growing shrub or leafy herbaceous plant. The less vigorous can be allowed to scramble up into climbing roses or other plants or they may be trained to wires or trellis. The vigorous kinds may be allowed to grow round trees, climb over sheds, or cover walls or fences.

All clematis can be pruned but it is sometimes rather difficult to prune the very vigorous kinds because of the tangle of growth they make. The method of pruning depends upon the group to which the clematis belongs.

Prune *Clematis alpina*, *C. macropetala*, and *C. montana* and their varieties in early August by shortening side growths to 3 or 4 in.

Prune varieties of the *florida* and *patens* groups immediately after flowering by shortening the flowering shoots to strong growth buds.

Prune varieties of the *jackmanii*, *texensis*, and *viticella* groups in February or March, by shortening to 3 or 4 in. each growth made the previous year.

Prune varieties of the *lanuginosa* group like *florida*, if early flowers are required, or like *jackmanii* for late flowering.

Retain all young growth of *C. armandii* but cut out old growth where possible after flowering.

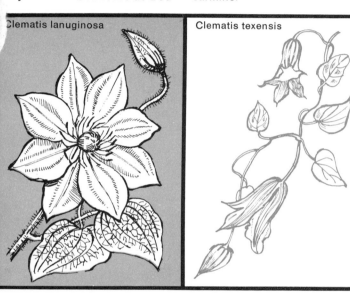
Clematis lanuginosa

Clematis texensis

Clematis macropetala

Clematis jackmanii

The large-flowered clematis are divided into several groups according to their parentage. One of these is the *viticella* group to which this variety, Ernest Markham, belongs

Clematis prefer to have their roots in the shade and their flowers and stems in the sun and they are often grown behind low-growing shrubs and herbaceous plants. This lovely variety is Countess of Lovelace

Cobaea and Others

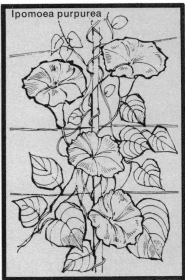
Ipomoea purpurea

Thunbergia alata

The three climbers cobaea, ipomoea, and thunbergia are often grown from seed and sometimes treated as annuals, being discarded in autumn and replaced by new seedlings in the spring.

Cobaea grows very rapidly, climbs by tendrils, and has bell-shaped, light purple or greenish white flowers in summer. Sow seed in February—March in loam and leaf mold with a scattering of sand, and later move to large pots or plant in a bed of good loamy soil. Water freely in spring and summer and do not shade. Water very sparingly in autumn and winter and protect from frost. The plants can be grown out of doors in summer from June to October.

Ipomoeas, commonly called morning glory, have blue or purple, wide, funnel-shaped flowers in summer, and climb by twining. Grow in exactly the same way as cobaea. Varieties of *Ipomoea purpurea*, such as Flying Cloud and Heavenly Blue, are annuals but *Ipomoea leari* is a perennial.

Thunbergia alata is a twining plant with white, buff, or orange black-centered flowers, for which reason it is known as Black-eyed Susan. It can be grown in the same way as cobaea, but it is much less rampant and can be used in hanging baskets. It is best treated as an annual and discarded each year after flowering.

Honeysuckles

The botanical name of honeysuckle is lonicera and it is under this that the various kinds of honeysuckle will be found in most nursery catalogues.

Honeysuckles enjoy good, well-cultivated soil, but will grow in most soils either in full sun or in shade. They all climb by twining so if planted against walls they should be provided with wires or trellis for support, but no tying will be needed.

The Common Honeysuckle has two useful varieties, Early Dutch, flowering in May and June, and Late Dutch, flowering from July onward. Both are very fragrant.

The Japanese Honeysuckle (*Lonicera japonica*), also very fragrant, has smaller creamy flowers in summer. There are several useful varieties such as *aureo-reticulata* with leaves netted with yellow and *halliana* with white flowers changing to dull yellow.

The Scarlet Trumpet Honeysuckle (*Lonicera brownii*) has very showy, scarlet flowers but no scent, and neither have either *L. tellemanniana* with coppery yellow flowers or *L. tragophylla* with large, bright yellow flowers. The last two are more successful in shade than in sun, and all honeysuckles are liable to be attacked by greenflies if planted in very hot, sunny places. The remedy is to spray with a systemic insecticide.

Thunbergia alata is better known to many gardeners as Black-eyed Susan. It succeeds best when treated as an annual and it makes a splendid plant for a hanging basket

There are several beautiful species of the ever popular honeysuckle. This one is *Lonicera periclymenum belgica*, the Early Dutch variety, and it has very fragrant flowers in May and June

Hydrangeas, Solanums

There are several climbing hydrangeas which cling like ivy by means of aerial roots. One, *Hydrangea petiolaris*, has flat circular heads of little creamy white flowers surrounded by a few large ones like a lace-cap hydrangea. A second, *Schizophragma hydrangeoides*, is similar, but the flower heads are more showy. Both are deciduous, flowering in June—July. A third, *Pileostegia viburnoides*, is evergreen, flowers from August to October, and has rather fluffy-looking heads of creamy white flowers. All like good, rich, rather moist soils, and will grow in sun or shade, though pileostegia really prefers a shady place.

The climbing solanums prefer warm, sunny places and like good, well-drained soil. *Solanum jasminoides* has very slender stems that ramble a long way and slaty blue flowers (white in variety *album*) produced from July to October. It is not very hardy and can be killed by hard frost. *Solanum crispum* is tougher, and its whippy stems grow to a height of 12 or 15 ft. The heliotrope blue flowers are produced from June to September in showy clusters.

Ivies

The botanical name of ivy is hedera, and it will usually be found under this name in nursery catalogues. There are a great many varieties, differing in the shape and color of their leaves, and there are also "bush" ivies, which do not climb at all but branch out like shrubs. This is the natural habit of ivy when it flowers and bush ivies are produced by taking cuttings from the flowering growths of ordinary ivies.

Ivies climb by roots which cling to any surface. They are hardy evergreens; they will grow in sun or shade—even quite dense shade—in practically any soil, and are among the easiest of climbers to grow. They can be cut back or clipped with shears in spring, and any dirt or debris lodged in them can be brushed out.

Good varieties of the common ivy are: Buttercup, with yellow leaves; *caenwoodiana*, with small leaves; Jubilee, dark green leaves with central golden splash; Silver Queen, leaves variegated with creamy white and pink; *sagittaefolia*, leaves with narrow lobes and *tricolor*, leaves gray green, white, and rose.

Hedera colchica variegata has very large, heart-shaped green and yellow leaves. The leaves of *H. canariensis variegata* are dark green, gray green, and white.

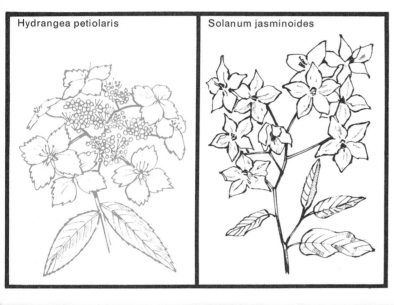

Hydrangea petiolaris | Solanum jasminoides

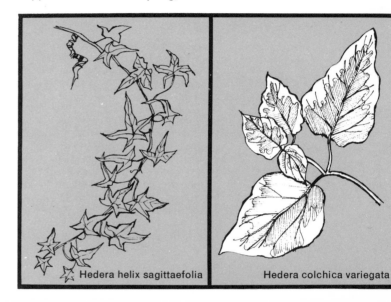

Hedera helix sagittaefolia | Hedera colchica variegata

Solanum crispum basking in the summer sun against a warm, sheltered wall. Solanums prefer a good, well-drained soil and they can be killed by a hard frost. Suitable for U.S. Zone 8

This large-leaved variegated variety of the Persian Ivy, *Hedera colchica dentata variegata*, has excellent decorative qualities. It makes a splendid cover for an old wall or tree stump

Jasmines

Jasminum polyanthum

There are two jasmines that are perfectly hardy and two others that can be grown out of doors in the mildest parts of the country and elsewhere in frostproof greenhouses. The hardy kinds are the Winter Jasmine (*Jasminum nudiflorum*) with yellow flowers on rather stiff green stems from November to February and the Summer Jasmine (*J. officinale*) with masses of white, sweetly scented flowers on thin twining stems in July and August. The two rather tender jasmines resemble these hardy ones in many respects, the Primrose Jasmine (*J. primulinum*), looking like a finer, double-flowered Winter Jasmine and *Jasminum polyanthum* being freer flowering and sweeter scented than *J. officinale*, with white flowers flushed with pink outside. The Primrose Jasmine flowers from March to May, *Jasminum polyanthum* from May to July.

All will grow in any reasonably cultivated soil. The Winter Jasmine will grow and flower equally well in sun or shade, but the others prefer sunny places. The Winter Jasmine and Primrose Jasmine must be tied to some kind of support, but the other two will twine themselves around any support, and the Summer Jasmine is especially good for covering fences or walls. Cut back the flowering stems of Winter and Primrose Jasmine when the flowers fade, and thin the others as necessary.

Nasturtium and Others

The Canary Creeper and the nasturtium are closely related, being different kinds of tropaeolum. They are annuals, useful for covering fences, walls, and sheds quickly but temporarily since they will die in the autumn after flowering.

Sow seeds of Canary Creeper (*Tropaeolum peregrinum*) in pots or pans in a warm greenhouse or frame in March; pot seedlings singly in 4-in. pots in peat-based potting mix and plant out in late May or early June in a warm, sunny place. The flowers are small, fringed, and canary yellow.

Sow seed of the Climbing Nasturtium (*Tropaeolum majus*), out of doors in April or May a few inches apart and 1 in. deep in a sunny place where the plants are to grow and thin the seedlings to 1 ft. apart. Spray the plants occasionally with insecticides to kill blackflies and caterpillars.

There is also an annual hop, *Humulus japonicus*, which is very quick growing and has attractive, light green leaves variegated with white in some varieties. This can be grown just like the Climbing Nasturtium, but the perennial hop, *Humulus lupulus*, should be planted where it can grow permanently. It is chiefly valued in gardens in its gold-leaved variety *aureus*.

Tropaeolum peregrinum

Humulus lupulus

The Winter Jasmine is a sprawling plant rather than a true climber and will need an occasional tie to keep its slender stems in position. It will grow and flower in shady places

Tropaeolum speciosum, the Flame Flower, is a slender climber with gracefully divided leaves and vividly colored flowers. It likes to grow through an evergreen shrub which will shade its roots

Wisteria

Wisterias are beautiful hardy twining plants which bear their pea-type flowers in long trails like laburnum, but usually in some shade of blue, lavender, or mauve. There are also white varieties and one rather rare pale pink wisteria. All flower in late May and early June.

Wisterias like sunny places and will grow well in most soils, though they like best a good, well-cultivated soil. They can be trained against walls or fences or over pergolas. To keep them tidy and encourage flowering, prune them in late July and shorten all the shoots made that summer to about five leaves. It is also possible to prune these shoots again in autumn to within about 2 in. of the main stems, and by this means wisterias may be grown as bushes in the open without any support.

The two most popular kinds are the very fine variety of the Japanese Wisteria (*W. floribunda*) named *macrobotrys* or *multijuga*, with trails of flowers sometimes 3 ft. long, and the Chinese Wisteria (*W. chinensis*) with shorter but very numerous trails of sweetly scented flowers. There are white-flowered varieties of both the Japanese and Chinese Wisteria, and also varieties with double, blue mauve flowers.

Woody Climbers

There are some shrubs which although not by nature climbing are readily adaptable for training against walls and fences. Of these there are numerous varieties of ceanothus, some evergreen and some deciduous, mostly with blue flowers in late spring or summer, though there are pink-flowered forms. Some are not very hardy and appreciate the protection of a sunny wall. Prune spring-flowering kinds to shape immediately after flowering, and the summer-flowering kinds in April.

The fire thorns (pyracantha) are also very popular evergreen shrubs which make excellent wall cover. They produce clusters of small white flowers in early summer followed by heavy crops of scarlet, orange red, or yellow berries in the autumn. All kinds are completely hardy and will thrive on shady as well as on sunny walls. Trim to shape in early summer when the flowering stems can be seen.

Some kinds of cotoneaster also make good wall or fence climbers, particularly the Fish-bone Cotoneaster (*C. horizontalis*), which spreads its fanlike branches against a wall to a height of 5 or 6 ft. without requiring any support or pruning. It has red berries and the leaves turn crimson in autumn.

Japanese Quinces (chaenomeles) with scarlet, crimson, pink, or white flowers in early spring also make good wall climbers and will thrive in sun or shade. Shorten misplaced shoots after flowering.

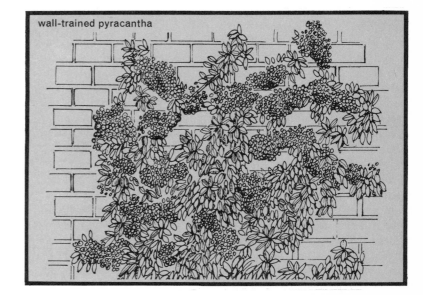

wall-trained pyracantha

In late May and June the magnificent trails of wisteria flowers are a very beautiful sight. Above is *Wisteria chinensis*, a vigorous free-flowering Chinese species

This fresh springtime scene is dominated by a magnificent wall-trained specimen of *Ceanothus impressus*. This species is the hardiest of the evergreen kinds. Suitable for U.S. Zone 7

Garden Trees

Trees can make or mar a garden. Too many of them, or unsuitable kinds, can rob the garden of light and the soil of food and moisture, making it impossible to grow anything else well. But a few well-placed and well-chosen trees can give a garden distinction and provide welcome summer shade.

Large trees, such as oak, elm, lime, poplar, beech, willow, cedar, pine, and fir, are only suitable for large gardens, but there are sometimes narrow, upright-stemmed, or fastigiate forms of large trees that can be planted in quite small gardens. Examples are the Dawyck Beech, fastigiate oak and fastigiate Tulip Tree (liriodendron). The Lombardy Poplar is a fastigiate form of the Black Poplar and its branches do not take up much room, but its roots penetrate too far to make it a good, small garden tree.

Conifers, of which cypress, cedar, juniper, fir, larch, and pine are familiar examples, differ from other trees in having narrow, sometimes needlelike leaves. Most, but not all, are evergreen. There are not many other evergreen trees, so conifers do play a rather special part in the garden, accentuated by the fact that many are conical in habit in contrast to the more rounded shapes of broad-leaved trees. Though naturally green leaved, some conifers produce varieties with leaves of different colors, usually blue gray or golden. Most conifers are allowed to branch from ground level, but other trees are often grown on a bare trunk and are known as standards.

Once trees are planted they are likely to remain for a great many years, during which time no further deep cultivation can be carried out. Initial soil preparation should therefore be thorough.

Planting holes must be of ample width and it is wise to drive a stout stake into the center of each hole. Plant so that the soil mark on the main trunk is about 1 in. below soil level. Firm the soil thoroughly around the roots and tie the main stem securely to the stake to prevent wind rocking.

Even if trees are to be grown in grass, a cultivated circle at least 4 ft. in diameter should be maintained around each for the first few years. In addition, young trees should be fed each spring as soon as the ground is warm enough with a topdressing of manure or a compound fertilizer used according to manufacturer's instructions. No ornamental tree requires regular pruning, but most will benefit from a little shaping in the early stages to maintain a good balance of growth on all sides while retaining a natural habit. Suckers—growths from the roots and from the main trunk below the head of branches—should also be removed. When removing branches, cut them close to a fork or where they join a larger branch of the main trunk.

Almonds, Peaches

Almonds and peaches are closely related and very similar in appearance and requirements. The Common Almond, *Prunus amygdalus*, is the first to flower, being at its best in March. It makes an open, shuttlecock-shaped head of branches up to 20 ft. high in the common form, and has light pink single flowers, though there are white-flowered and double pink-flowered forms.

The Peach is *Prunus persica*, and it makes a smaller tree, rarely over 15 ft. high, often considerably less. It flowers in April, and the most popular variety, Clara Meyer, has double rose pink flowers. Iceberg is semi-double and white, and Russell's Red, double crimson.

Both almonds and peaches like good, fairly rich, well-cultivated soil and a sunny position. Both are subject to a disease known as leaf curl, which causes the young leaves to turn red, pucker and curl. This is most likely to occur in exposed places and in cold weather. It can be controlled by spraying with Bordeaux mixture or a copper fungicide when conditions are warm enough.

These are first-rate town trees as they do not take up too much room and appreciate the shelter of neighboring buildings. Any pruning necessary should be done immediately after flowering and then kept to a minimum.

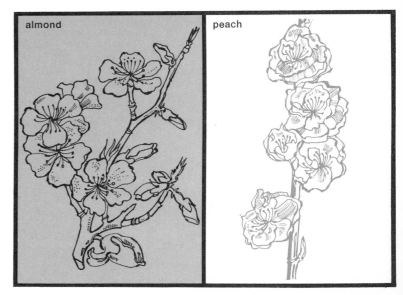

almond

peach

This ornamental peach, *Prunus persica* Clara Meyer, is a very popular small tree. During April it is covered in a wealth of beautiful pink double flowers. It grows well in town gardens

Beeches, Birches

The Common Beech, *Fagus sylvatica*, is too large to be grown as a tree in gardens of ordinary size, though it can be hard pruned and used as a hedge. The Dawyck Beech is a fastigiate variety making a very narrow tree, tapering top and bottom, so that it can be accommodated in quite a limited space. The Copper Beech and the Purple Beech are of normal habit with bronze-colored and deep beetroot-red foliage respectively. They make a splendid contrast to green-leaved trees where there is room for them, but in 20 years may easily be 40 ft. high and 30 ft. in diameter.

The Silver Birch, *Betula pendula*, is one of the few forest trees suitable for planting in fairly small gardens. It is very variable and care should be taken to purchase good forms with really silver-white bark color and drooping branches. The variety *tristis* is reliable and *youngii* is a smaller tree making a dome of slender branches weeping to ground level.

Both birch and beech will grow in most soils, with birch preferring light, rather sandy or peaty soils, and beech limestone soils. They can be pruned in autumn or winter, but great care should be taken with birch not to destroy the natural graceful habit of the tree.

Cherries

Together with the crab apples, cherries are the most valuable flowering trees for gardens.

Cherries thrive in a wide variety of soils with a particular liking for those of a limy nature, and though they prefer open, sunny places they will grow in shade. Their one slight drawback is their susceptibility to bacterial canker disease which may be aggravated by pruning. Nothing much can be done when trees do become infected, indicated by small circular holes in the leaves, dying branches, and masses of gum exuding from the bark, and they are best dug up and burned. Any pruning necessary should be done after flowering.

Representative varieties are as follows, but there are many more equally good varieties available.

Amanogawa, double soft pink, April—May, narrow columnar habit; Fugenzo, double deep pink, April—May, spreading habit; Kwanzan, double deep pink, April, shuttlecock habit; Cheal's Weeping, double deep pink, April, small tree with weeping branches; Shimidsu, double white, May, low, spreading habit; Ukon, double pale greenish yellow, April, well branched; *Prunus sargentii*, single pink, April, shuttlecock habit; *Prunus subhirtella autumnalis*, small, semi-double pale pink flowers, November to February, well branched; *Prunus yedoensis*, single white, March—April, well branched.

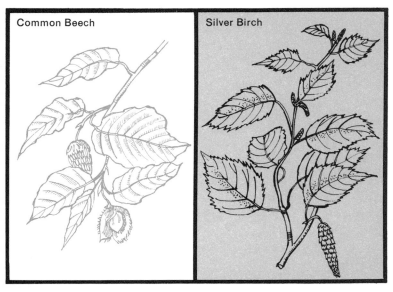

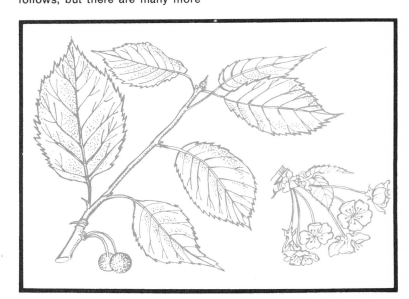

Care should be taken when buying Silver Birches from a nursery to get good bark color and attractive drooping branches. This variety, *Betula pendula youngii*, is always reliable

Cherries are very valuable flowering trees and Kwanzan is just one of the many lovely forms available. It has a shuttlecock habit, though, as the trees age, the branches tend to droop and spread more widely

Crab Apples

These are magnificent ornamental trees, some grown primarily for their spring flower display, others for their highly colored fruits. All are hardy and easy to grow in a wide variety of soils, though they prefer reasonably good, well-cultivated, adequately drained soil, and sunny, open places. All can be pruned at any time in autumn or winter as necessary.

Malus floribunda, the Japanese Crab, is one of the first to flower, opening its small but very abundant crimson and pink flowers in April. It makes a small, densely branched tree, 15 ft. or so high.

Malus lemoinei has deep wine red flowers in April and May and grows to 20 ft. or thereabouts. *M. purpurea*, *M. aldenhamensis*, and *M. eleyi* closely resemble it, but vary slightly in flowering time. *M. eleyi* also usually carries good crops of small red purple fruits in autumn.

The Red Jade crab apple has an all-year interest, being of a graceful pronounced weeping habit with floral beauty of white mantle in spring and is most picturesque with its cheerful burden of red fruits lasting well into the winter—which suggested the name. Originated at the Brooklyn Botanic Garden. Hardy from Zone 4 south.

There are many others in this group of superb flowering trees for the temperate zone.

The white blossom of the crab apple John Downie is followed by a striking display of fruit in the autumn. Crab apples are easy to grow given a reasonably good soil and a sunny, open position

Cypresses

Cypresses are evergreen conifers, mostly conical in shape though varying considerably. Many make excellent hedges and windbreaks and all can also be planted as individual specimens.

Cypresses grow in a wide variety of soils, but prefer reasonably good, well-cultivated and adequately drained soil. All can be pruned in spring or early summer as necessary. Some kinds transplant rather badly and should be purchased in containers from which they can be taken without root injury, or with their roots bound in sacking.

Lawson Cypress (*Chamaecyparis lawsoniana*) is tall, green, pyramidal, and very hardy. It has numerous varieties such as *allumii*, deep blue gray; *columnaris*, dark blue gray, columnar habit; *fletcheri*, light blue gray, feathery leaves, slow growing; *erecta viridis*, light green, narrow pyramidal habit; and *lutea*, golden leaved.

The Arizona Cypress (*Cupressus arizonica conica*) makes a narrow, blue gray column.

The Monterey Cypress (*Cupressus macrocarpa*) is bright green, fast growing, but not very hardy. It has a beautiful golden-leaved form.

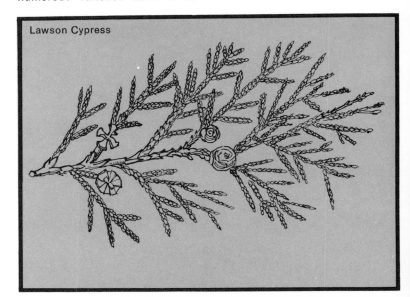

Lawson Cypress

Chamaecyparis obtusa is a Japanese cypress with numerous varieties of which this golden-leaved form named *crippsii* is one of the most attractive with its rich coloring

Hawthorns

Hawthorns are small, densely branched deciduous trees, some of which are grown solely for their flowers and some for both flowers and berries. They are very hardy, growing almost anywhere, and will withstand pruning well so they can be thinned or cut back as necessary in autumn or winter.

The most showy flowering hawthorns are varieties of the English Hawthorn, *Crataegus oxyacantha*. Paul's Double Scarlet Thorn (also known as *coccinea plena*) has clusters of fully double, light rosy red flowers in May. *Rosea plena* has double pink flowers and *alba plena* double white, also in May.

Crataegus carrierei is a hawthorn without thorns, a neat tree 15 to 20 ft. high, with white flowers in June, followed by large, orange red berries which are not attractive to birds.

The Cockspur Thorn, *Crataegus crus-galli*, has white flowers, scarlet berries and leaves which turn yellow, orange, and scarlet in autumn.

Crataegus prunifolia makes a rather broad, low tree, has white flowers in June followed by scarlet fruits and also gives fine autumn foliage color.

Judas Tree, Black Locust

The Judas Tree, *Cercis siliquastrum*, makes a small, rather slow-growing tree with elegant, rounded leaves and little clusters of rosy purple pea-type flowers all along the branches in May and early June. It is often raised from seed and since seedlings may differ in the quality and color of their flowers it is desirable to select specimens while in flower.

This is an excellent deciduous tree for small gardens. It will grow in most reasonably well-drained soils and sunny positions, but is not suitable for planting in very cold, exposed places as the young growth is rather tender.

The Black Locust, *Robinia pseudoacacia*, has ferny leaves, each composed of a number of small round leaflets, and white pea-type flowers in hanging clusters rather like those of a laburnum, but appearing in June. It grows rapidly into a large, open-branched tree, but does not take a lot of light from the garden. A variety named *frisia* has golden leaves and is much slower growing. Both grow well in almost all well-drained soils and are excellent town trees.

The Rose Acacia, *Robinia hispida*, is little more than a shrub, with fine rose pink flowers. It needs good, well-drained soil and a sheltered, sunny position.

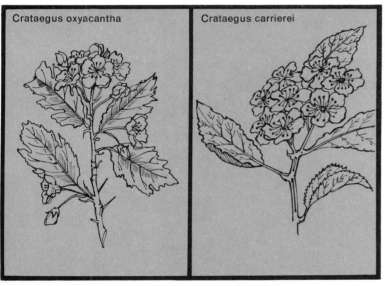
Crataegus oxyacantha — Crataegus carrierei

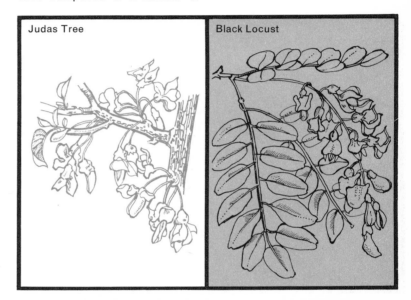
Judas Tree — Black Locust

Hawthorns are small deciduous trees, some grown for the flowers alone and some also for berries. This variety of hawthorn, Paul's Double Scarlet Thorn, bears clusters of double flowers in May

The attractive flowers of *Robinia hispida*, the Rose Acacia. This small tree has brittle stems which are easily damaged by the wind, so it is best grown in a sheltered place

Junipers

The junipers are evergreen conifers with a very wide range in style and size, some being low, spreading shrubs and others tall, columnar trees. They thrive in most soils, even those that are very limy, and they include some particularly good small trees.

One of the very best is the Irish Juniper, *Juniperus communis hibernica*, which makes a dense, narrow column of gray green leaves. Even after many years it is unlikely to be more than 10 ft. high and 2 ft. through. Another form, *Juniperus communis compressa*, is so slow in growth that it can be used to simulate tree growth in miniature in a rock garden.

The Chinese Juniper, *Juniperus chinensis*, also has many different varieties. One named *aurea*, or Young's Golden Juniper, makes a slender pyramid of yellow foliage.

Juniperus sabina, known as Savin, is a spreading shrub of which the best form for garden planting is *tamariscifolia*. This makes layer upon layer of wide-spreading horizontal branches, densely set with gray green leaves. The juniper called Pfitzer's Juniper (*Juniperus pfitzeriana*) makes a larger bush with wide-spreading, but slightly ascending branches, and is very useful as a contrast to the columnar conifers. It is improved by annual trimming out of small shoots between the main branches.

Laburnums

No deciduous trees make a more concentrated flower display than the laburnums, and few grow so rapidly without becoming excessively large. Laburnums do not as a rule live to a great age, but they are relatively cheap to buy. They will grow in almost any reasonably well-drained soil, with a special liking for limy soils though they are not suitable for planting in wet places. The seeds, usually produced very freely, are poisonous so care should be taken to see that young children do not pick them up and eat them.

The Common Laburnum, *Laburnum anagyroides*, makes an open-branched tree about 20 ft. high with abundant yellow flowers in late May.

The Scotch Laburnum, *Laburnum alpinum*, is similar in size but has longer trails of yellow, fragrant flowers in early June. It is probably the best kind for general planting.

The laburnums known as *vossii* and *watereri* are hybrids between the Common Laburnum and the Scotch Laburnum, and are much like the latter, *watereri* particularly so. Both are excellent garden trees.

Laburnums do not require regular pruning, but if overgrown may be thinned and reduced in autumn.

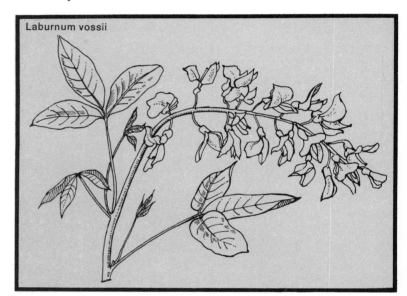
Laburnum vossii

Some junipers make especially attractive trees for the small garden. This one, the Irish Juniper, makes a dense narrow column which is unlikely to reach a height of more than 10 ft. or exceed 2 ft. through

Laburnums are one of the most popular of spring-flowering trees. Though superficially alike there are several varieties of which the one illustrated, *L. vossii*, is distinguished by its extra-long flower trails and vigorous arching habit

Magnolias

Many people call magnolias Tulip Trees, because of their tulip-shaped flowers, but this name belongs to the liriodendron.

Magnolias like good, well-cultivated soil, preferably free of lime, though some kinds will tolerate such soils. They thrive in sunny, sheltered places and benefit from an annual spring topdressing of peat or leaf mold and on limy soils may be fed with iron and manganese chelates. All have an open, branching habit and some spread widely.

The best evergreen kind is *Magnolia grandiflora*, with large, shining green leaves and fragrant white flowers, rather like water lilies, from July to September, though usually few at a time. It is often grown effectively as a wall shrub.

Magnolia soulangeana is the most popular deciduous magnolia. Its white, purple-flushed flowers are freely produced in late April and early May. *Alba* is a variety with pure white flowers; *lennei* has flowers white inside and purple outside; and both *rubra* and *nigra* are all purple and flower in May.

Magnolia sieboldii is a small, slender-branched tree with hanging, cup-shaped flowers each with a crimson central boss, produced from late May to July. *Magnolia wilsonii*, *M. sinensis*, and *M. high-downensis* are similar, the last being particularly suitable for limy soil.

Maidenhair Tree and Others

The Maidenhair Tree, or gingko, the Dawn Redwood, or meta-sequoia, and the Swamp Cypress, or taxodium, are all deciduous conifers, beautiful and rather uncommon.

The Maidenhair Tree is so called because its light green leaves are the shape of maidenhair fern leaves, but greatly enlarged. They turn yellow in autumn. The best variety, *fastigiata*, makes a tall but rather narrow column or pyramid and it is slow growing, for which reason it can be planted in relatively small gardens even though it may eventually reach 40 ft. or more.

The Dawn Redwood, by contrast, is very fast growing, sometimes adding 3 ft. or more each year, but it makes a fairly narrow pyramid of ferny, light green leaves which turn russet brown before falling in the autumn.

The Swamp Cypress closely resembles the Dawn Redwood in appearance but has even more feathery leaves, is much slower growing, and turns a light cinnamon red in autumn.

All three thrive best in good loamy, well-cultivated soil, but will grow in most soils, though the Swamp Cypress dislikes lime. It thrives in moist soil and is an excellent tree to plant beside a stream or lake.

Magnolia soulangeana

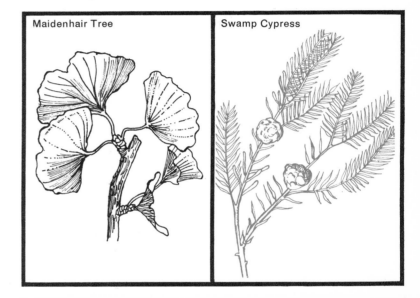

Maidenhair Tree   Swamp Cypress

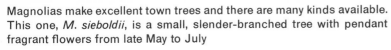

Magnolias make excellent town trees and there are many kinds available. This one, *M. sieboldii*, is a small, slender-branched tree with pendant fragrant flowers from late May to July

The handsome bark and ferny foliage of the Swamp Cypress, *Taxodium distichum*. Though this will eventually make a large tree it is slow growing and very decorative when young

Maples

There are many different kinds of maple, or acer, including such familiar trees as the Norway Maple, *Acer platanoides*, and the Sycamore, *A. pseudoplatanus*, which are too large for the average-sized garden. By contrast the Japanese maples are very small bushy trees or large shrubs and are very suitable even for small gardens.

All maples are deciduous and many color well before the leaves fall in autumn. The Japanese maples are outstanding in this respect, the variety Ozakazuki turning scarlet and *lutescens* yellow. The leaves of *atropurpureum* are bronzy crimson from spring to autumn; those of *dissectum* are deeply cut into a lacy pattern and those of *dissectum atropurpureum* are both lacily cut and colored.

Acer negundo variegatum makes a tree of moderate size with light green leaves variegated with white. It grows well in towns.

Crimson King is a purple variety of the Norway Maple, a fine tree where there is space for it. *Brilliantissimum* is a slow-growing variety of Sycamore Maple with coral pink young leaves.

The Snake Bark Maples (*Acer davidii*, *hersii*, and *pennsylvanicum*) have sage green bark, striped with light green and white.

All succeed in most soils and in sun or shade, but the Japanese maples prefer well-drained soils and rather sheltered places.

Mountain Ash, Whitebeams

There are many kinds of sorbus, the Common Mountain Ash being *Sorbus aucuparia*, and the Common Whitebeam, *S. aria*. They are excellent garden trees of small to medium size, thriving in almost any reasonably well-drained soil, and the whitebeams succeed particularly well on limy soils.

Mountain Ash makes a neat pyramidal tree 20 ft. or so high with rather ferny leaves and small white flowers in May and June followed by large clusters of orange scarlet fruits. There are numerous varieties, one named *xanthocarpa*, with yellow fruits; another, *asplenifolia*, with even more fernlike leaves.

There is also the Chinese Mountain Ash, *Sorbus hupehensis*, with white fruits which turn pink, and the Japanese Mountain Ash, *S. matsumurana*, with very fine orange scarlet fruits.

The Common Whitebeam also makes a neat, pyramidal tree, with leaves that are bright green on top and white beneath. The clusters of white flowers in May are followed by bunches of red fruits. Again there are several varieties, *pendula* having a weeping habit, and *lutescens* leaves which are creamy white beneath. There is also the Swedish Whitebeam, *Sorbus intermedia*, with lobed leaves, and the Chinese Whitebeam, *S. zahlbruckneri* (or *S. alnifolia submollis*), a very small, narrow tree.

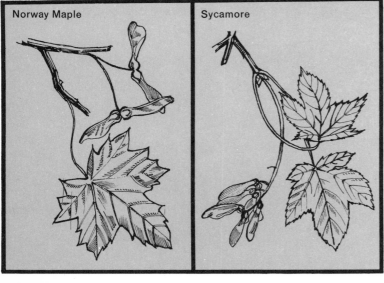

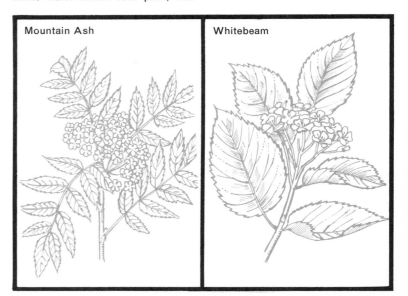

Japanese maples are very attractive foliage trees suitable for quite small gardens since they grow slowly. This is *Acer palmatum dissectum* with much divided purple leaves

These handsome berries of *Sorbus aucuparia*, the Common Mountain Ash, follow the white flowers. This tree is easily raised from seed sown in the spring and thrives on all well-drained soils

Plums, Shadbush

The ornamental plum most commonly planted in gardens is the Purple-leaf Plum, *Prunus cerasifera atropurpurea*. It is often sold as *Prunus pissardii*, and it has beetroot-purple leaves and small, pale pink flowers in early spring. A variety named *nigra* is similar, but has even darker purple leaves. Both make trees 20 ft. or so high which will grow almost anywhere.

Prunus blireiana is similar but makes a smaller, slower growing tree and has larger, semi-double rosy pink flowers and copper red leaves. It is the most beautiful plum but needs sun and a good, well-cultivated soil.

There are also ornamental varieties of the Blackthorn or Sloe, *Prunus spinosa*. *Purpurea*, the Purple-leaved Sloe, has red young leaves which later turn purple, and small white flowers in March—April. *Rosea* is similar but has pale pink flowers. Both make big bushes or small trees and will grow almost anywhere.

The Shadbush, *Amelanchier canadensis*, makes a round-headed tree, 20 ft. or so high with bronzy young leaves turning crimson in autumn and masses of tiny white flowers in April. It will grow in any well-cultivated soil.

All these trees are deciduous and none needs regular pruning, though suckers should be removed. Trees can be thinned in August or September.

Sweet Gum, Indian Bean

The Sweet Gum, *Liquidambar styraciflua*, has maple-like leaves which turn to rich shades of crimson before they fall in the autumn. It makes a shapely, pyramidal tree rather narrow in proportion to its height. It likes good, well-cultivated soil and an open position as its color is not so well produced in the shade. As a rule it does not thrive so well on limy soil.

The Indian Bean Tree, *Catalpa bignonioides*, is remarkable for the size of its rounded, yellowish green deciduous leaves, and stiff, upstanding sprays of white, gold, and purple flowers rather like those of a Horse Chestnut, but produced in July and August. Variety *aurea* has yellow leaves. They make rounded trees of medium size.

Both will grow in most places but prefer good, well-cultivated, well-drained soils and a sunny position. They succeed well in town gardens and can be pruned hard early each spring, which helps to keep down the size of the trees and increases the size of the leaves. All the previous year's growth can be cut to within an inch or so of the older branches, much as when pollarding a willow.

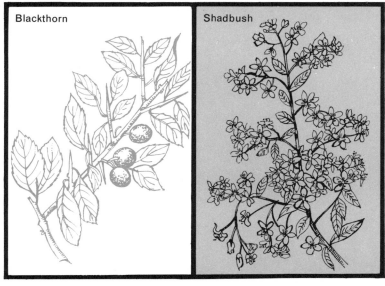

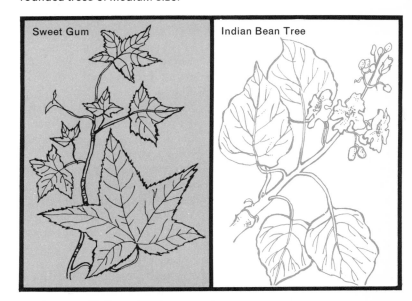

Amelanchier canadensis, the Shadbush, is a graceful tree of medium size with abundant small white flowers in April. The foliage turns a brilliant crimson color in the autumn

The showy flower clusters of the Indian Bean Tree appear in July and August. The large leaves and the broad, spreading habit make it an excellent shade tree. It succeeds well in town gardens

Garden Hedges

Planting

Like other shrubs, hedges, once planted, will grow in the same place for many years without anything more than surface cultivation, so initial preparation should be thorough. If the ground has not already been well dug, take out a trench at least 2 ft. wide and 1 ft. deep for the whole length of the hedge, throw in some well-rotted manure or compost and break up the bottom of the trench with a fork, thus working the manure or compost in.

Plant the hedge shrubs in this trench, if necessary first returning some soil to enable them to be placed at the correct depth. The soil mark on each plant, that is, the mark indicating where the soil came to in the nursery bed, should be about 1 in. below soil level. With container-grown hedging plants the top of the soil ball should be 1 in. below soil level.

Stretch a line tightly to mark the exact center of the hedge and use this as a guide to planting, spacing the plants as recommended for the different kinds of hedging shrub. Return most of the soil around the roots and tread firmly, then scatter the remaining soil over the surface and level with a fork or rake.

When planting in spring, water for a few weeks if the weather is hot or dry until the plants are growing freely, especially if the hedge borders a drainage ditch.

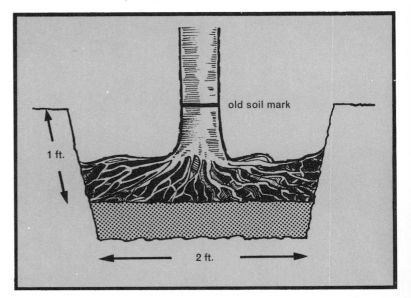

Hedges serve both a decorative and a utilitarian role in the garden. They can be used to give privacy and to keep out intruders, to separate one part of the garden from another or to provide a fine background for a border of flowers or a handsome ornament. They can be clipped in simple or elaborate shapes or they can be permitted to grow freely—an informal mode of treatment that suits flowering shrubs, including shrub roses.

Formal hedges will need to be clipped from both sides so, if they are located on the boundary, sufficient room must be left to give convenient access without trespassing on neighboring property. It is not possible to insist that a neighbor trim a hedge for you, nor can he be compelled to permit access through his property to a hedge located too close to the boundary.

All hedges cast some shade, interfere with the free movement of air, and take food and moisture from the soil, sometimes for several feet on each side. Allowance should be made for this when locating hedges and planting other things near them. There are plenty of plants that enjoy shade, provided the soil is good and reasonably moist, but not so many that thrive in the dry shade found close to well-grown hedges. Often it is better to have a path or a lawn, rather than a flower border, immediately alongside a hedge to permit easy access for trimming and reduce interference with the roots of other plants. The roots of a hedge will grow quite happily beneath gravel, paving slabs, or bricks.

On sloping ground hedges will break the flow of cold air down the slope which occurs during still, frosty weather. In consequence, cold air accumulates on the slope above each hedge and may cause injury to tender plants growing there. It is better to place hedges down, rather than across, slopes or to leave gaps in the bottom of the hedge through which cold air can trickle downward.

In rose gardens, close encircling hedges may encourage mildew by restricting the natural movement of air, but there are other plants which are readily damaged by high wind and for which the shelter of a hedge is highly beneficial. Hedges give better protection against wind than either walls or fences of similar height, since they filter the wind rather than divert it and therefore cause far less air turbulence.

Though evergreen shrubs are most popular for garden hedge making, deciduous kinds can also be used. Hawthorn is the most widely used of all hedge-making plants, but for farm fields rather than for gardens. Beech, though a large tree, stands clipping well and when grown as a hedge retains its dead leaves all winter, making an excellent windbreak.

Berberis thunbergii atropurpurea makes a splendid hedge up to 6 ft. high with richly colored, crimson foliage. Its densely branched habit and prickly stems make an impenetrable barrier

Care and Trimming

Do not neglect hedges after planting. They need care and feeding just like any other plants. Do not fork or dig near hedges as this destroys many of their roots. Keep the weeds down by hand weeding, shallow hoeing, or the use of approved weed killers but be careful to apply weed killer as instructed and not in excess nor on the leaves of the hedging plants.

Feed each spring with well-rotted manure or garden refuse spread for a foot or so on each side of the hedge, or with a good compound fertilizer lightly peppered on the soil.

Trim young hedges three or four times each year from early June to late August to keep well furnished with growth right to the base. As they grow older one or two clippings each summer may suffice. Flowering hedges are best trimmed after flowering. Beech and hornbeam can be trimmed in summer or winter. Small-leaved shrubs such as privet, box, lonicera, cypress, and yew may be trimmed with shears but larger-leaved shrubs, such as aucuba and laurel, are best pruned with special lopping shears so as not to disfigure the leaves.

When trimming, hold the shears so that the blades lie flat against the surface to be cut and the handles slope conveniently to the hands.

Conifer Hedges

The three principal kinds of conifer used for hedging are cypress, thuja, and yew. All are evergreens which stand frequent clipping and yew, like box, is much used for topiary specimens.

The most popular hedging cypress, *Chamaecyparis lawsoniana* (Lawson Cypress), with rather ferny, green foliage will make good hedges up to 10 ft. high. It is fairly quick growing, hardy, and will grow in most soils. Plant 2 to 2½ ft. apart. There are numerous varieties of this cypress, some with lighter green foliage, some blue green, and some golden, all suitable for hedges either by themselves or in mixtures.

Leyland Cypress, *Cupressocyparis leylandii*, resembles Lawson Cypress but grows almost twice as fast.

Thuja plicata also resembles Lawson Cypress and has handsome dark green leaves. It grows well in heavy soils and may be treated as for Lawson Cypress.

Yew is available in dark green and golden-leaved varieties which may be planted separately or in mixture. It is slow growing and so does not need frequent clipping, is very durable, and will grow in most conditions including limy soils. Plant 1½ to 2 ft. apart.

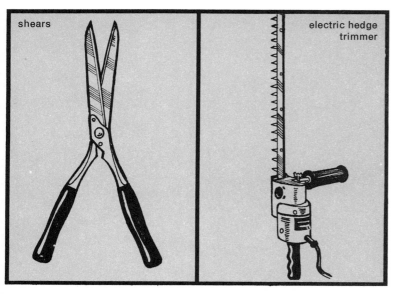

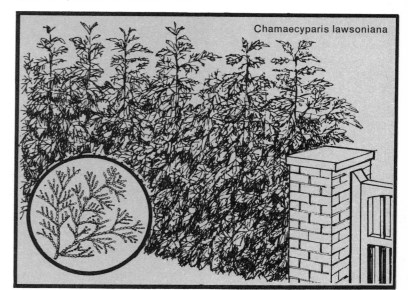

Chamaecyparis lawsoniana

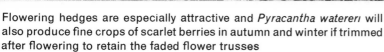
Flowering hedges are especially attractive and *Pyracantha watereri* will also produce fine crops of scarlet berries in autumn and winter if trimmed after flowering to retain the faded flower trusses

The Golden-leaved Yew, *Taxus baccata aurea*, makes a thick evergreen screen but is a slow grower. It is long lasting and suitable for most soils, including lime

Deciduous Hedges

These are hedges made of shrubs that do not retain their leaves all the year. Their appearance changes with the seasons and this can add interest to the garden.

European Beech makes an interesting deciduous garden hedge. It grows rapidly, has such strong stems that it can be used to make a tall yet narrow hedge, and, when trimmed, retains its reddish brown dead leaves throughout the winter. Plant shrubs 1 ft. apart for a good dense hedge. Beech grows in all well-drained soils, and especially well in limy soils. For a tapestry effect, Copper and Purple Beech may be mixed with green-leaved beech.

The European Hornbeam closely resembles beech and is better in wet soils. Plant in the same manner.

Myrobalan Plum has green leaves and small white flowers in April, and it makes a strong, quick-growing but not very ornamental hedge. Plant 1 ft. apart.

Prunus cistina is a purple-leaved plum which makes an excellent small hedge of up to about 4 ft. high. It is much neater and more decorative than Myrobalan Plum. Plant 18 in. apart and trim in April.

We call *Crataegus monogyna* the English Hawthorn, the British simply, Hawthorn. Grows wild all over Europe except Iceland. It makes a thorny deciduous hedge that can readily be trimmed. Plant 9 in. apart. The following winter cut back hard to promote branching.

Small-leaved Evergreens

Lonicera is the most popular small-leaved, fully evergreen hedge shrub. Two kinds are commonly used, *Lonicera nitida* with very slender stems and little round leaves and *L. yunnanensis* (or *L. nitida fertilis*) with stiffer stems. Both thrive in most soils and situations and will make good hedges up to 5 ft. high. Plant 1 ft. apart and prune tops immediately to encourage branching from base.

Box also has small, round, fully-evergreen leaves. It is stiffer in growth than lonicera, and thus much favored for topiary specimens such as cones, peacocks, etc. Handsworth Variety, planted 2 ft. apart, is best for hedges up to 8 ft. high and for topiary; *suffruticosa*, purchased by the yard (enough when split up to plant a yard), is most suitable for low box edgings to beds.

Privet is only fully evergreen in mild winters. The best varieties are Oval-leaf, which is all green, and Golden which has bright yellow leaves and is slow growing. Both will grow practically anywhere and are excellent for hedges from 4 to 8 ft. high. Plant 1 to 1½ ft. apart and prune tops immediately to encourage branching from ground level.

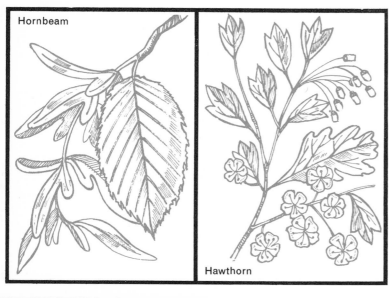

Hornbeam

Hawthorn

box

privet

The Purple Beech, *Fagus sylvatica purpurea*, is, like the Common Beech, one of the best plants for a tall narrow hedge. These two and the Copper Beech, *F.s. cuprea*, can be mixed to give added interest

Lonicera nitida aurea is a golden-leaved form of this normally green-leaved shrub. Thriving in most soils, this lonicera will be well branched from the base if the tops are pruned immediately after planting. Suitable for U.S. Zone 7

Large-leaved Evergreens

Common Laurel (*Prunus laurocerasus*), has large, shining, dark green leaves, will grow well in most soils in full sun or dense shade and is excellent for large, broad hedges. It is a hungry shrub and not suitable for small gardens. Plant 2 ft. apart.

Portugal Laurel (*Prunus lusitanica*) has smaller, darker green leaves and is also excellent for a big, thick hedge, but is not recommended for small gardens. It will thrive in most soils in sun or shade. Suitable for U.S. Zone 7.

Aucuba has large, light green leaves, heavily spotted with yellow in the most popular species, *Aucuba japonica*, sometimes called Spotted Laurel. It will grow anywhere, succeeding especially well in the shade even in grimy industrial surroundings, and is excellent for large hedges. Plant 2 ft. apart.

Holly makes a dense, impenetrable hedge. There are dark green-leaved, golden variegated and silver variegated varieties which may be planted separately or in combination. Holly succeeds in most soils in sun or shade and will make good hedges from about 5 to 10 ft. in height. It is very hardy and long lived, but rather slow growing. Plant 1½ ft. apart and trim in August.

Common Laurel

Shrub Hedges

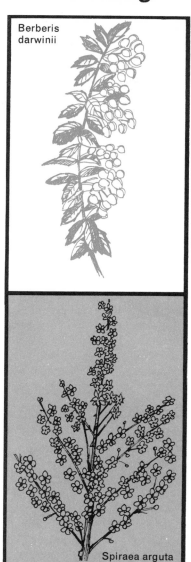

Berberis darwinii

Many flowering or fruiting shrubs make excellent informal hedges.

Berberis darwinii is neat, evergreen, and prickly and has orange flowers in April; *B. stenophylla* is yellow flowered and less tidy. Both will make hedges to 6 ft. high and through. *B. verruculosa* resembles *B. darwinii* but is shorter and will make a good 4-ft. hedge. Plant all three 2 ft. apart and trim immediately after flowering.

Berberis thunbergii atropurpurea is deciduous, spiny, and has small purple leaves and yellow flowers in early summer. Planted 2 ft. apart and pruned in March it makes a good 4- to 6-ft. hedge.

Cotoneaster simonsii is deciduous, stiffly erect, and has scarlet berries in autumn and winter. Plant 1½ ft. apart and prune in March for a 4- to 5-ft. hedge. *C. henryana* is evergreen, scarlet berried, looser in habit, and will make a 6- to 8-ft. hedge. Plant 2 ft. apart and prune in spring.

Laurustinus (*Viburnum tinus*) is a good evergreen, much like Portugal Laurel in leaf and habit, but slow growing with pink and white flowers in winter and spring. Plant 2 ft. apart and prune in spring.

Spiraea arguta is deciduous, twiggy, and has small white flowers in April. Planted 2 ft. apart and trimmed after flowering it makes a good 3- to 4-ft. hedge.

Spiraea arguta

This fine holly with cream-edged leaves is named *Ilex aquifolium aurea marginata*. It is a female variety which will produce good crops of berries if a male holly is planted with it

Laurustinus (*Viburnum tinus*) makes a good dense evergreen hedge, 7 to 10 ft. in height. It has the added attraction of producing flowers from late autumn to early spring and it succeeds well in town gardens. Suitable for U.S. Zones 7 and 8

Colorful Perennials

Most herbaceous perennials, like trees and shrubs, live for many years and do not have to be frequently renewed from seed or cuttings like annuals or many bedding (temporary display) plants. Unlike trees and shrubs they have soft stems which in many kinds die down in the autumn and grow again the following spring, though a few have evergreen leaves and an even smaller number grow in winter and die down in the summer. Not all herbaceous perennials are hardy but here we are only concerned with those that are.

Hardy herbaceous perennials, to give them their full title (though they are often referred to simply as perennials or hardy plants) are very valuable in the garden since most are relatively cheap, grow quickly and can be readily increased by seed, division, or cuttings. Many kinds grow so fast that it is desirable to dig them up every two or three years, divide them into smaller pieces, and replant after digging the soil and enriching it with manure or fertilizer. Spring is usually the most favorable time to do this, though if herbaceous plants are quickly replanted and are well looked after subsequently, they can be moved at almost any time of the year. A few herbaceous perennials dislike root disturbance and are best left for many years. Examples of this kind are Japanese anemones, hellebores, and peonies.

Most herbaceous plants will grow well in any reasonably good, well-cultivated soil. All enjoy moderate dressings of well-rotted manure or garden refuse and a sprinkling of bonemeal before planting, and this feeding can be repeated each spring as a topdressing, lightly forked in.

Herbaceous perennials may be used in a variety of ways in the garden. Where space permits, whole borders or beds may be devoted to them or they can be used with shrubs, annuals, or bedding plants or as isolated plants or groups of plants. An open, reasonably sunny position is best for beds or borders devoted exclusively to herbaceous perennials since this will suit the majority, but there is no shortage of kinds that will grow in shade that is not too dense.

Most herbaceous plants flower for only three or four weeks each year, so if a bed or border devoted exclusively to them is to remain interesting for a long period, plants with differing flowering periods must be selected and placed with due regard to their color, height, and flowering time. As a rule they are planted in irregular groups of a variety, the taller kinds at the back of a border or in the middle of a bed, shorter kinds in front or around the edge. It is better to make individual groups long and narrow rather than broad since they will be less conspicuous when out of bloom.

Planting

Plant small- to medium-sized plants with a trowel, large plants with a spade, being careful to make all holes sufficiently large to accommodate roots naturally spread out. Plant so that the crown, i.e., the point where leaves or stems join the roots, is ½ to 1 in. below the surface. Make soil firm around the roots.

Plant tall or fast-spreading herbaceous plants about 2 ft. apart, plants of medium height or growth 15 to 18 in. apart and small plants 9 to 12 in. apart. When planting in groups of a kind, make each group an irregular shape and use an odd rather than an even number of plants, i.e., groups of 3, 5, 7, or more of each variety. Place the plants in each group a little closer than the recommended spacing and leave a rather greater space between groups; e.g., if the recommended spacing is 15 to 18 in. space plants in a group 15 in. apart and leave at least 18 in. between this and neighboring groups. In this way, each group will grow together to form what appears to be one large plant clearly defined from neighboring "plants."

March and April are good planting months and so is October for many kinds. Herbaceous plants grown in containers can be planted from these at almost any time, provided soil conditions are favorable.

A summer border of hardy perennials which has been carefully planned and planted to include many herbaceous plants such as delphiniums, salvia, irises, campanula, goldenrod, and *Stachys macrantha*

Care and Feeding

Weeds must be kept down at all times by hoeing, hand weeding, or the use of suitable weed killers. Extra care, however, is required in using weed killers in herbaceous beds and borders since the plants often have leaves right down to soil level and roots very near the surface. It is, therefore, sometimes difficult to restrict chemical applications to weeds alone and to keep them off the plants, to which they are likely to be equally fatal. Forking is not desirable because it disturbs surface roots.

If possible, apply an annual top-dressing of well-rotted manure or compost in spring and, at the same time, give a light scattering (about 3 oz. per sq. yd.) of a compound fertilizer. A second applica-tion of fertilizer at 2 oz. per sq. yd. may be beneficial about mid-summer.

Remove faded flower heads or stems and thin out growth where it is overcrowded. Water plants freely in dry weather, if possible by placing a sprinkler to play on them until the soil is well moistened to a depth of at least 2 in.

Water young plants individually from a watering can until they are established and are growing well.

Staking

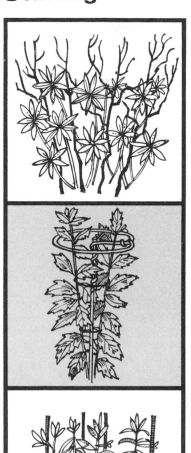

Herbaceous plants up to about 2 ft. in height are usually self-supporting, but taller kinds may require some extra support.

One simple and effective means of support is to use short bushy branches such as those sold as pea sticks and to thrust two or three of these firmly into the ground around each plant or group of plants when growth is still only a few inches high. The plants will grow through the twigs, obtaining support from them and at the same time concealing them from view.

Alternatively, squares of netting (string, nylon, or wire) may be stretched between stakes about 18 in. above ground level so that the stems will grow through them and be held securely. Special wire supports are available which work in the same way and are both neat and durable.

A few plants with very long stems, e.g., delphiniums, holly-hocks, and verbascums, may require staking with canes, one to each main stem. These should be thrust well down into the soil and should be sufficiently long to come to the base of the flower spike. The stems must be tied securely, but not too tightly. Make a double twist in the tie between stem and cane to allow for expansion.

The handsome flower spikes of kniphofia justify its popular name of the torch lily. It is also aptly known as the red-hot poker. It likes a well-cultivated, well-drained soil and an open, sunny position

Verbascum chaixii is a very useful herbaceous plant which thrives in dry soils and sunny positions. It has showy spikes of flowers during July and August and is not usually long lived

Lifting and Dividing

Many herbaceous plants spread outward so that they progressively occupy more and more ground, and as they grow the center portion of each plant gets more and more starved. To overcome this, plants are lifted, split up, and replanted, i.e., divided.

Very fast growing plants, such as Michaelmas daisies and sunflowers, really need to be divided every second year for the best results, and most plants benefit from division at least every fourth year. Usually, the most convenient compromise is to remake herbaceous beds and borders every third year, dividing as necessary.

March and April are good months for dividing most herbaceous plants, though it can also be done in October. Lift the plants carefully with a strong fork or spade and shake off as much soil as possible. Some plants can easily be divided with the fingers, but for tough old clumps thrust two forks (border forks or hand forks, according to the size of the clump) back to back through the center of the plant and lever them apart. Repeat as necessary to reduce plants to manageable size. Occasionally a knife may be needed to cut through tough crowns but it is better to rely on leverage only where this will work.

Discard the hard, starved center portions and replant only the young pieces from the edges of the plants. Make sure that each piece which is retained has both shoots and roots.

Seed and Cuttings

Many herbaceous plants can be raised from seed and this is often the cheapest way of producing a large number of plants. However, seedlings usually take at least a full year to attain flowering size and do not always resemble their parents in every detail.

Seed may be sown in boxes or pots in a cool greenhouse or frame as soon as it is ripe in summer, or stored and sown the following spring. Most kinds can also be sown outdoors in May or early June. Seedlings are pricked off or are transplanted when sufficiently large to be handled and are usually grown on in a reserve bed until they have attained flowering size.

Some herbaceous plants can also be raised from either stem or root cuttings and this has the advantage that the plants produced do resemble their parents in every detail. Stem cuttings are usually prepared in March and April from firm young shoots and are rooted in sandy soil in a frame or cool greenhouse. Root cuttings are prepared from the thicker roots cut into short pieces and either inserted right way up in pots of sandy soil or strewn over the surface of sandy soil in seed boxes and covered with about $\frac{1}{2}$ in. of the same mixture. Taken in winter or early spring, such cuttings will usually produce shoots by early summer when they can be transplanted to a nursery bed.

Beds of herbaceous perennials can be colorful for several months with the added interest of a good variety of leaf shapes and colors. Many kinds grow rapidly and need to be divided every few years

Solidago, popularly known as goldenrod, is an easily grown herbaceous plant which readily seeds itself around. The branching sprays of tiny flowers appear in late summer and early autumn

Acanthus and Others

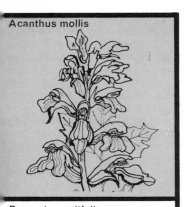
Acanthus mollis

Bergenia cordifolia

Bocconia cordata

Acanthus, bergenias, and bocconias are plants which have leaves as decorative as their flowers and all are very easily grown.

The bear's-breech, or acanthus, has very large, shiny, green, deeply divided leaves, which were used by the ancient Greeks as models for the scrolls on their Corinthian columns. The flowers are hooded, light purple and white, carried in late summer in stiff spikes 4 to 5 ft. high and when cut and dried they can be used for winter decoration. In *Acanthus mollis* the lobes of the leaves are broad and waved, and in *A. spinosus* they are much narrower and spiny.

Bergenias are also sometimes called megaseas or giant-leaved saxifrages. They have big, rounded, rather leathery, shining green leaves and stiff, crowded sprays of pink or purple flowers on 1-ft. stems in spring. *Bergenia cordifolia* has light pink flowers; Silverlight is palest pink and Evening Glow reddish purple. All can be left undisturbed for years or can be divided if required.

Bocconia cordata is known as the Plume Poppy and also as macleaya. The leaves are large, rounded, deeply lobed and grayish and the little pinkish buff flowers are borne in large sprays on 7-ft. stems in August and September.

All three plants spread steadily but need not be disturbed unless desired, when they can be lifted and divided.

Anemones, Globeflowers

Japanese anemone

globeflower

Japanese anemones are good plants for herbaceous beds and borders, flowering in late summer. They have pink or white saucer-shaped flowers carried in small sprays on slender but rigid stems 2 to 3 ft. high.

These plants will grow in most soils in sun or shade but they do not transplant well, so it is wise to purchase small plants in pots or other containers from which they can be planted with roots unbroken. They should then be left undisturbed for as long as possible and will slowly spread outward to form large clumps.

Some good varieties of Japanese anemone are: Alba, white; September Charm, soft pink; Louise Uhink, white; and Profusion, deep rose.

The globeflowers are so called because their bright yellow or orange flowers are almost ball shaped. All are varieties of trollius and have attractive light green, deeply divided leaves, make neat clumps which do not spread too rapidly and enjoy moist places, though they will grow in any good, well-cultivated soil that does not dry out too rapidly in hot weather. They can be divided every three or four years. Most are 2 ft. high and flower in May, but Golden Queen is 3 ft. and has more open, orange flowers in June.

An early-flowering season and handsome, almost evergreen foliage make *Bergenia cordifolia* a fine garden plant. It is not fussy about soil and will grow in sun or shade

Globeflowers are excellent herbaceous plants for a moist situation. The yellow or orange blooms, which appear in May, resemble enormous buttercups and the foliage is deeply divided

Bergamots, Sages

These are related plants and they are among the most useful of medium height for the border, as they are easily grown in most places and make good masses of color from July to September.

The bergamots, or monarda, grow 2½ ft. high with a bushy habit and carry their pink, scarlet, or purple flowers in little clusters all over the top of the plants. There are several varieties differing mainly in color. Representative examples are: Cambridge Scarlet, scarlet; Croftway Pink, rose pink and Blue Stocking, violet. All grow rapidly and should be divided every second or third year.

monarda

The best sage for the herbaceous border is *Salvia superba*, with slender violet-purple spikes from July to September. There are several good varieties differing mainly in height; Superba is 3 ft., Lubeca 2 ft., and East Friesland only 1½ ft. All will grow almost anywhere with a preference for good, well-drained soils and sunny places. They should be divided every second or third year.

Two other sages, sometimes planted in herbaceous borders, are *Salvia haematodes* with slender 3-ft. spikes of lavender blue flowers in July and August and *Salvia uliginosa*, with short spikes of sky blue flowers on wiry 4-ft. stems in September and October.

salvia

Bell and Balloon Flowers

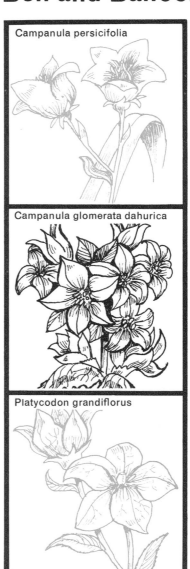

Campanula persicifolia

Campanula glomerata dahurica

Platycodon grandiflorus

There are many bellflowers, or campanulas, some of which are rock plants. But there are also first-rate kinds for herbaceous borders and beds, all easily grown in almost any soil in sun or partial shade. They should be divided every third or fourth year.

Campanula persicifolia carries its flowers in slender 2- to 3-ft. high spikes in June and July. Telham Beauty is single and blue; Wirral Belle, double and deep blue and Fleur de Neige, double and white.

Campanula glomerata dahurica carries its violet purple flowers in compact heads on 18-in. stems in June and July; *C. grandis* has 2-ft. spikes of blue flowers in June and July; and the tallest at 5 ft. with loose sprays of light blue flowers in July and August is *C. lactiflora*, of which Loddon Anna is a variety with mauve pink flowers and Pouffe makes a 1-ft. high mound of lavender flowers.

The balloon flowers are varieties of *Platycodon grandiflorus*, very like bellflowers but slower growing, needing well-cultivated soil and not to be divided unless absolutely necessary. They are 18 in. high, flower in July and August and have inflated buds opening to cup-shaped flowers, commonly light blue, though there are soft pink and white varieties.

A refreshing corner of a garden which has been created by including many foliage plants of differing shapes and colors in and around a pool. The purple sage contrasts well with the surrounding plants

This bellflower, *Campanula glomerata dahurica*, flowers on 18-in. stems in early summer. Its rich coloring adds distinction to any herbaceous border and it is a valuable front row plant

Catmint, Heuchera

The Catmints, or nepeta, are gray-leaved plants with spikes of little lavender blue flowers more or less continuously from June to September. The most popular kind is the Common Catmint, *Nepeta faassenii*, and since it only grows 18 in. high it is excellent for the edge of a bed or border. Six Hills Giant is a little taller and is a dark lavender-blue variety.

Catmints enjoy well-drained soils and sunny places, though they will grow almost anywhere. They spread rapidly and should be divided at least every third year. Bees are attracted by the flowers.

Heucheras are also primarily edging plants, but with small pink or red flowers in elegant sprays in June and July. The leaves are round, often with zones of different shades of green, and remain all the winter when the plants still make a good effect.

They need well-drained soil and succeed best in a sunny place, though they will grow in partial shade. They tend to get "leggy" with age, and more soil can then be placed around them or the plants can be lifted, divided, and replanted.

Representative varieties are: Coral Cloud, coral pink; Red Spangles, crimson scarlet; and Scintillation, bright pink.

nepeta

heuchera

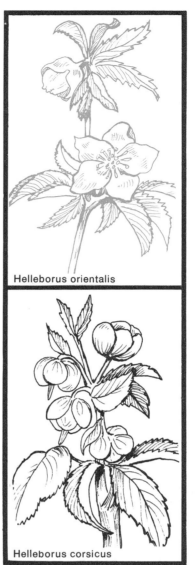

Christmas Roses and Others

Helleborus orientalis

Helleborus corsicus

Neither the Christmas nor the Lenten Roses are in any way related to true roses, but are herbaceous plants belonging to the buttercup family and known as helleborus or helebores. The popular names have arisen because the flowers have a slight resemblance to single roses and appear in midwinter or early spring. It is this early flowering that makes them so valuable in the garden. The plants in this group make slowly spreading clumps of dark green—more or less evergreen—deeply divided leaves which are themselves quite decorative. All thrive in shady places, enjoy good, well-cultivated soil, and should be left undisturbed for as long as possible. It is best to start with fairly small plants.

The Christmas Rose, *Helleborus niger*, has white flowers on 1-ft. stems from December to February. There are several varieties, such as St. Brigid and Potter's Wheel, with extra-fine flowers.

The Lenten Rose, *Helleborus orientalis*, is 1½ ft. tall, and has flowers varying from ivory white to deep maroon from March to April.

The Corsican Hellebore, *Helleborus corsicus*, has large clusters of yellowish green flowers on 2- to 3-ft. stems in January and February. Its leaves are particularly decorative as are those of the Green Hellebore, *Helleborus foetidus*, with jade green flowers at the same time.

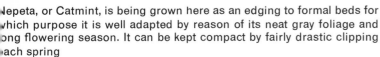
Nepeta, or Catmint, is being grown here as an edging to formal beds for which purpose it is well adapted by reason of its neat gray foliage and long flowering season. It can be kept compact by fairly drastic clipping each spring

The Corsican Hellebore, *Helleborus corsicus*, has pleasant lime green flowers carried on large heads in January and February and handsome divided leaves. It will thrive in sunny as well as shady places

Columbine, Monkshood

The columbines, or aquilegias, are delightfully graceful plants with ferny leaves and fragile-looking flowers, some with long spurs containing nectar poised on slender stems, and the varied colors are often as delicate as the shape.

Columbines grow readily from seed sown in a greenhouse or frame in March or out of doors in May and come into flower in the June of the following year. They range in height from 1 to 3 ft. They like well-drained soils and will grow in sun or shade. Although not usually long lived, they will often maintain themselves by self-sown seedlings. Double-flowered varieties are also available, and the McKana Hybrids include a wide range of colors.

Monkshood, or aconitums, also have unusually shaped flowers, like little cowls, blue, white, or yellow, and carried in spikes. These plants thrive in any reasonably good soil and in sun or shade, and as they do not usually spread very fast they need dividing only every four or five years.

There are numerous varieties of which the following are representative: Bressingham Spire is violet blue, 3 ft., in July and August; Spark's Variety, indigo blue, 4 ft., June—July; Barker's Variety, deep blue, 5 ft., August—September; *Aconitum lycoctonum*, creamy yellow, 4 ft., July—August; *Aconitum napellus bicolor*, blue and white, 3 ft., July.

Coneflowers

The coneflowers are closely allied to the sunflowers and they get their name because in some kinds the central disk, flat and button-like in the sunflowers, is raised into a cone. All are easily grown in most places. The yellow-flowered varieties are all rudbeckias, but the purple coneflowers are varieties of *Echinacea purpurea*.

Autumn Sun, also known as Herbstsonne, is one of the tallest of the rudbeckias, 6 or 7 ft. high with bright yellow flowers, each with a green central cone, in August and September. It is a fine plant for the back of a border, but needs staking.

Rudbeckia sullivantii Goldsturm is only 3 ft. high, stiff stemmed and self-supporting. Its orange yellow flowers have a black center and are freely produced in August and September. *Rudbeckia speciosa* is similar but not quite so showy.

Goldquelle is 3 ft. high and has double, deep yellow flowers in September and October.

Golden Glow has double lemon-yellow flowers, is 5 ft. tall, and flowers in August and September.

The purple coneflowers are 3 to 4 ft. high, have rosy purple flowers on very stiff stems in August and September. The King is a reliable variety.

All coneflowers grow fast and should be divided every second or third year.

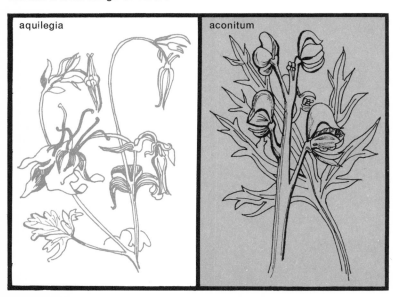

Long-spurred aquilegias. Many other colors are available and there are also short-spurred and double-flowered varieties as well as short kinds suitable for rock gardens

Rudbeckia sullivantii Goldsturm grows 3 ft. high and makes a handsome and accommodating border plant. It is ideal for cutting and arranging during August and September

Cornflowers, Scabious

The common cornflower is an annual but there are other useful kinds that are perennial herbaceous plants, quite hardy and easily grown in almost any soil and reasonably open situation. They vary greatly in size and in flower color but all are fairly vigorous plants that are the better for being lifted and divided every three or four years.

The Mountain Cornflower, *Centaurea montana*, has leaves that are silver gray when young and blue flowers on 18-in. stems in May and June. *Centaurea dealbata* is 2 ft. high and has rosy magenta flowers from June to August; *Centaurea macrocephala* is 3 ft. high, with big thistlelike yellow flowers in June and July; and *C. ruthenica* is 4 ft.

high with lemon yellow flowers in June and July.

The Caucasian Scabious (*Scabiosa caucasica*) makes an excellent cut flower, bearing its blue, purple, or white flowers on good 3-ft. stems from July to October. It enjoys lime in the soil, and if this is lacking it should be added before planting, and be given as an annual topdressing each spring—say 4 oz. per sq. yd. of hydrated lime.

Plants should be divided every three years, but only in the spring as this scabious does not transplant well in autumn. Clive Greaves and Sarah Cramphorn are good blue varieties; Miss Willmott a good white.

Centaurea montana

Scabiosa caucasica

Delphiniums

Delphinium elatum

Delphinium belladonna

Delphiniums are among the noblest of herbaceous plants, their tall spikes of flowers dominating beds and borders in June and July. They require good, fairly rich, well-cultivated and well-drained soil for in cold, wet soils they are apt to rot away in winter or be destroyed by slugs. They like open, sunny places.

Good delphiniums can be raised from seed, though the flowers may vary in color and form. If sown in a greenhouse in March and planted out in June many seedlings will give small flower spikes in August and full-sized spikes the following June or July.

Cuttings can be taken of firm young shoots in March—April for rooting in a frame and planting out of doors in June or July. Old plants can also be divided in spring, but this is not so satisfactory.

There are two main types of delphinium, the large-flowered, or Elatum, 4 to 6 ft. high, with long spikes of bloom, and the Belladonna, about 3 ft. high, with smaller spikes or sprays of bloom. There are many varieties of the elatum type, single flowered, semi-double and fully double in colors from white, pale blue, and lilac pink to bright blue and deep purple.

There are fewer belladonna varieties though the color range is similar. Good seed strains are available of elatum delphiniums only.

Among the most attractive of all border flowers for cutting are the varieties of *Scabiosa caucasica*. In addition to the mauve and violet purple kinds there are white varieties

A charming display of large-flowered delphiniums and anthemis. Delphiniums thrive in an open, sunny position and rather rich but well-drained soils. They are not usually very long lived

Day and Torch Lilies

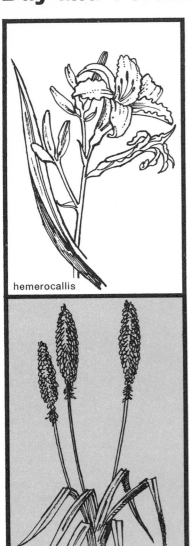

hemerocallis

kniphofia

The day lilies, or hemerocallis, are so called because each of their lilylike flowers lasts only for one day, though a succession of buds ensures a display for weeks. They make big clumps of narrow leaves and carry their flowers in July and August on stout, branched stems, 2 to 3 ft. high.

Day lilies will grow practically anywhere, though for the best results they should be planted in well-cultivated soil and be divided every second or third year. There are many varieties in a color range from lemon yellow to deep orange and mahogany crimson.

Torch lilies, or kniphofia, are also known as red-hot pokers, both popular names referring to the close heads of typically scarlet flowers surmounting a stout stem. There are, however, many varieties differing in color, height, and flowering time. Representative varieties are: Gold Else, golden yellow, 2 ft., July and August; Maid of Orleans, ivory, 3 ft., July to September; Royal Standard, scarlet and yellow, 3 ft., July, and *Kniphofia uvaria grandiflora*, coral and yellow, 4 ft., August and September.

All like well-cultivated, well-drained but not dry soil, and an open, sunny position. Only lift and divide when overcrowded. The stiff, grassy leaves are evergreen and may be tied together over each plant in autumn as a protection against frost. Untie again in the spring.

Dicentra, Polygonatum

The dicentras are very graceful plants with ferny, light green leaves and pendant heart-shaped flowers. The largest is *Dicentra spectabilis*, or Bleeding Heart, 2 ft. high with arching stems and rose and white flowers in April and May. These plants will grow in most places, but like a reasonably good, well-cultivated soil and an open, sunny position.

Dicentra formosa is 18 in. high and has smaller, more clustered flowers very freely produced from April to June. There are rose-colored and white varieties. This and the still smaller *D. eximea*, 1 ft. high, also available in white and pink varieties, are very adaptable and will grow in most places in sun or shade. All these plants can be divided every three or four years.

Solomon's Seal, *Polygonatum multiflorum*, enjoys shady places. It has creeping roots which send up long, arching, leafy stems from which the tubular green and creamy white flowers hang in May and June. It will grow in most soils, is an excellent plant for woodlands as well as for shady town gardens, and can be left undisturbed for years. When it spreads too far the outer portions of each colony can simply be dug out.

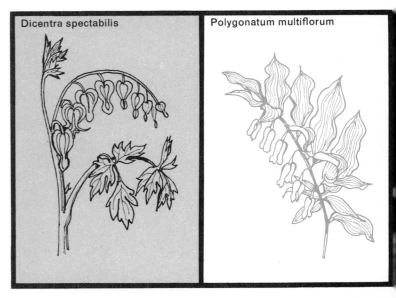

Dicentra spectabilis

Polygonatum multiflorum

The handsome flowers of Black Prince, a variety of the day lily, or hemerocallis. These are easily cultivated plants which will grow in almost any soil and a sunny or partially shaded position

The graceful arching stems and ferny foliage give added charm to *Dicentra spectabilis*. The pendant, heart-shaped flowers give this plant its common name, Bleeding Heart

Geums, Potentillas

Both geums and potentillas are sun-loving plants and both flower for most of the summer. They enjoy well-drained soils, and though geums in particular are very short lived in cold and damp places, both plants are extremely easy to grow.

Geum borisii has single orange-red flowers on 1-ft. high stems, but most garden varieties are 2 ft. high and have ruffled, semi-double flowers. Fire Opal, brilliant red, copper sheen; Lady Stratheden, yellow, and Mrs. Bradshaw, scarlet, are typical varieties. Some of these can be raised fairly true to color from seed, but for complete accuracy in reproduction plants must be divided and it is wise to do this every two or three years.

Potentillas resemble the herbaceous geums in many respects, but are low shrubs. Farreri, deep yellow flowers, also known as Gold Drop. Jackman's Variety, bright yellow flowers. Katherine Dykes, primrose yellow. Maanely's, pale yellow, also called Moonlight. All these are carried by a number of nurseries.

Potentillas require the same conditions of well-drained soil and open, sunny positions that suit geums and, like them, they are best divided every second or third year.

geum   potentilla

Golden Daisies

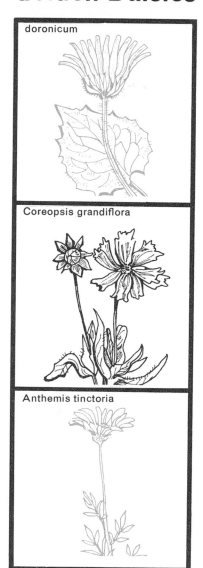

doronicum

Coreopsis grandiflora

Anthemis tinctoria

Three different kinds of herbaceous plant are included under this heading: the doronicum, or leopard's-bane; coreopsis, and anthemis.

Doronicums are the first to flower, opening their big yellow daisies in March and continuing into May. There are several kinds, two of the best being *Doronicum plantagineum* Harpur Crewe, 3 ft. high and excellent for cutting, and *Doronicum cordatum*, which is only 6 in. high and a good edging plant. Both will grow in almost any soil, in sun or partial shade, and should be divided every second or third year.

There are also several different kinds of coreopsis, all thriving in well-drained soils and sunny places. *Coreopsis grandiflora* has good-sized flowers on 3-ft. stems from June to August and makes an excellent cut flower. Mayfield Giant has even larger flowers and *auriculata* has a spot of crimson at the base of each petal. *Coreopsis verticillata* is very distinctive, being only 18 in. high and with narrow leaves and lots of little yellow flowers from June to August. It should be divided every three or four years.

Anthemis tinctoria is a bushy 2-ft. plant with ferny gray green leaves; it flowers on long stems from July to August. Likes well-drained soils and sunny places and cannot be divided.

Flowering throughout the summer in a light, well-drained soil and sunny position, geums are gay but not as a rule long-lived herbaceous plants. This variety is Red Wings

Doronicum plantagineum Harpur Crewe is one of the showiest early-flowering perennials. The daisylike flowers are excellent for cutting besides being highly decorative in the border

Erigerons, Geraniums

The erigerons look like low-growing perennial asters, but they start to flower in June and continue all summer. Most are very easy to grow in almost any soil and a fairly open place, but orange-flowered varieties such as B. Ladhams and *Erigeron aurantiacus* do not like wet soils and are liable to die in winter. Reliable varieties are: Charity, light pink, 2 ft.; Foerster's Liebling, cerise pink, 2 ft.; Merstham Glory, lavender blue, 2 ft.; and Vanity, pink, 2½ ft. They should be divided every two or three years.

The herbaceous geraniums are quite hardy and not very like the bedding geraniums or pelargoniums to which they are related. There are numerous varieties, some with blue and some with magenta flowers. They are also easily grown in almost any soil in full sun or partial shade, and make good, bushy plants. They should be divided every two or three years.

Geranium armenum is 2 ft. tall with showy magenta flowers in June and July. *G. endressii* is 18 in. high, spreads rapidly, and has pink flowers from June to September. Wargrave Pink is an improved variety.

Geranium grandiflorum has large blue flowers in June and July on a compact plant and is one of the best. Johnson's Blue has smaller light blue flowers from June to August on 18-in. stems. Russell Pritchard is crimson, 9 in. high, and flowers from June to August.

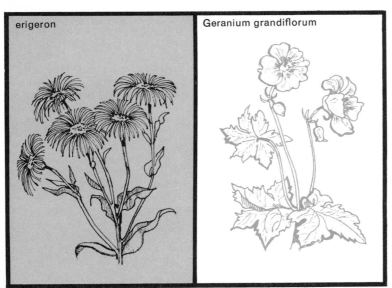

erigeron

Geranium grandiflorum

Herbaceous geraniums have showy, saucer-shaped flowers which are freely produced in summer. This is *G. armenum*, one of the most strongly colored kinds. There are others with blue or lavender flowers

Gray Leaves, Everlastings

artemisia

santolina

anaphalis

Gray and silver foliage is valuable in herbaceous beds and borders as a foil to brighter colors, and the wormwoods or artemisias are particularly good for the purpose. Nearly all tend to be a little woody, not quite shrubs yet not really true herbaceous plants either. Representative are: *Artemisia ludoviciana*, 2 ft.; *A. nutans*, 2 ft.; and Silver Queen, 3 ft. Odd man out is *Artemisia lactiflora*, 4 ft. tall, which is green leaved and fully herbaceous, with creamy plumes of tiny flowers from July to September. It enjoys good, rich soil and can be grown in sun or shade, whereas the other varieties thrive in light, well-drained soils and like sunny places. All can be divided every two or three years.

The lavender cottons, or santolinas, are also half shrubby and do best in well-drained soils and sunny places. *Santolina incana* is 18 in. high and silver gray; variety *nana* is similar but under 1 ft. tall.

The herbaceous everlasting flowers are mostly different kinds of anaphalis, and they, too, have gray leaves and are good border plants, liking sunny places and well-drained soils. Recommended kinds are: *Anaphalis margaritacea*, with silver flowers in August, 1½ ft.; *A. triplinervis*, creamy flowers in August, 1 ft.; and *A. yedoensis*, creamy flowers in August, 2 ft.

Gray and silver foliage in the herbaceous border complements well the gay colors of other hardy plants. *Santolina incana* is an excellent example and it can be clipped each spring to keep a compact habit

Galega, Everlasting Pea

These are among the easiest plants to grow, and they are very useful for rough places, but since they grow very vigorously care must be taken to place them where there is no chance of their smothering weaker plants.

Goat's rue, or *Galega officinalis* and varieties, makes a bushy plant 4 to 5 ft. high with little divided leaves and small clusters of vetch-like flowers very freely produced in June or July. All will grow practically anywhere and should be divided every second or third year.

The Everlasting Pea, *Lathyrus latifolius*, resembles old-fashioned varieties of sweet pea and is a sprawling or climbing plant with stems 6 to 7 ft. long which die back in the autumn and grow again the following spring. There are both pink and white-flowered forms, blooming in July and August.

The Everlasting Pea will grow in practically any soil but likes warm, sunny places. It can be trained up walls, fences, or tripods or allowed to sprawl over sunny banks. Division is not necessary and plants are easily raised from seed, though seedlings may vary in color.

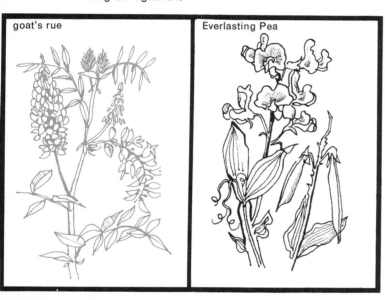

goat's rue

Everlasting Pea

Goldenrod, Yarrow

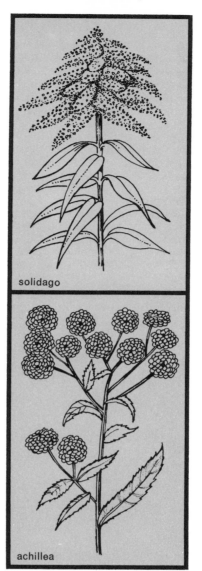

solidago

achillea

The goldenrods (solidago) flower in summer and early autumn and all have dense sprays of very small yellow, daisy-type flowers. There are numerous varieties, differing in height and shade of yellow.

Representative varieties are: Lemore, primrose, 2 ft.; Goldenmosa, golden yellow, 3 ft.; and Golden Wings, golden yellow, 4 ft. *Solidaster luteus* is similar but stiffer and is 2 to 3 ft., with light yellow flowers in August and September.

All will grow in almost any soil and place and are among the easiest of herbaceous plants to grow. They spread rather rapidly and should be lifted and divided every second year.

There are many yarrows (achillea); some dwarf plants for the rock garden, some larger plants for herbaceous borders and beds. These latter fall into three main groups as regards flower character, but all are equally easy to grow in almost any soil, though they prefer reasonably sunny, open places. They can be divided every third year.

Gold Plate has flat heads of yellow flowers on stiff 4-ft. stems in July and August. Coronation Gold is similar but smaller and flowers from June to September.

Cerise Queen has flat heads of carmine flowers on 2½-ft. stems from June to August.

The Pearl and Perry's White have sprays of little double white pompon flowers on 2½-ft. stems from June to August.

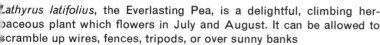
Lathyrus latifolius, the Everlasting Pea, is a delightful, climbing herbaceous plant which flowers in July and August. It can be allowed to scramble up wires, fences, tripods, or over sunny banks

Achillea Coronation Gold is a very good plant for the herbaceous border, flowering throughout the summer in a well-drained, sunny place. It also makes an excellent cut flower

Gypsophila, Meadow Rue

When plants are massed together the effect can be heavy and wearying to the eye without the filmy texture provided by the gypsophilas and meadow rues.

The herbaceous *Gypsophila paniculata* is even lighter in effect than the annual gypsophila, with foaming masses of tiny white flowers from June to September in a 3-ft. dome over narrow, silvery gray leaves and slender stems. It is most effective in its double-flowered forms, of which Bristol Fairy is typical. Flamingo repeats this effect in lilac pink and Rosy Veil, also pink, is more sprawling and only 1 ft. high. All varieties like sunny places and well-drained soils and are particularly happy on lime. The plants should be left to grow completely undisturbed.

The meadow rues, or thalictrums, are equally slender and airy, with fernlike leaves and sprays of flowers. The loveliest is *Thalictrum dipterocarpum*, 5 ft. high, with very open sprays of little lavender and pale gold flowers in July and August. In Hewitt's Double each flower is a tiny, fully double pompon of lilac petals. *Thalictrum aquilegifolium* has closer, fluffy heads of purple flowers and is 3 ft. high and *T. glaucum*, 5 ft. high, is yellow.

The last two can be divided every three or four years, but *T. dipterocarpum* and Hewitt's Double should be left undisturbed. All like good, well-drained soils and sunny places.

Heleniums, Gaillardias

Both heleniums and gaillardias have daisy-type flowers but they produce a quite different effect when grown in the garden. Heleniums have quite stiff stems terminating in close-packed clusters of medium-sized flowers, so that when in bloom they make solid masses of color in the borders. These flowers may be all yellow, yellow splashed with dull red, or entirely crimson or mahogany red. Heights, too, vary from 2 to 5 ft. and flowering time is from July to September. All are easily grown in any reasonably well-drained soil and open position. They spread rapidly and should be divided every second or third year.

The flowers of gaillardia are much larger individually and are borne on more slender stems which are inclined to twist if not supported. Typically, the flowers are yellow with a broad central zone of red, but there are also all yellow varieties or all reddish orange or reddish bronze varieties. Heights vary from 2 to 3 ft. and the flowering period from June to September.

Gaillardias like well-drained soils and sunny places. They are apt to die in winter if the soil is wet and heavy and are seldom very long lived, though good strains can be raised quickly and cheaply from seed. The flowers are useful for cutting.

Thalictrum dipterocarpum, a lovely meadow rue that can be readily raised from seed. Its dainty flowers are borne on thin, wiry stems in large loose sprays and are as delightful cut as in the garden

The showy, daisylike flowers of *Gaillardia* Wirral Flame. Unusual colors such as this are not reproduced entirely true from seed and so are propagated by division or root cuttings

Hostas, Rodgersias

Although hostas and rodgersias are grown largely for their handsome foliage, some also have very attractive flowers.

Hostas are also known as funkias and as plantain lilies. They make bold clumps of unusually broad, lance-shaped leaves, green in some varieties, blue gray in others, variegated with silver or gold in others. The flowers, produced in July and August, are tubular and carried in spikes. Hostas will grow in either sun or shade, in almost any place, though for the best foliage effects they should be given good, well-cultivated soil.

There are numerous species of which the following are representative: *Hosta albomarginata* has leaves edged with white; *H. for-*tunei has gray blue leaves and lilac-blue flowers; *H. lancifolia* has rather narrow green leaves; *H. sieboldiana* has gray green leaves and white flowers; *H. undulata variegata* has silver variegation.

The rodgersias have rounded or deeply divided leaves, and the small flowers are produced in branched heads on stout stems. They like moist soils and shady places and look well near water. They should be left undisturbed and divided only if overcrowded.

Representative kinds are: *Rodgersia pinnata superba* with bronzy leaves and pink flowers in July and August; *R. tabularis*, with platelike leaves and creamy white flowers; and *R. aesculifolia*, with divided leaves and white flowers.

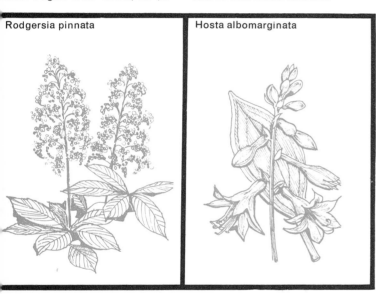

Rodgersia pinnata   Hosta albomarginata

Irises

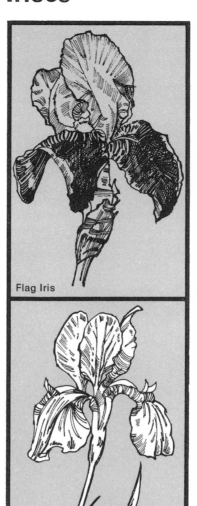

Flag Iris

Siberian Iris

Some irises have bulbous roots and some are plants for the waterside. However, the Bearded Iris (also known as German, June-flowering, and Flag Iris) and the Siberian Iris are useful plants for herbaceous borders and beds.

There are a great many varieties of Bearded Iris, all flowering in May and June, with stout, branched flower stems each carrying several large flowers. Heights vary from $2\frac{1}{2}$ to 4 ft., and the color range is immense, including many shades and blends not commonly found in other plants.

These irises make rhizomes, i.e., fleshy stems lying flat on the ground from which the roots grow. Plants should be lifted every second or third year immediately after flowering and only a small portion of healthy young rhizome retained with each leaf cluster for replanting. Plant with the rhizome barely covered with soil and do not pile soil over it later. Bearded Irises thrive in good, well-cultivated and sunny places, and like limy soils.

The Siberian Iris (*Iris sibirica*) has taller, more slender stems, smaller, more numerous blue, purple, or white flowers in June, and no rhizomes. It should be divided every second or third year.

The Algerian Iris (*Iris unguicularis*) has pale blue flowers on short stems in winter, likes a sunny place, and well-drained soil and may be left undisturbed for many years.

Hostas are chiefly grown for their handsome leaves though a few species have a good display of flowers. They will thrive in damp, shady places and look especially attractive by water

There are a great many varieties of the Bearded Iris differing in height and coloring. This one is Snow Tracery which reaches a height of 3 ft. and flowers in late May and early June

Incarvillea, Penstemon

Incarvilleas are remarkable plants with trumpet-shaped flowers like those of the greenhouse gloxinia and an exotic appearance, but in fact they are quite hardy if planted in well-drained soil and an open, sunny place. They are slow starters, should not be disturbed unnecessarily, and are best increased by seed, though the seedlings take a few years to reach flowering size.

Incarvillea delavayi is deep rose, 1½ ft. high, and flowers in June. Bees' Pink resembles it, but has clear pink flowers, and *I. grandiflora*, only 1 ft. tall, has larger deep rose flowers. Bees' Pink must be increased by careful division in spring.

Penstemons also have trumpet-shaped flowers, but smaller. They are more numerous, and carried in slender spikes continuously from July to October. There are many varieties differing in color and flower size and not all are equally hardy, but it is very easy to root stem cuttings during the summer months and overwinter them in a frame to offset losses. Otherwise penstemons are easily grown in any reasonably good, well-cultivated soil, in sun or partial shade.

Representative varieties are: Evelyn, rose pink, 1½ ft.; Firebird, scarlet, 2½ ft.; and Garnet, ruby red, 1½ ft. *Penstemon barbatus* has smaller, tubular, scarlet flowers in 4-ft. spikes. *P. heterophyllus* True Blue is 1 ft. high and has small, light blue flowers.

Liatris, Lobelia

Both liatris and lobelia are spike-flowered plants of medium size and striking color, self-supporting, and very useful for the middle positions in herbaceous beds and borders.

Liatris is sometimes known as blazing star, though the reason is not very obvious since the rather feathery purple flowers are crowded together in stout, stiff spikes with the peculiarity that they begin to open at the top and continue downward. Gay feather, another popular name, seems more appropriate. Kobold is a particularly good variety with rosy purple flowers in 2-ft. spikes in July and August.

These plants enjoy good, well-cultivated soils and sunny places, and can be left undisturbed for several years.

Some lobelias are annuals but several more are herbaceous plants, though not always fully hardy in all parts of the country. It is, however, very easy to lift them in autumn and transfer them to a frame for the winter, and in cold exposed gardens this precaution should be taken with at least a few plants to maintain a reserve. Otherwise lobelias are easy to grow, enjoying good, well-cultivated soil and plenty of water in summer.

Lobelia cardinalis and *L. fulgens* both have slender 4-ft. spikes of brilliant scarlet flowers from July to October. *Lobelia vedrariensis* has deep purple flowers and a similar habit.

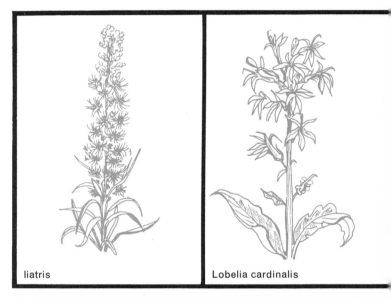

liatris

Lobelia cardinalis

The big gloxinialike flowers of incarvillea have an exotic appearance and yet the plants are completely hardy when given good winter drainage and plenty of sunshine

The small flowers of liatris are crowded together on handsome, stiff, stout spikes and are peculiar in that they open from the top downward. This kind is named *L. callilepis*

Loosestrife, Sidalcea

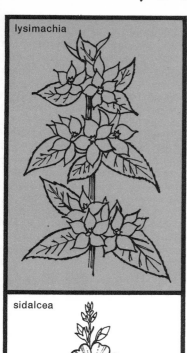

lysimachia

sidalcea

These are all spike-flowered plants, useful as a contrast to the flat or rounded heads of flowers that can easily dominate a herbaceous border.

The Yellow Loosestrife, *Lysimachia punctata*, has stiff 2- to 3-ft. spikes of bright yellow flowers in July and August and the Purple Loosestrife, *Lythrum salicaria*, has more slender 3- to 4-ft. spikes of rosy carmine flowers at the same period. The Beacon is a deeper colored variety and Robert a clear pink. Another kind of Purple Loosestrife, *Lythrum virgatum*, is shorter, 1½ to 2 ft. tall, and also has pink and carmine varieties.

All these will grow almost anywhere, and do not mind wet soils. They grow rapidly and should be divided every second or third year.

The herbaceous sidalceas have narrow, tapering 3- and 4-ft. spikes of pink, rose, or mallow purple flowers in August and September. There are numerous varieties differing in shade, representative examples being: Elsie Heugh, pale satin pink; Rev. Page Roberts, rose pink, and Mrs. Galloway, rose red.

All will grow almost anywhere, but prefer reasonably good, well-cultivated soil and open places. They should be divided every second or third year.

Lupines

lupine

The stout spikes of lupines are among the gayest flowers in the garden in June and if they are cut as soon as they fade, many plants will produce a few smaller spikes later in the season. It is, anyway, desirable to remove the faded flower spikes as they soon look untidy. Also, the heavy crops of seed they produce will weaken the plants, and if the seed is left to be naturally dispersed, seedlings of inferior quality may soon dominate the garden.

Lupines like deep, well-drained soils, but they do not thrive on limy soil on which their leaves turn yellow. Nor do they like much manure in the soil, though an annual dressing of a good compound fertilizer at about 3 oz. per sq. yd. in March will improve their quality.

Unlike many other herbaceous plants they cannot be divided and are increased either by cuttings or seeds. Cuttings of firm young shoots in spring provide the only means of raising plants exactly resembling the parents. Seedlings can be disappointing, but from commercially produced seed a good percentage of high quality plants will be obtained. Seed may be sown in a greenhouse or frame in February or March or outdoors in April or May. Early sown seedlings will often flower the same year, but they will be later than established plants.

Sidalcea is an excellent border plant, easily grown in any ordinary soil and reasonably open situation. The slender spikes of flowers are at their best in August. This variety is called Rev. Page Roberts. Suitable for U.S. Zone 8

Lupines make a gay splash of color in the herbaceous border in June and there is often a second flush of blooms later in the season. They are easily grown from seed or from cuttings of young shoots

Peonies

Although one of the most sumptuous of flowers in late spring and early summer, peonies are rather slow to start and do not like interference. They should, therefore, be placed where they can remain undisturbed for years even when plants around them are being lifted. Peonies like rather rich, well-cultivated soil and rotted manure. Garden refuse can be worked in during preparation and applied each spring. These plants thrive best in a sunny, open place, but will grow in partial shade.

The common peony, *Paeonia officinalis*, flowering in May, has very full double blooms, crimson in the variety *rubra plena*, deep rose in *rosea plena*, and white in *alba plena*. All are 2 ft. high.

The Chinese Peony, *Paeonia lactiflora*, flowers in June, is fragrant, and has single, semi-double, and fully double varieties. Representative of these are: Albert Crousse, double pink and crimson, 3 ft.; Bowl of Beauty, semi-double rosy pink and lemon, 3 ft.; Duchesse de Nemours, double white, 3 ft.; Felix Crousse, double carmine red, 3½ ft.; *festiva maxima*, double white, 3 ft.; Lady Alexandra Duff, soft pink, 3 ft.; Sarah Bernhardt, double bright rose, 3 ft., and Solange, double soft salmon, 2½ ft.

Other fine peonies are Defender, single crimson, June, 3½ ft., Sunshine (also known as *P. peregrina* and *P. lobata*), single flame red, May, 3 ft., and *Paeonia mlokosewitschii*, single primrose, May, 2½ ft.

common peony   Chinese Peony

The magnificent flowers of *Paeonia officinalis*. This single form is not as common as the fully double varieties which are great favorites with home gardeners

Perennial Asters

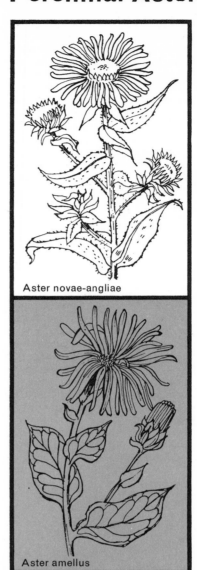
Aster novae-angliae

Aster amellus

Perennial asters, or Michaelmas daisies, grow in any reasonably cultivated soil and in sun or partial shade. Because they grow so fast it is wise to lift, divide, and replant at least every second year, though some gardeners do it annually.

The garden varieties may be divided into five main groups.

The Novi-belgii group is the most popular. Varieties have smooth shiny leaves, grow from 2 to 6 ft. high, and have single, semi-double or double flowers in large sprays in September and October. Color range is from white, pink, and pale lavender to crimson and purple.

The Novae-angliae group is similar in general appearance but the leaves are slightly downy and not shiny. All varieties are tall (4 to 6 ft.) but colors include only the pink, rose, and purple range.

The Dwarf, or Dumosa, group resembles the Novi-belgii group except that no variety exceeds 2 ft. in height and most are 1 ft. or less. They are excellent for the front of a bed or border.

All varieties in the Amellus group have rather large, single flowers carried in broad, rather flat sprays. Most are 2 to 3 ft. high and flower in August and September. Colors are mauve, soft pink, blue, and violet. Plant these in the spring; they do not transplant well in the autumn.

A miscellaneous group includes varieties with very small starry flowers freely produced in large sprays or clusters.

A variety of *Aster amellus*, an early flowering type of perennial aster with quite large single flowers during August and September. Plants are bushy and of medium height

Phlox, Garden or Summer

These perennial phlox (*Phlox paniculata*) bear their honey-scented flowers in fine heads from July to September, and at that time are among the showiest plants in the garden. They will grow almost anywhere but enjoy good, well-cultivated soil into which decayed manure or garden refuse has been worked, and which is kept well watered in dry weather. They will grow well in full sun or partial shade.

Phlox are sometimes badly attacked by eelworms. These are almost microscopic pests which enter stems and leaves and feed within them. As a result, stems become swollen, leaves are contorted and plants make little or no growth. Healthy stocks of new plants can often be produced from infected plants by root cuttings, since the roots do not become infected by eelworms, but if these healthy plants are then planted on eelworm-infested land they will soon be attacked again.

Phlox spread fairly rapidly and should be divided every third or fourth year.

There are a great many varieties differing in height from 1 to 4 ft. and in color from white, pink, and lavender to crimson, purple, and violet. Suggested varieties are: Beltsville Beauty, 3 ft. high, which can be had in a wide assortment of colors; Olive Seymons-Jeune, rich rose tinted with orange.

Pinks, Campions

These are related plants, both thriving in open, sunny places and well-drained soils. Some kinds are not long lived but they are usually easily raised from seed or cuttings, and it is wise to maintain a stock of young plants to make good losses and to replace plants that have become straggly with age. Garden pinks, which are all varieties of the hybrids of *Dianthus plumarius*, have a special liking for limy soils.

The narrow, gray leaves of pinks are decorative in themselves and look well at the front of a bed or border. There are a great many varieties, those classed as Allwoodii flowering most of the summer and the ordinary garden pinks flowering mainly in June. Many are highly fragrant. Representative varieties are: Constance, bright pink; Doris, salmon pink; Mandy, cochineal pink; Inchmery, pale pink; Mrs. Sinkins, white; and White Ladies, white.

The Rose Campion, *Lychnis coronaria*, makes a well-branched plant 2 ft. high with gray leaves and magenta crimson flowers from May to August. It is sometimes known as *Agrostemma coronaria*, and is readily raised from seed.

So is the Jerusalem Cross, or Maltese Cross, *Lychnis chalcedonica*, a slightly taller less-branched plant, with heads of vivid scarlet flowers in July and August. Both will grow well in hot, dry places and in relatively poor sandy soils.

phlox

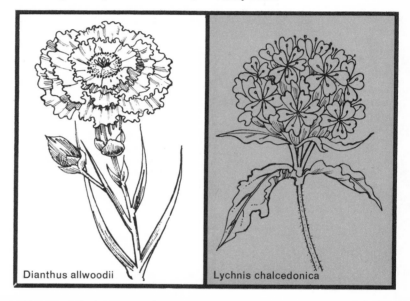

Dianthus allwoodii

Lychnis chalcedonica

Windsor, a typical variety of border phlox. Many other colors are available and varieties also differ in height and flowering time but all are sweetly scented

Lychnis chalcedonica, the Maltese or Jerusalem Cross, is a 3-ft. high herbaceous plant which is readily raised from seed. It prefers open, sunny positions and well-drained soils

Polygonums and Others

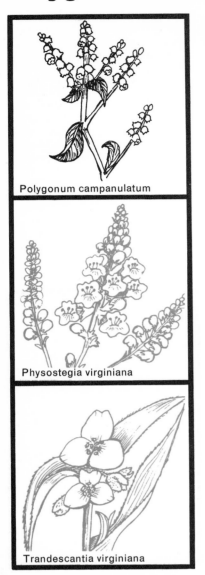

Polygonum campanulatum

Physostegia virginiana

Trandescantia virginiana

Polygonums, physostegias, and tradescantias are useful for their ability to thrive in the more difficult places and to keep on flowering for a very long time.

The herbaceous polygonums all relish damp soils and most will grow in shady as well as open situations. *Polygonum bistorta superbum* and *P. amplexicaule* both have close little spikes of bloom, pink in the former, red in the latter, on slender 2- to 3-ft. stems from July to October. *P. campanulatum* creeps about on the ground and covers itself in filmy sprays of palest pink flowers, also from July to September.

Physostegia virginiana is called the Obedient Plant because its pink tubular flowers, carried in slender spikes, can be moved about as if hinged. The commonest form is rather tall and straggly, but a variety named Vivid is only 18 in. high, quite self-supporting, and a good, deep rose color. It flowers in September and October and is well matched by Summer Snow, a pure white, slightly taller variety. Both will grow almost anywhere. *Tradescantia virginiana*, often called Spiderwort, is 18 in. tall and has clusters of three-petaled flowers from June to October, with rushlike leaves. There are several varieties such as J. C. Weguelin, light blue; Isis, dark blue; Osprey, white and blue; and *rubra*, rosy red. They will grow almost anywhere.

All these plants spread fairly rapidly and may be divided every two or three years.

Poppy, Evening Primrose

Some poppies are annuals or biennials but the Oriental Poppy, *Papaver orientale*, is a herbaceous perennial with large, immensely showy flowers in May and June. It likes deep, well-drained soil and a sunny place, and tends to rot in winter in heavy, wet, cold soil. Typically, the flowers are blood red with a black blotch at the base of each petal, but there are also scarlet-, pink- and white-flowered varieties, all about 3 ft. high. The Oriental Poppy is readily raised from seed sown outdoors in May and June but seedlings may vary in color. Selected varieties can be increased by root cuttings.

The common evening primrose, *Oenothera biennis*, is a biennial but there are other perennial kinds, the best for herbaceous borders and beds being *Oenothera fruticosa* and *O. tetragona*. These produce rather fragile-looking yellow flowers on 18-in. stems from June to August. There are several varieties differing chiefly in the exact shade and size of the flowers; Fireworks has bronzy red buds and deep yellow flowers, and Yellow River has extra-large yellow flowers. All grow readily in most soils, but prefer open sunny places. They should be divided every second or third year.

Oriental Poppy

evening primrose

The flowers of tradescantia, which are produced in succession from June to October, are unusual in that they only have three petals. Isis is one of several good varieties

The Oriental Poppy, *Papaver orientale*, is a herbaceous perennial easily raised from seed which it produces freely. Red, pink, and white varieties are available as well as some with fringed petals

Sea Holly, Globe Thistle

The sea hollies, or eryngiums, have handsome leaves and sprays of distinctive teazlelike flowers, each surrounded by a stiff ruff of bracts often in distinctive metallic shades of blue. These plants are accustomed to sandy soils and throw long taproots deep into the ground in search of water. In gardens they need good, well-drained soils and are apt to die in winter if at all waterlogged, but some kinds are more tolerant than others. One of the best and easiest is *Eryngium tripartitum*, 3 ft. high with wide sprays of small blue flowers in July and August. *E. oliverianum* has large metallic blue flowers, and Violetta is violet blue.

The globe thistles, or echinopses, are equally distinctive, with spherical heads of blue or white flowers on stiff stems in July and August. They also push stout roots down into the soil and like well-drained, sunny places. Taplow Blue is a good variety, 3½ ft. high and light blue; *Echinops ritro* is 3 ft. high and steely blue; *E. humilis nivalis* is white flowered, 5 ft. tall, and *E. sphaerocephalus* has gray green leaves, silvery gray flowers, and is 6 ft. tall.

Neither sea hollies nor globe thistles can be divided easily and are best left undisturbed. They can be increased by seed and by root cuttings.

Shasta Daisy, Pyrethrum

Shasta Daisies, or Moon Daisies, as they are often called, are big white daisies on 2- to 3-ft. stems. They are very useful for cutting in July and August, and make a fine foil to the brilliant colors of other garden flowers which are out then. They are all varieties of *Chrysanthemum maximum* and those with double flowers such as Esther Read and Wirral Supreme do slightly resemble some of the greenhouse chrysanthemums. There are a number of varieties, some single flowered, some semi-double, some fully double, and a few with a slight flush of yellow.

All are quite hardy and easily grown in most places, though for the best results they should have well-cultivated soil and an open situation. They grow so rapidly that they should be divided every second year.

Pyrethrums resemble Shasta Daisies in flower shape and size, but differ in that they make clumps of ferny leaves, their main flowering season is May and June, and they have a color range from white and pale pink to crimson. They are more difficult to grow as they need well-drained soil and a sunny situation, and may rot away in damp dark places in winter. They should be planted in spring or July and August, but should not be disturbed in autumn or winter. There are both single- and double-flowered varieties, all excellent for cutting.

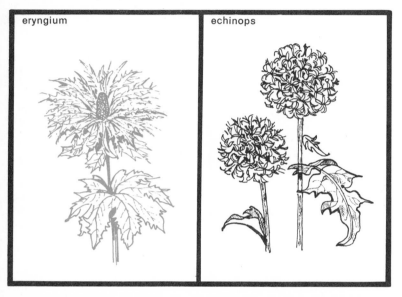

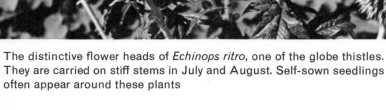

The distinctive flower heads of *Echinops ritro*, one of the globe thistles. They are carried on stiff stems in July and August. Self-sown seedlings often appear around these plants

Pyrethrums (*Chrysanthemum coccineum*) produce a first-class display in the garden and are excellent as cut flowers but they need very well-drained soil. This variety is Marjorie Robinson

Spiraea, Meadow Sweet

Spiraeas and meadow sweets enjoy cool, rather moist places, with peat or leaf mold in the soil, growing well by streams and pools or in shady parts of the garden where they do not get scorched and dried out in summer. They can be divided every three or four years.

The herbaceous spiraeas are more correctly known as astilbes to distinguish them from the shrubby spiraeas. They make clumps of ferny leaves with elegant pyramidal plumes of white, pink, or carmine flowers in June and July. Some of the numerous varieties, differing in color and height, are: Ceres, rosy lilac, 3 ft.; Fanal, ruby red, 2½ ft.; Professor van der Wielen, white, 3½ ft.; and Red Sentinel, turkey red, 2½ ft. *Astilbe simplicifolia* is only 9 in. high and has deep pink and pale pink varieties.

The meadow sweets, or filipendulas, are closely allied and enjoy similar conditions, but their plumes of flowers are more spreading or even flat topped. *Filipendula hexapetala plena* has little double, creamy white flowers on 18-in. stems in June and July and is exceptional in growing well in quite hot, dry places. *Filipendula purpurea* has deep rose flowers on 2½-ft. stems in July and August and *F. rubra* is similar but 4 ft. tall.

The Goat's Beard, *Aruncus sylvester*, grows 5 to 6 ft. high and produces large plumes of ivory flowers in June—July. It prefers moist soils but will grow almost anywhere.

astilbe

meadowsweet

Meadow sweets are admirable plants for a cool, moist corner. The delicate plumes of flowers are accompanied by fernlike leaves. Above is *Filipendula purpurea*

Spurges, Stonecrops

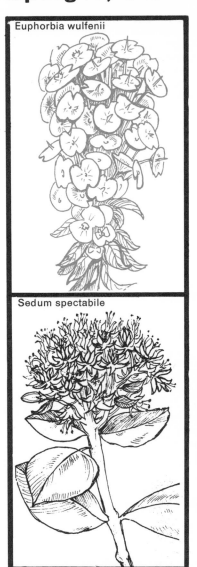

Euphorbia wulfenii

Sedum spectabile

There are many different spurges, or euphorbias, and in general they are not showy plants, but their foliage is often striking.

Euphorbia cyparissias has little narrow leaves, is 1 ft. tall, and turns bright yellow in the autumn. It loves hot, rather dry places. So does *E. epithymoides* (also known as *E. polychroma*) which is 18 in. tall and has lemon yellow flowers in April and May. *E. griffithii* is 2½ ft. high and has reddish orange flowers in May and June. *E. sikkimensis* is 3 ft. and produces a similar color effect with its foliage. Both will grow in shady places. *E. wulfenii* is semi-shrubby, 3 ft. tall, with large heads of yellowish green flowers in April and May. It is best left undisturbed, but most of the other varieties can be divided every three or four years.

The stonecrops, or sedums, also have good foliage. Many are rock plants, but the taller kinds are useful herbaceous plants for sunny places and well-drained soils. *Sedum spectabile* has fleshy gray green leaves and flat heads of pink flowers on 18-in. stems in August and September. The hybrid Autumn Joy is similar in habit, but the flowers, in September and October, are reddish pink deepening to russet red. *Sedum maximum atropurpureum* has fleshy, beetroot purple leaves and creamy flowers on 18-in. stems in August and September. All these plants can be divided every two or three years.

Euphorbia griffithii is a native of the Himalayas. Its fiery flowers are produced mainly in May and June but side branches continue to flower throughout the summer

Sunflowers

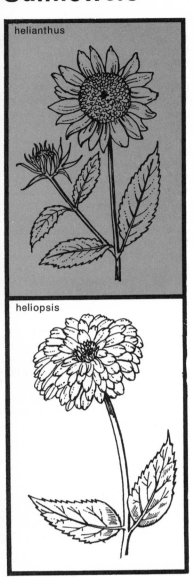

The true sunflowers are all helianthus, but here the name includes heliopsis which closely resemble sunflowers and have no popular name of their own. Both helianthus and heliopsis are vigorous, strong-stemmed, easily grown plants thriving in almost all soils but preferring sunny places. All herbaceous perennial sunflowers have yellow flowers but they differ in height, flowering time, shape of bloom, and shade of yellow.

Representative varieties are: Teddy Bear, 3 ft. tall with many laterals, flowers 5 in. across; Sungold, 7 ft. tall with flowers 6 to 8 in. across, double; Dwarf Sungold, only 15 in. high, even in dry weather or in poor soils supplies bright shot of color all summer, easy to grow; Red Sunflower, of various shades of red, some with some yellow, 5 to 6 ft.; Sutton's Red, 6 ft., chestnut red; Color Fashion, a wide range of colors; Italian White, unusual shades white to primrose yellow, 4 ft.; Autumn Beauty, sulfur yellow, copper, bronze, 5 ft.

In the heliopsis there is Summer Sun, 3 ft. high, flowers mostly doubles, 4 in. across, early to bloom the first season; Gold Greenheart, green-centered, golden yellow flowers.

Sunflowers should be divided every second year; the variety Monarch every year.

Verbascums, Veronicas

Verbascums are also known as mulleins, and are valuable because of their long, slender spikes of flowers. Some are very tall and may require support in exposed gardens. Few are long lived, but many renew themselves by self-sown seedlings, particularly when grown in light, well-drained limy soils and warm, sunny places. They should be left undisturbed, and can be increased by root cuttings. Representative varieties are: Broussa, with leaves covered in white down and yellow flowers in a 6-ft. spike in June and July; Cotswold Beauty, biscuit and lilac, June—July, 4 ft.; Gainsborough, primrose, June—July, 4 ft.; Pink Domino, mauve pink, June—July, 3 ft., and *Verbascum vernale*, yellow, July—September, 5 ft.

Veronicas also bear their flowers in spikes, but these are freely produced on bushy plants which are true perennials. Most kinds will grow almost anywhere, but prefer well-cultivated soil and an open situation. All can be divided every three or four years. Representative varieties are: Barcarolle, rose pink, 1½ ft., July to August; Minuet, gray green leaves, pink, 1½ ft., June to August; Shirley Blue, clear blue, 1 ft., June to July; Wendy, silver gray leaves, deep blue, 1½ ft., July to August; *Veronica gentianoides*, light blue, 2 ft., April to May; *V. longifolia subsessilis*, deep blue, 1½ ft., July to August, and *V. virginica alba*, white, 3½ ft., July to September.

Perennial sunflowers are excellent plants for the middle or back of the herbaceous border. This variety is Soleil d'Or and it flowers from July to September

Veronica gentianoides is one of the earliest of the herbaceous kinds and by mid-May it is fully out. The bright blue flowers are set off by shining green foliage

Practical Rose Growing

Types of Roses

hybrid tea

floribunda

dwarf polyantha

For garden purposes, roses are divided into a number of different types, each with its own characteristics of growth and flower.

Hybrid Teas have large, shapely flowers produced singly or in small clusters from June to October, with peak-flowering periods in June—July and September.

Floribundas have smaller flowers in large clusters produced over the same period. They make more display in the garden, but the flowers are not individually so beautiful.

Grandiflora is a name applied to varieties that are intermediate between hybrid teas and floribundas. They have medium-sized, shapely flowers, produced in fairly large clusters. They are becoming increasingly popular as the best all-purpose roses for garden and cutting.

Polyanthas are roses with small rosette flowers produced in large clusters from June to October. The first floribundas were produced from them.

Any of these types can be grown as standards, but usually nurserymen offer only the more vigorous kinds in this form.

Roses are the most popular of all flowers. They captivate gardeners by the variety of their colors, shapes, and perfumes, the ease with which they can be grown, the freedom with which they flower. A great industry has grown up in the production of rosebushes for gardens and also in the breeding of new roses both to meet the demand for novelty and also to replace old favorites that have become less satisfactory with age. The new roses, being raised from seed, start with a fresh lease of life whereas established varieties, which must be increased by cuttings or budding to keep them true to type, tend to become progressively debilitated by diseases which are passed on from one batch of plants to another. Nevertheless, it does not follow that the newest and most publicized roses are necessarily the best. Many old favorites show remarkable stamina and continue to delight successive generations of gardeners. There are even roses hundreds of years old that are still admired and planted and some of these have flower shapes and colors not commonly found in modern roses. However, few of these old-fashioned roses have the long flowering season of the new roses.

When planning a rose garden or border it is wise to bear in mind that some types, notably the wild roses (species), the ramblers, and some of the shrub roses, flower only once each year, whereas other roses, often collectively known as bedding or display roses, flower for a much longer period, not as a rule continuously, but in two or three bursts or flushes from June to September. Each type has its place in the garden, but their uses are different, and it is disappointing to plant, unwittingly, a nonrepeat flowering rose in a place where one had expected a succession of blooms during most of the summer.

It is unwise to choose roses solely on the character of their flowers, however desirable these may seem. Some of the most magnificent blooms are produced sparingly on plants of deplorable habit. Flower shows are not, therefore, the best places in which to choose roses, nor are nursery gardens if all they have to show are the young plants being grown for sale. It is only in older plants that the true character of the plant can be seen; whether it is sufficiently well branched to cover a reasonable area of ground, whether it is of reasonable height and has abundant as well as attractive foliage. Many rose nurseries maintain display beds of older bushes, and these can also be seen in many public gardens and parks as well as in the gardens of friends and neighbors and those so frequently and generously opened to the public for charity. These are the best places in which to decide which varieties to buy and which to leave alone.

The prize-winning rose, Piccadilly, grows about 3 ft. tall. The flowers pale to pink and soft gold as they age and the foliage, which is reddish when young, becomes a dark green

The Site

climber

rambler

old-fashioned

Climbers have long, fairly stiff stems and medium to large flowers produced singly or in clusters. Some varieties flower from June to October with peaks in June—July and September, but some flower only once in June and/or July.

Climbing Sports resemble climbers in habit but are derived from bush varieties whose names they bear and which they resemble in every aspect except the greater length of their stems. Thus Climbing Étoile de Hollande has large, shapely, crimson flowers like those of Étoile de Hollande of which it is a sport.

Ramblers are vigorous climbing or trailing roses with small flowers often of rosette type, carried in large clusters in July or August.

Shrub Roses are vigorous, bushy varieties, 5 ft. or more in height, usually with small- to medium-sized flowers produced in small or large clusters. They have various flowering times.

Old-fashioned Roses are varieties raised before the 20th century or with an appearance characteristic of these old varieties.

Miniatures are varieties which are 1 ft. or less in height with small flowers produced in clusters from June to October.

Species are wild roses, unaltered by hybridization in the garden. They are extremely variable in appearance and habit, but nearly always have single flowers.

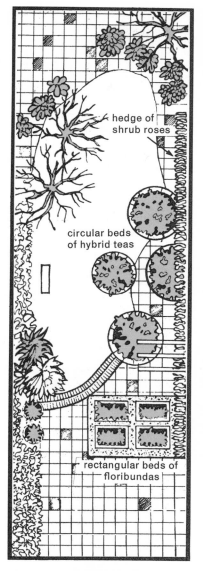

hedge of shrub roses

circular beds of hybrid teas

rectangular beds of floribundas

Roses thrive in most soils that are not very dry, very wet, very acid, or very alkaline. They prefer good loamy soils, i.e. soils consisting of a mixture of clay, sand, and decaying organic matter. In thin chalky soils, leaves are liable to become yellow through lack of green coloring matter; and in poorly drained soils some roots may die each winter, thus weakening the plants and shortening their life.

The more open the situation the more suitable it is for roses. In enclosed places, where there is little movement of air, roses may suffer badly from mildew. Some varieties will grow in the shade, but most prefer sun for at least part of the day.

Roses are frequently given beds to themselves or even a section of the garden designed specially as a rose garden. This suits them well, but they can also be grouped with other plants. Floribunda roses look well with herbaceous perennials, and vigorous shrub roses may be associated with other shrubs.

Climbing and rambler roses require the support of walls, fences, pergolas, arches, or poles. They do not climb of their own accord, but make long growths which will sprawl about if not tied in.

The main attraction of *Rosa rubrifolia* is the almost thornless growth, which is purplish copper when young. The gray and mauve tinted foliage has a coppery sheen, and the flowers are followed by brownish red hips

Baby Masquerade is a fine representative of the miniature type of rose suitable for edging or for massing in small beds such as these used to decorate a cobbled courtyard

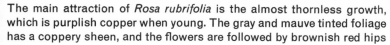

The Plan

standard

half-standard

bush

trelliswork screen

rose pyramid

Everyone will have individual ideas on how a rose garden should be planned, but a few general suggestions may be borne in mind.

Since every variety of rose has its own distinctive habit it is better to give each variety a bed to itself rather than to make beds of mixed varieties. However, standard roses look very effective planted among bush roses, so that they give a second tier of bloom. These standards may be of another variety to give contrasting color.

Beds should be sufficiently large to make a good display but not so large that they cannot be looked after without walking on them. Beds from 3 to 6 ft. wide are most convenient and effective.

A pergola or screen covered with climbing roses can make a very pleasing background to rose beds. Rose-covered arches, poles, and pyramids (three or four poles lashed together at the top) can be used to break up the level of the rose garden.

Mown grass makes a delightful background for rose beds, but in a small garden, paving will withstand the wear better.

Soil Preparation

Once planted, roses may occupy the same ground for many years, so the soil must be well prepared. Dig the site thoroughly and remove all perennial weeds, such as couch grass, bindweed, docks, thistles, and nettles. Roses like a rich soil, so work in well-rotted manure or decayed garden refuse (compost) freely. One hundredweight (a good barrowload) of either of these to every 6 sq. yd. will not be too much. If possible, complete digging at least a month before planting. If neither manure nor compost is available, use substitutes such as peat, covering ground with about 3 in. of it and working it in.

Leave ground rough after digging to "weather," but immediately prior to planting give it a dusting of bonemeal, after which break down the surface with a fork and rake to leave a level, crumbly surface.

If water readily collects on the surface, improve drainage by laying pipe drains and connecting to a ditch, or by working in coarse grit to improve the texture of the soil.

Chaplin's Pink Climber is a vigorous variety ideal for growing on a pergola. In a smaller garden it could be trained along a fence or screen or up a pillar

Brasilia, an attractive, large-flowered bicolor rose opening loosely with petals resistant to rain. It has abundant glossy foliage, which is crimson when young, and a vigorous upright habit

Planting Lifted Roses

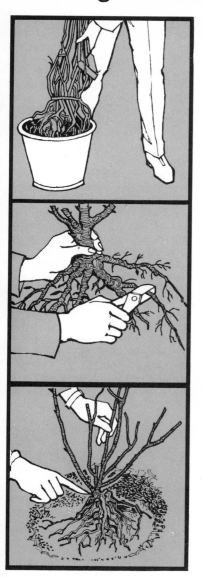

Plant roses lifted from the open ground mid-November or in spring in April. If they arrive from the nursery when the ground is frozen or too wet for planting, open the bundle or bag sufficiently to expose the stems, but not the roots, place in a shed or garage and wrap burlap, straw, or newspapers around the roots for additional protection. Plant at the first favorable opportunity.

If the roots appear dry, soak for a few minutes in a bucket of water. Cut off any damaged portions of root and the ends of long thin roots.

Plant bush roses from 18 to 24 in. apart according to the vigor of the variety. Plant standard roses 4 to 8 ft. apart, climbers and ramblers 6 to 10 ft. apart, and vigorous shrub roses at least 4 ft. apart.

Make each hole sufficiently large to accommodate all roots when naturally spread out and to allow the point of union between stems and roots to be $\frac{1}{2}$ to 1 in. below the surface. Break up the soil as it is returned, work it around the roots, and make it thoroughly firm. Plant standards so that their uppermost roots are covered with 1 in. of soil and stake immediately.

The First Pruning

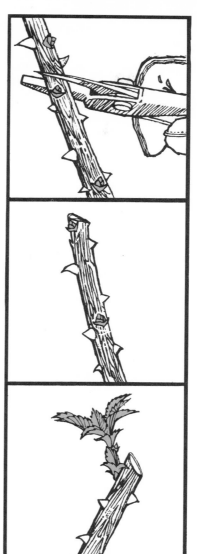

Roses that have been lifted for planting so that all or most of the soil has fallen from their roots must be pruned hard in the first year. Do this in April and cut each good stem down to about 6 in. of soil level. Cut damaged stems to healthy wood.

Prune with really sharp shears so as not to bruise the stems and make each cut just above a growth bud. These will appear as little swellings on the stems, each with a shallow semicircular scar beneath it where a leaf stalk was attached.

It is from these buds that the new shoots will grow in April. Examine them toward the end of that month and if some stems have started to grow from the lower buds leaving the uppermost bud dormant, prune again to just above the uppermost of these shoots. If this is not done, the end of the stem, lacking new growth to draw sap through it, will die and the decay may continue down the stem.

This popular rose well deserves its name of Fragrant Cloud, for the large, well-formed flowers are particularly fragrant. They are borne on strong upright stems, with dark green, glossy foliage

Queen Elizabeth is a very vigorous rose which can become excessively tall unless carefully pruned. After planting it should be hard pruned like other roses that have suffered root disturbance

Container-grown Roses

Roses grown in containers, such as pots, polyethylene bags, or tins, can be planted at any time of the year when the soil is in good condition, provided the plants are sufficiently established in the containers to be removed from them intact, with the soil around the roots.

Plant in holes sufficiently large to take the complete ball of soil as it comes from the container, with a little room to spare, so that some more fine soil can be worked in around it and also on top to a depth of about half an inch. Make this soil firm and if planting when the soil is fairly dry, water the plants well.

Container-grown roses purchased in full growth in spring or summer need not be pruned until the following winter or spring, but container-grown roses planted in autumn or winter should be pruned the following March. It is not necessary to prune so severely as for lifted roses. Cut strong stems to 5 or 6 in.; thinner stems to about 2 in.

Pruning Bush Roses

After the first year, pruning of all bush roses can be done at any time between November and April inclusive. First remove any very old, weak, diseased, or damaged stems. Old stems can be distinguished by their darker and rougher bark. Disease may show as purple or black spots or patches on the bark, or as cankers.

Prune the remaining healthy and vigorous stems according to variety and the purpose for which the roses are required. Naturally vigorous roses need lighter pruning than those that make less growth. Roses required for exhibition need harder pruning than those primarily required for garden display. Hybrid tea roses need more severe pruning than floribunda and shrub roses, and rose species.

For hard pruning shorten every strong stem to a length of about 6 in. For medium pruning (applicable to most hybrid tea roses grown for garden display) prune strong stems to 12 in. For light pruning, shorten strong stems to about 18 in.

In all pruning, make each cut just above a growth bud and make clean cuts by using sharp shears.

Whisky Mac has fragrant, shapely deep yellow blooms, freely produced. Its dark green glossy foliage is tinted bronze when young. Like other popular varieties it can usually be purchased in containers for out-of-season planting

Frühlingsmorgen, a hybrid shrub rose, produces many delicate single blooms in May and June and a few later in the season. Growth is naturally vigorous and pruning should be relatively light

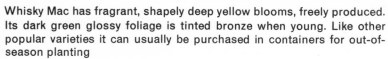

Pruning Climbers

Ramblers planted from the open ground, i.e., purchased with more or less bare roots and not in containers, must be hard pruned the first April after planting, just like bush varieties. Make an exception, however, for those varieties known as "climbing sports." These are always distinguished in catalogues by the word Climbing before their names, e.g., Climbing Étoile de Hollande, Climbing Ophelia, etc. Only shorten strong stems of these by about one-third, and weaker stems by half to two-thirds.

In subsequent years prune all climbing roses after final flowering (October to frost). With rambler roses this may be after flowering (July and August), but with many modern perpetual flowering climbers it will be between November and April as for bush varieties.

First cut out all diseased or damaged stems and as much old wood as possible without sacrificing strong young stems. These can be retained at nearly full length or be shortened as necessary to fill the available space.

Some ramblers make so much young, canelike growth from the base each summer that it is possible to cut out annually all the old stems that have just flowered and retain the young stems to flower the following year.

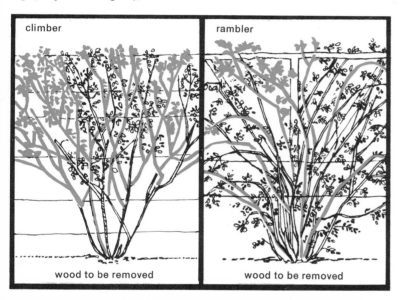

climber

rambler

wood to be removed

wood to be removed

Pruning Standards

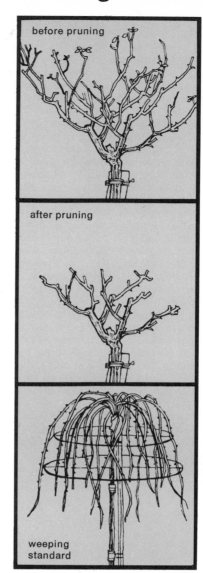

before pruning

after pruning

weeping standard

Standards are grown on a bare stem which may be anything from 2 to 4 ft. in height, with a head of branches on top so that the appearance is rather like that of a miniature tree. The main stem must be kept entirely free of growth at all times and if any shoots do appear they should be removed at once.

Prune the heads in April after frost, following the same general principles as those described for bush roses but pay greater attention to shaping the head. Make each cut immediately above a growth bud facing outward from the center of the head so that stems tend to grow outward. Remove inward pointing stems and maintain a good balance of growth all round the head.

In April rub out any new shoots that are badly placed and likely to crowd the center of the head or unbalance it.

Weeping standards are rambler roses budded on top of a 6 or 7 ft. stem from which stems cascade all round. Climbers can also be used, but these form stiffer growths and are not true weeping standards. Prune after flowering as for climbers and ramblers, but again pay particular attention to the balance of the head. A crinoline-like wire trainer can be attached to the top of the stake used to support the main stem and young growths can be tied down to it.

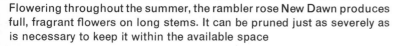

Flowering throughout the summer, the rambler rose New Dawn produces full, fragrant flowers on long stems. It can be pruned just as severely as is necessary to keep it within the available space

The floribunda rose Sarabande, grown here as a standard, is one of the most brilliant of vermilion varieties. Standards require careful pruning to keep the heads of branches well balanced all round

General Care

Keep rose beds free of weeds by hand weeding, hoeing, or by using suitable weed killers, such as Dactal or diquat.

For large individual flowers, thin out young shoots in spring, retaining the best two or three per stem. Later, when flower buds develop, thin these also to one per stem, retaining the central flower bud and removing the others (unless it is damaged when the best side bud should be retained). This thinning and disbudding is not necessary when roses are grown primarily for garden display and is never necessary for floribunda or climbing roses, which should be permitted to produce their flowers in clusters.

As flowers fade, cut them off with a short length of stem to encourage new growth and further flowering.

It is wise to spray roses as a matter of routine, whether or not pests and diseases are seen. Special combined insecticides and fungicides for use on roses can be purchased and should be used according to manufacturer's instructions about once every two weeks from May to October. Or use a mixture of a systemic insecticide, such as Isotox, with a fungicide, such as folpet (Phaltan).

Feeding

It is the natural habit of roses to replace old growth with new, and much pruning is intended to assist this end. It can only be successful if the roses are growing strong, and to ensure this they must be well fed.

Each spring, spread well-rotted manure or garden compost over the surface of the bed at about 1 cwt. (a good barrowload) to 6 sq. yd. After pruning, scatter a compound fertilizer or a specially blended rose fertilizer all over the surface of the rose beds, or for a couple of feet around each isolated rosebush, at the rate of 3 oz. per sq. yd. This fertilizer topdressing can be repeated at 2 oz. per sq. yd. at the end of May and again about six weeks later, but it should be well watered if the weather is dry.

If leaves turn yellow in summer on limestone or other alkaline soils it is probable that the soil is deficient in iron and magnesium. To rectify this, apply iron sequestrene (iron chelate) as recommended by the manufacturer and also sulfate of magnesium (Epsom salts) at 1 oz. per sq. yd.

If neither manure nor compost is available for spring application, use peat as a substitute and increase the spring fertilizer application to 4 oz. per sq. yd.

Escapade, a rather unusual color in the floribunda range. The fragrant flowers are semi-double and are borne on well-spaced trusses. A vigorous grower with glossy foliage

Christian Dior, a large-flowered rose with full shapely flowers borne on long stems. Like most of its kind it responds well to generous feeding coupled with fairly hard pruning

Suckers

Almost all commercially produced roses are budded on to a stock. The roots of the purchased plant are therefore of a different kind of rose from the stems, and if allowed to produce shoots these will bear flowers of a different and inferior kind (usually single, wild roses). Such shoots, growing direct from the roots or from the main stem below the head of branches, are referred to as suckers and must be removed as soon as they are seen.

Suckers can be recognized by the fact that they come from below the main branches of the bush or standard and that they have a slightly different appearance. Usually they are thinner, with smaller leaves which are a different shade of green from the rest of the plant.

Thorns are also usually of a different character from those on the true garden rose stems. A comparison of the two shoots side by side usually reveals these differences quite plainly.

Cut off suckers at the place from which they grow. If they come straight from the roots, scrape away some soil with a trowel so that they can be cut off cleanly where they join the roots. Do not chop them off with a spade or a further crop of suckers will appear.

Any shoots arising partway up a standard rose stem are also certain to be sucker growths, and should be rubbed off as soon as they appear.

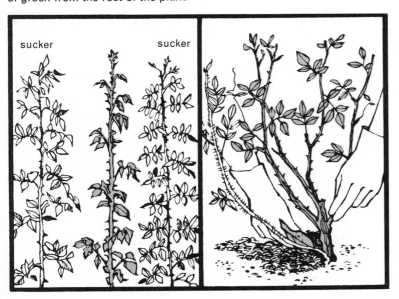

Rose Hedges

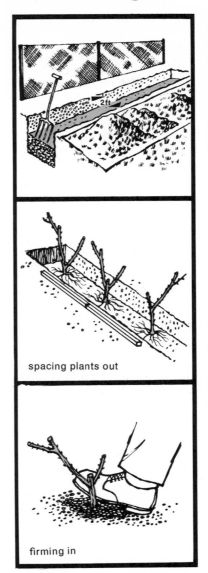

spacing plants out

firming in

Many vigorous varieties of roses make excellent ornamental hedges in good, well-cultivated soil and open places, though few are suitable for close and regular clipping, which interferes with flowering. However, the sweetbriar, *Rosa rubiginosa*, is grown mainly for the fragrance of its leaves and so can be pruned repeatedly. It makes a dense, thorny, impenetrable hedge to about 5 ft. Plant 1½ ft. apart and prune hard to encourage branching from ground level.

Any of the shrub roses may be planted 2 ft. apart to form informal hedges, which can be pruned to shape in winter or early spring and again in summer after each flush of flowers. According to their vigor they are suitable for hedges 4 to 6 ft. high and nearly as much through.

Floribunda and grandiflora roses can be used in the same way. Plant vigorous varieties, such as Frensham, crimson; Queen Elizabeth, pink, and Daily Sketch, pink and silver; 2 ft. apart. They will make good hedges of 4 to 6 ft. in height. Plant less vigorous varieties, such as Iceberg, white; Masquerade, yellow and red; Spartan, 3 ft., red coral; Valentine, 1½ ft., red; and Circus Parade, 3 to 4 ft., multicolor, 1½ ft. apart to make hedges 3 to 5 ft. in height.

The beautifully scented hybrid tea rose Wendy Cussons, a valuable asset to any garden. It produces many perfectly formed blooms, which are able to withstand rain

Extremely attractive rose hedges can be made by using vigorous varieties but careful pruning is required to preserve some regularity in shape without interfering with flowering

Roses on Walls

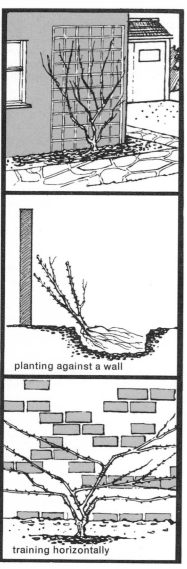

planting against a wall

training horizontally

Suitable roses can be found to be grown against walls whatever their location, even those facing north which get no direct sunshine. Since roses are not natural climbers some means of support must be provided. This may be wires trained between "vine eyes" fixed in the masonry, trelliswork, or nylon-coated netting. Whichever method is chosen, make sure that it is securely fastened, for roses in full growth can be very heavy. Also, attach it 2 or 3 in. away from the wall so that it will be easy to tie the rose stems to it, for this will have to be done several times each summer to keep them tidy.

Plant at least a foot away from the wall, not close against it where the soil is sure to be dry. If plants do not make sufficient growth from low down to clothe the wall properly, cut one or two good stems back to within a foot of ground level at pruning time or train one or two shoots almost horizontally. This will check the rise of sap through them and encourage dormant buds to start into growth.

With climbing sports, retain the best of the older stems and shorten side shoots which have already flowered to about 1 in. to encourage fresh growth.

Underplanting

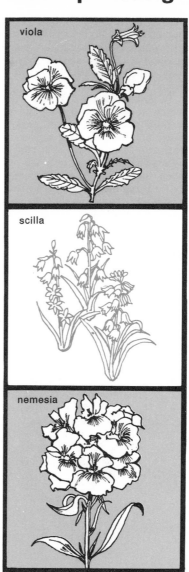

viola

scilla

nemesia

Though the less vigorous hybrid teas undoubtedly thrive best when planted in beds on their own, a great many modern roses, including most floribunda varieties, do not suffer from the competition of suitably chosen underplanting and this can be very useful to supplement the display made by the roses and continue it over a longer season.

Select plants not above 1 ft. in height, that are fairly shallow rooting, and that will look attractive with the roses when they are in bloom. Violas and pansies are very suitable; the Lavender Cotton, or santolina, makes a good, silver gray background for scarlet and crimson roses. Most low-growing annuals and bedding plants may be used, particularly Sweet Alyssum, ageratum, lobelia, nemesia, and verbena. Spring-flowering bulbs such as short tulips, hyacinths, crocuses, scillas, and chionodoxas may be planted for a spring display.

Creeping rock plants, such as arabis, aubrieta, and *Veronica prostrata*, may be used to carpet beds, and small herbaceous plants, such as *Hosta albo-marginata*, *Geranium* Johnson's Blue, variegated sage, nepeta (Catmint), and *Tiarella cordifolia* make excellent border plants for rose beds.

Madame Gregoire Staechelin, a climbing rose, trained up the wall of a house. Plastic-coated netting attached to the wall provides support for the rose, and is soon hidden by the leaves and branches

A border of shrub roses, with Catmint, pinks, and other perennials to prolong the flowering season. Vigorous roses accept this dual planting without ill effect provided they are well cared for

Pests

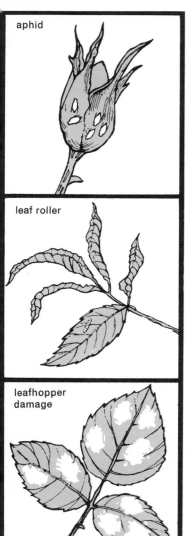

aphid

leaf roller

leafhopper damage

Aphids may appear at any time from spring to autumn, and they will multiply very rapidly. The young shoots and leaves are attacked first and the green insects cluster around these, sucking sap from them. At the first sign of attack, spray with an aphid insecticide and repeat as necessary.

Leafhoppers live on the undersides of leaves, sucking sap from them, as a result of which the leaves become mottled with white. Empty white skin cases may be found sticking to the undersides of leaves. Spray as for aphids.

A mass of froth is produced for protection by young spittlebugs. When only a few, remove the insect inside the froth by hand, otherwise spray forcibly with malathion.

One kind of leaf roller eats the surface of the leaves so that only a skeleton remains, while another causes the leaves to roll up. For either, spray at the first sign of attack, with Isotox.

Insects of various kinds eat holes in rose leaves and can also be killed by spraying with Isotox.

Thrips are small, narrow, active, yellowish or nearly black insects which attack leaves and flowers, particularly in hot weather. Leaves become mottled and flowers fail to open or are disfigured and petal edges turn brown. Spray as soon as damage is seen with Isotox or malathion (when used, Isotox above 80°F. causes burning).

Diseases

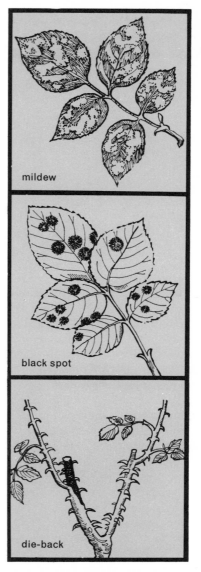

mildew

black spot

die-back

Mildew produces a powdery white coating on stems, leaves, and flowers. Some rose varieties are more susceptible than others and the disease is particularly troublesome where there is little air movement. Spray with Benlate (benomyl) as a protection before the disease appears and repeat every few weeks.

Black spot produces roundish black spots on the leaves, which rapidly increase in size until the leaf falls prematurely. Some varieties are especially susceptible. Spray as a protection with Phaltan wettable powder or other recommended fungicide, starting in mid-April and continuing at 10- to 14-day intervals until September.

Rust is identified by the small, orange-colored pustules it produces on the lower surface of the rose leaves. Spray every two weeks as a preventive with Phaltan, starting in May and continuing until October.

Stem canker attacks the stems, producing dark patches which eventually burst open to form large wounds. Cut out and burn all infected growth. For canker, spray with lime sulfur early in spring when dormant. In summer use Phaltan and Isotox.

Vera Dalton is a particularly good pink cluster-flowered rose which seldom gives much trouble in the garden. However, it must be protected from aphids, a universal rose enemy

This rosebush has been badly attacked by mildew, a disease which can be particularly troublesome where there is little movement of air. Effective fungicides are available to control it

Bulbs for Garden Display

Buying Bulbs

"single-nosed" bulb

"double-nosed" bulb

"mother" bulb

Bulbs, corms, and tubers are all storage organs which enable plants to survive periods of drought or inactivity. Most can be kept dry for quite long periods in cool, airy frostproof sheds or rooms and are usually sold in this condition by bulb merchants.

Many of the most commonly grown kinds, such as daffodils, tulips, crocuses, and gladiolus are usually carefully graded by size before sale. Some are sold according to the maximum circumference of the bulb, which is usually measured in inches.

Daffodils are graded according to the number of "noses," or growing points, they have. Thus a "single-nosed," or "round," has only one growing point and is unlikely to produce more than one flower, a "double-nosed" bulb may produce two flowers and a "mother bulb" will have more than two growing points. Large bulbs are worth more than small bulbs of the same variety, since in general they will produce better plants.

The two principal seasons for buying bulbs are in autumn for the hardy kinds and in spring for those that are more tender. There are also a few autumn-flowering bulbs that need to be planted in July or August.

Most plants that produce bulbs or other storage organs (collectively known as bulbs) become almost completely dormant at some time of the year. Foliage dies and the bulbs can then be dug up and stored for weeks or even months. It is not essential that this should be done, but it does provide a convenient method of marketing bulbs which can be sold "dry" in shops. Those bulbs that flower in the spring or early summer mostly die down sometime between June and August and are then planted in the autumn. Bulbs that flower in late summer mostly die down in the autumn and are planted in the spring. Bulbs that flower in autumn die down in May or June and are planted in July or early August. Bulbs are of many different kinds and can be grown in various ways. Tulips and hyacinths are particularly useful for spring bedding displays and for cultivation in pots, window boxes, and other containers. Daffodils, crocuses, and snowdrops are usually planted more informally and may be naturalized in grass, provided it is not mown until their leaves are beginning to ripen and turn yellow in May or June. Small bulbs such as grape hyacinths and scillas are often grown on rock gardens or used to make carpets of spring color beneath taller plants.

A special tool can be obtained for planting bulbs in grass. It has a spadelike handle and a small circular blade which cuts out a neat core of turf just large enough to enable a bulb to be dropped in. Then the core is replaced, leaving little or no trace of the operation. Naturalized bulbs are usually permitted to grow undisturbed for years. They benefit from an annual early spring topdressing of a good compound fertilizer or bonemeal at 3 oz. to each square yard and this will also feed the grass.

Because spring-flowering bulbs die down in summer they can be used effectively with deciduous shrubs, which are bare of leaves when the bulbs are growing and flowering, or with herbaceous plants, most of which have hardly started to grow so early in the year. By such means a double display can be obtained from the same piece of ground without need for any extra work or replanting. Winter Aconite (eranthis), snowdrops, crocuses, scillas chionodoxas, muscaris, and daffodils are particularly recommended for this kind of two-tier planting since they do not have to be lifted annually but can be left undisturbed for years until they get overcrowded.

Bulbs that are dormant in summer are also sometimes useful in hot, dry situations since they are at rest when conditions are most unfavorable to growth. The thorough ripening the bulbs get under these conditions is often just what they need to make them flower freely.

Columbine, a primulinus gladiolus with upper petal curved over the flower like a little hood. Gladiolus corms are sold by size but it is not necessarily the largest that produce the best flowers

Increasing Bulbs and Corms

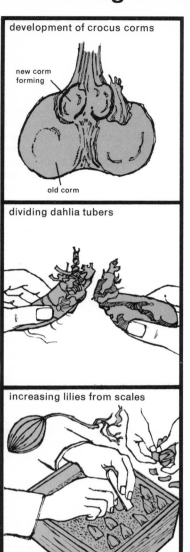

development of crocus corms

new corm forming

old corm

dividing dahlia tubers

increasing lilies from scales

Almost all bulbs can be increased by seed sown in spring in pots, frames, or sheltered borders outdoors, but seedlings take several years to flower and often differ markedly from their parent plants in flower color, form, etc. New varieties are raised from seed in this way.

Selected varieties are usually increased by division of the bulb clusters when these are lifted for cleaning and replanting.

Corms form new corms on top as the old corms wither away and also cormels (tiny corms) are formed around them. Both corms and cormels can be separated but cormels should be planted in a reserve bed to grow on longer as it is unlikely that they will flower for a year or more.

Tubers can be increased by careful division, which is best done when they start into growth and it can be seen just where the new shoots are. Each division must have both a portion of tuber and at least one shoot or growth bud. A sharp knife may be required to divide the tubers cleanly; dust wounds with sulfur.

Many lilies can be increased from mature bulb scales detached in autumn and kept in damp sand and peat in a frame or cool greenhouse. Some lilies, e.g. Tiger Lily, produce bulbils up the flowering stems. If collected when about to fall off in early autumn, and pressed gently into the surface of pans of seed compost, these root readily. Grow on as for cormels.

Allium, Ornithogalum

Allium ostrowskianum

Allium neapolitanum

Ornithogalum umbellatum

The onion and leek are both alliums and some of the ornamental species, grown for their handsome flower heads, have a similar odor when crushed. Alliums are easily grown in sunny places and reasonably good well-drained soils. Among the most decorative are *Allium ostrowskianum*, with globular heads of lilac pink flowers; *A. neapolitanum* with looser heads of white flowers; *A. moly* with yellow flowers; *A. rosenbachianum* with very large heads of purplish flowers, and *A. sphaerocephalum* with small heads of plum purple flowers. All flower in summer.

Ornithogalum umbellatum has sprays of white flowers on foothigh stems in June, and is known as Star of Bethlehem. *O. thyrsoides* has 15-in. spikes of papery, white everlasting flowers in May and June and is the South African Chincherinchee. The flowers are excellent for cutting and will last many months.

Plant all alliums and ornithogalums except the Chincherinchee in autumn 3 in. deep and 6 to 9 in. apart. Plant the Chincherinchee in April 3 in. deep and 4 in. apart in a specially warm and well-drained place or grow in pots, five or six bulbs in a 5-inch pot in a sunny, unheated greenhouse.

Poppy Anemones provide a riot of color in the garden in spring or early summer and are also useful for flower arranging in the home. They can be increased from seed or by the small tubers they produce

Ornithogalum umbellatum, the Star of Bethlehem, is an attractive bulbous plant for June display. It can be allowed to grow for many years without disturbance and will often spread considerably

Amaryllis, Crinum

Crinum powellii

Some people call hippeastrum by the name of amaryllis, but here the name is used for the Belladonna, or Jersey Lily, *Amaryllis belladonna*. It produces fine heads of trumpet-shaped pink and white flowers on stout 2-ft. stems in September. Plant the bulbs in autumn in well-drained soil and in warm, sunny, sheltered places, such as in a border near the foot of a south-facing wall. Cover only just the tip of the bulb, and in cold places, protect in winter with a covering of chopped straw or salt hay. Leave undisturbed for years. Or plant one bulb in a 6- or 7-in. pot of potting mix and grow in a frost-proof greenhouse in winter, standing the pots outdoors from June to September. Water moderately in winter, freely from March to June, and then keep the soil almost dry until flowering shoots appear in August.

Crinums have large, trumpet-shaped pink or white flowers on 3- to 4-ft. stems in summer, and are grown in the same way as the Belladonna Lily except that they should not be kept dry in summer as they are growing freely then, and not resting.

Anemone, Ranunculus

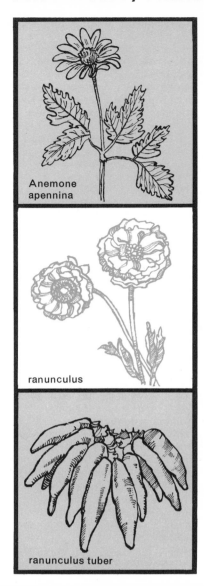

Anemone apennina

ranunculus

ranunculus tuber

Poppy Anemones produce showy flowers in shades of pink, red, and blue in spring and early summer. They make first-rate cut flowers. St. Brigid varieties have double flowers, and De Caen varieties single flowers.

Plant from October to April for successive flowering in good, fairly rich, well-drained soil and a sheltered, sunny place. Soak tubers in water for a few hours before planting. Plant 2 in. deep and 4 in. apart and protect early plantings in winter with a scattering of peat or chopped straw. Lift tubers when foliage dies down in summer and store till planting time or leave undisturbed and protect in winter.

Other tuberous-rooted anemones are *A. blanda* with blue or pink flowers; *A. apennina* with blue flowers; and *A. nemorosa* with white or pale blue flowers; all flower from March to May. They are suitable for cool, partially shaded rock gardens, as edgings for beds, beneath thinly planted shrubs or for woodland. Plant 2 in. deep in rather leafy or peaty soil in September or October.

Giant-flowered ranunculus have showy double or semi-double flowers on foot-high stems from May to July.

Plant tubers claw side downward, 2 in. deep in specially sunny and sheltered places in rich, well-drained soil. Lift tubers when foliage dies down and store until planting time. They are not suitable for cold gardens.

Amaryllis belladonna, the Belladonna Lily, bears its magnificent, fragrant flowers on strong 2-ft. high stems in late summer. If planted near a sunny wall, they will flower freely every year

Anemone blanda produces its pretty, starlike flowers early in the spring. It can take more sunshine than its ally, the British wood anemone (*A. nemorosa*), and is often planted in rock gardens

Chionodoxa, Muscari

Grape Hyacinth

Chionodoxa is known as Glory of the Snow, because its sprays of brilliant little blue and white flowers come so early in the spring, sometimes almost before the snow has gone. It is a fine plant for rock gardens, for edging borders, or for planting under trees. Plant in autumn, 3 in. deep in reasonably good soil and leave undisturbed until overcrowded.

Muscari is known as Grape Hyacinth, because the little spikes of blue or white flowers look like tiny half-opened hyacinths or the newly formed bunches of grapes. They spread rapidly and are excellent for rock gardens or beds or as edgings to paths. Plant in autumn, 3 in. deep in any reasonably good soil, and in a sunny or partially shaded place. There are several different varieties, of which Heavenly Blue is one of the brightest and fastest growing. *Muscari tubergenianum* is known as the Oxford and Cambridge Grape Hyacinth because its spikes (8 in. high) are dark blue above and pale blue at the base. *M. botryoides album* is white flowered. *M. comosum plumosum* is known as the Feather or Tassel Hyacinth because its blue flower sprays are loose and feathery. As they naturally flop about, this plant looks best on a sunny ledge in the rock garden.

Crocus, Colchicum

Though crocus and colchicum are unrelated, their flowers have a superficial resemblance, and colchicums are often known as Autumn Crocuses. A better popular name is Meadow Saffron since there are true crocuses that flower in the autumn.

Both crocus and colchicum thrive in most soils, but the wild species of crocus prefer light, well-drained soils. All thrive in open, sunny places and colchicums will grow in partial shade.

Prepare ground by thorough digging. Work in some well-rotted manure or compost and scatter bonemeal at 3 oz. per sq. yd. over the surface.

Plant spring-flowering crocuses in September or October, autumn-flowering crocuses and colchicums in late July or August. Make holes for corms 2 to 3 in. deep; for colchicums 6 in. deep. Space crocus corms 3 to 4 in. apart; colchicums 6 to 8 in. apart.

Both crocus and colchicum can be naturalized in grass. Plant with a special bulb-planting tool, or remove turfs, plant with a trowel or spade and replace the turfs. Grass must not be cut until crocus and colchicum foliage has died down in May or June.

Leave plants undisturbed until overcrowded, then lift as soon as foliage dies down. Divide the clusters of crocus corms or colchicum bulbs and replant at normal planting time. Feed each spring with bonemeal, 2 oz. per sq. yd.

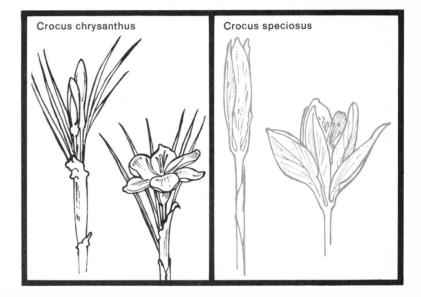
Crocus chrysanthus

Crocus speciosus

Muscari Heavenly Blue spreads rapidly to form a carpet of brightly colored blooms which are attractive in bedding displays or in a rock garden. In the background is *Narcissus* Scarlet Elegance

Colchicum speciosum flowering in the autumn long before its broad leaves appear. The large bulbs are totally unlike the much smaller corms of crocus to which the flowers have a superficial resemblance

Cyclamen

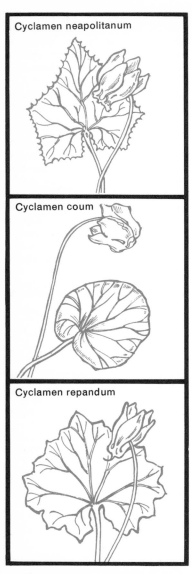

Cyclamen neapolitanum

Cyclamen coum

Cyclamen repandum

The fine greenhouse cyclamen are too tender to be grown out of doors, but there are also a number of small wild cyclamen that are quite hardy, and are delightful plants for cool, shady places in rock gardens, on banks or under trees. All like plenty of leaf mold or peat and dislike disturbance. When the site is congenial they spread by self-sown seedlings.

All make flattish corms which are sold dry, or they may be purchased growing in containers. Start dry corms into growth in damp peat in a frame or greenhouse and plant out when they have a few leaves. Container-grown plants can be planted at any time, with the tops of the corms just covered with soil.

Cyclamen neapolitanum has indented, dark green leaves marbled with white. The pink flowers on 6-in. stems are produced from August to October. The variety *album* is white flowered.

Cyclamen orbiculatum has smaller, rounded, dark green leaves, sometimes with a silver zone or markings, and the flowers, on 3-in. stems, come from January to April. There are pink, crimson, and white varieties, some of which may be sold as *C. coum, C. atkinsii*, or *C. hiemale. C. repandum* has marbled, ivylike leaves and pink, crimson, or white flowers in March and April.

Daffodils

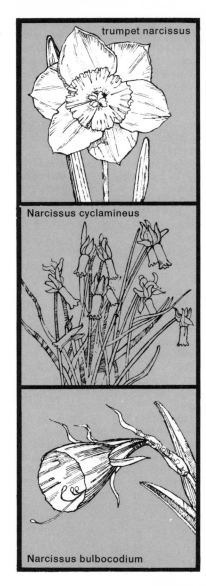

trumpet narcissus

Narcissus cyclamineus

Narcissus bulbocodium

Daffodils are botanically known as narcissus. In popular garden usage "narcissus" is reserved for varieties with a cup or eyelike center to the flower, and "daffodil" for those with a trumpetlike center.

For garden purposes daffodils are divided into 11 types according to the character of the flower:

1. Trumpet Narcissus, e.g., Beersheba, Golden Harvest, King Alfred, Mount Hood, Queen of Bicolors, Rembrandt, Spellbinder, Unsurpassable.

2. Large-cupped Narcissus, e.g., Carbineer, Carlton, Eddy Canzony, Fleurimont, Fortune, John Evelyn, Rustom Pasha.

3. Small-cupped Narcissus, e.g., Chungking, Firetail, Matapan, Mystic, Verger.

4. Double-flowered Narcissus, e.g., Golden Ducat, Inglescombe, Mary Copeland, Van Sion, White Lion.

5. Triandrus Narcissus, e.g., Silver Chimes, Thalia.

6. Cyclamineus Narcissus, e.g., Beryl, Dove Wings, February Gold.

7. Jonquilla Narcissus, e.g., Lanarth, Trevithian, Waterperry.

8. Tazetta Narcissus, e.g., Cheerfulness (double), Cragford.

9. Poeticus Narcissus, e.g., Actaea, Pheasant's Eye (recurvus).

10. Species Narcissus (wild forms), e.g., *N. bulbocodium, N. pseudo-narcissus* (English Wild Daffodil), *N. triandrus albus* (Angel's Tears).

11. Any other kind, e.g., Orchid-flowered, Butterfly-flowered.

Cool, shady corners of a rock garden can be filled to advantage with *Cyclamen repandum*, where pink, crimson, or white flowers will develop amidst marbled ivylike leaves

Verger is typical of the small-cupped type of narcissus. Not all varieties have a similar strong contrast between the color of the cup or corona and the surrounding petals or perianth segments

Eranthis, Erythronium

Daffodils grow in most soils but prefer a rich, well-drained loam. They thrive in full sun or partial shade and many kinds can be naturalized in grass.

Prepare beds by thorough digging. Add rotted manure or garden compost and finish by scattering bonemeal over the surface at 3 oz. per sq. yd. Plant bulbs at least 6 in. apart in August, September, or October (the earlier the better). Use a trowel and plant so that the bulbs rest firmly on the soil at the bottom of the hole, and are covered by their own depth of soil.

Daffodils can be lifted in late June when the leaves have died down, but it is not necessary to lift every year. Store lifted bulbs in shallow boxes in a cool, dry place until it is time to replant. Clusters of bulbs may be split into individual bulbs, but plant undersized bulbs in a reserve bed to gain size.

Daffodils also grow well in pots in unheated or moderately heated greenhouses, frames, etc. Pot in August or September, shoulder to shoulder, in 6- or 7-in. pots, or place two layers of bulbs staggered one above the other in an 8- or 9-in. pot. Plunge pots beneath 2 in. of sand, peat, or sifted ashes in a shady place and leave for at least ten weeks. Then take the pots into a greenhouse or under other protection and keep well watered. After flowering allow bulbs to complete their growth, then shake away the soil and store ready to plant out in the autumn. Do not force bulbs a second year.

Eranthis is a delightful little plant with yellow, buttercuplike flowers each surrounded by a green ruff. They appear in midwinter when little else is in flower, and the plant is popularly known as Winter Aconite. It will grow in shade, and can be used to carpet the ground beneath shrubs or as an edging to a shady border. Plant in autumn 2 in. deep in good, rather moist soil, and leave undisturbed for years to spread into a low carpet of growth which dies down completely in summer but reappears in January.

Erythronium is equally delightful, and because the commonest kind, *E. dens-canis*, has little mauve pink nodding flowers in early spring it is known as Dog's-tooth Violet, though it is really more like a cyclamen. There are several other kinds; one named Pagoda has yellow flowers on foot-high stems.

Erythroniums will also grow in shade, but not such dense shade as Winter Aconite. A north-facing rock garden or bank suits them well.

Plant erythroniums in autumn 2 in. deep in soil with which plenty of peat or leaf mold has been mixed, and leave undisturbed for years.

correctly positioned bulbs

storing bulbs

bulbs planted in a double layer

Dog's-tooth Violet

The delicate reflexed petals of *Narcissus* Dove Wings are a characteristic of the cyclamineus group, to which it belongs. This variety is suitable for the rock garden or mixed border

Eranthis tubergenii, a charming hybrid form of Winter Aconite. If left undisturbed, these plants will in time make a carpet beneath trees or shrubs that are not too closely planted

Fritillaries

Crown Imperial

The Snake's head Fritillary, or *Fritillaria meleagris*, is so called because its nodding, bell-shaped flowers, carried on slender foot-high stems, are spotted and checkered rather like the skin of a snake. They are in shades of purple and white and are produced in April and May. This fritillary thrives in good, loamy soil and partially shaded places and can be naturalized in grass that is not cut until about midsummer. Plant in autumn 4 in. deep and 6 in. apart and leave undisturbed for many years.

The Crown Imperial is also a fritillary, named *Fritillaria imperialis*, but it is very different in appearance. It makes a stout stem 3 ft. high, terminating in a cluster of nodding yellow or reddish orange bell-shaped flowers surmounted by a tuft of green leaves. It thrives in rich, loamy but well-drained soils and open, sunny places and is not suitable for naturalizing in grass. Plant the bulbs in autumn in holes 6 to 8 in. deep and 12 in. apart and leave undisturbed. Alternatively, the bulbs may be planted on their sides to prevent water collecting in the hollow on the top, and causing decay. This is a useful precaution on damp, heavy soils and in wet climates.

Galtonia, Camassia

Camassia cusickii

Camassia esculenta

Galtonia candicans is known as the Summer Hyacinth because its 4-ft spikes of nodding, ivory white flowers do look rather like a greatly enlarged hyacinth and they are produced in late summer (August and September). Plant the bulbs in autumn or early spring 6 in. deep and at least 1 ft. apart in fairly rich soil and a sunny position. Plants may be left undisturbed until overcrowded, or may be lifted, separated into single bulbs, and replanted in autumn or spring.

Camassias produce their starry blue or white flowers in long narrow spikes 2 to 3 ft. high in early summer, and are good plants for a sunny border. They associate well with other early-flowering herbaceous perennials and are not fussy about soil so long as it is reasonably well drained.

Plant the bulbs in autumn 3 in. deep and about 12 in. apart in an open or partially shaded bed or border. Lift and divide in autumn when overcrowded.

Recommended kinds are *Camassia cusickii*, lavender, 2 ft.; C. *esculenta*, deep blue, 2 ft.; C. *leichtlinii*, blue, 3 ft.; C. *leichtlinii alba*, white, 3 ft.

The Snake's-head Fritillary, *Fritillaria meleagris*, with its spotted petals reminiscent of a snake's skin, will naturalize well in shady places. White-flowered forms are also available

Galtonia candicans produces spikes of bell-like, fragrant flowers in August and September on 4-ft. high stems. The bulbs should be planted in rich soil and a sunny position

Hyacinths

Hyacinths are sold either as "ordinary" or "specially prepared" bulbs, the latter having been given special treatment to make them grow rapidly. Such bulbs are useful for forcing in greenhouses or indoors, but only ordinary bulbs should be planted outdoors.

Cynthella Hyacinths (also known as Roman Hyacinths) and Miniature Hyacinths have smaller, looser flower spikes and are most useful for indoor and greenhouse culture.

Prepare soil by thorough digging and working in some well-rotted manure or compost. Finish off with a scattering of bonemeal at 3 oz. per sq. yd. Improve drainage if soil is liable to lie wet in winter. Hyacinths succeed best in moderately rich, well-drained soils in sunny, sheltered places.

Plant in September or October with a trowel, making holes twice as deep as the bulbs, and spacing them 6 to 8 in. apart. Scatter peat, chopped straw, or dead leaves over the surface of the bed in winter as a protection against frost.

Lift bulbs in June when the foliage has died down and store in shallow trays in a cool, dry place until replanting time.

Hyacinths for greenhouse and indoor culture may be grown in drained pots in ordinary potting soil, or in undrained bowls in special bulb fiber.

Roman Hyacinth

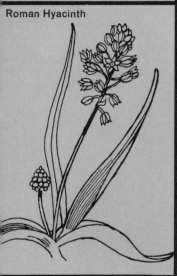

Bulbous Irises

Spanish Iris

Iris reticulata

Iris danfordiae

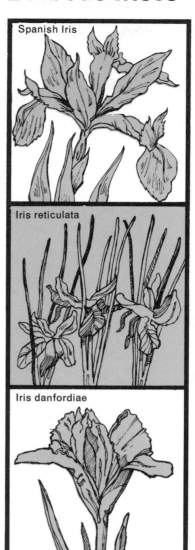

There are numerous kinds of iris with bulbous roots, and all should be planted as dry bulbs in September or October. They like good, well-drained soil and an open, sunny position.

Prepare ground by thorough digging and work in a moderate quantity of well-rotted manure or garden compost. Scatter bonemeal over the surface at 3 oz. per sq. yd.

Plant with a trowel 3 in. deep and 4 to 6 in. apart. When overcrowded, lift in summer as soon as the foliage has died down, separate bulb clusters and store in a cool, dry place until normal planting time.

English, Dutch, and Spanish Irises all produce fine flowers on long stems in May and June. There are white, blue, yellow, orange, and bronze purple varieties and all make excellent cut flowers.

Iris histrioides has blue flowers on 4-in. stems in January to February; *I. reticulata*, violet purple flowers on 6-in. stems in February to March; *I. danfordiae*, yellow flowers on 4-in. stems in January to February. All are best planted in the rock garden or in sheltered borders as their flowers are easily damaged by frost and rain. *I. danfordiae* requires particularly rich, light, well-drained soil and is more difficult than the other two.

ixed hyacinths used as bedding plants are well suited to the formality f this paved garden. After flowering the bulbs should be lifted and anted in a less conspicuous place until the leaves have died

The Spanish Iris flowers well in a sunny border in May and June. It is an excellent flower for cutting and arranging, as well as being very decorative in the garden. Suitable for U.S. Zone 7

Lilies

Trumpet Lily

Turk's Cap Lily

Upright-flowering Lily

Lilies may be classified according to the shapes of their flowers and the way in which they are borne.

Trumpet Lilies have long funnel-shaped flowers usually produced in clusters, e.g., Black Dragon, white and purple, 6 ft.; Golden Clarion, yellow, 4 ft.; Limelight, lemon, 4 ft.; *Lilium longiflorum*, white, 3 ft.; *L. candidum*, white, 3 ft.; Olympic Hybrids, cream to pink, 4 ft.; Pink Perfection, pink, 4 ft.; *L. regale*, white and yellow, 4 ft.

Turk's Cap Lilies have pendant flowers, the petals of which are curved back. They are usually borne in large sprays, e.g., Bellingham Hybrids, yellow to red, 6 ft.; Bright Star, orange and white, 4 ft.; Fiesta Hybrids, yellow to maroon, 3 ft.; *L. hansonii*, yellow, 4 ft.; *L. henryi*, orange, 4 ft.; *L. martagon*, white to maroon, 4 ft.; *L. pardalinum*, orange and maroon, 4 ft.; *L. speciosum*, pink and white, 4 ft.; *L. tigrinum*, orange, 4 ft.; *L. davidii willmottiae*, orange red, 4 ft.

Bowl-shaped lilies have large, widely opened flowers which may be broadly funnel shaped or nearly flat, e.g., *L. auratum*, white and gold, 5 ft.; Green Dragon, green and white, 3 ft.; Jamboree Strain, white and red, 5 ft.

Upright-flowering lilies have clusters of flowers facing upward and outward, e.g., Cinnabar, maroon, 2½ ft.; Mid-century Hybrids, lemon to crimson, 2 to 3 ft.; *L. hollandicum*, yellow to blood red, 12 to 18 in.

½ in.

3 in.

Lilium candidum

Lilium testaceum

other lilies

Lilies prefer deep, moderately rich, well-drained soil, and dappled shade. They associate well with rhododendrons and azaleas.

Prepare soil by thorough digging; work in some well-rotted manure or garden compost. Peat may also be used freely, especially on light sandy and heavy clay soils.

Plant dry bulbs in September or October (but *Lilium candidum* in August); growing bulbs can be lifted and transplanted carefully in March. Bulbs delivered after October should be potted and grown in a frame until spring when they can be planted out.

Plant with a trowel or spade, making holes amply large enough to contain the bulbs and sufficiently deep to allow bulbs to be covered with 3 in. of soil (*Lilium candidum* and *L. testaceum* ½ in. only). Place a handful of sharp sand and another of peat under and around each bulb.

Do not hoe or fork around growing lilies. Remove weeds by hand or spread peat or leaf mold over the surface to smother weeds. Stake tall varieties individually.

Do not disturb after flowering. Lilies establish themselves slowly and give their best display after several years. Lift only when overcrowded and then do so in September or October, replanting as quickly as possible.

Feed lilies each spring by spreading well-rotted manure or garden compost around them.

Lilium auratum is known as the Golden-rayed Lily of Japan. It reaches a height of 5 to 7 ft. and carries several of its large heavily scented flowers on each stem

Lilium Honeydew is a hybrid trumpet lily which can produce 15 or more of its funnel-shaped blooms on each 5-ft. stem. It is suitable for growing in pots or in a partially shaded place out of doors

The Montbretias

Curtonus paniculatus

Tritonia crocata

The common montbretia is a very familiar plant with branched spikes of orange red flowers on stiff but slender 2-ft. stems in late summer. It will grow in a great variety of soils and situations including quite poor, sandy soils and hot, sunny places. Improved varieties with larger flowers in various colors from yellow to coppery red are available, but they are not so hardy or so vigorous. Plant all montbretias 3 in. deep in spring, the choicer kinds in good, well-drained soil and a sunny position. In cold gardens, lift the choice kinds in late October and place in a frame for the winter, planting out again in the spring.

Crocosmia masonorum looks like an extra-fine montbretia with larger, redder flowers and more handsome leaves. It needs the same treatment as the common montbretia and will grow in any good, well-drained soil and sunny place.

Curtonus paniculatus was once known as Antholyza, from which it derived the popular name of Aunt Eliza. It is like a taller montbretia with smaller, almost scarlet flowers and needs the same treatment as the common montbretia.

Tritonia crocata is also allied to montbretia, but it is much smaller and more tender. The orange cup-shaped flowers are borne on 12-in. stems in summer. Plant the corms in spring 2 in. deep in sandy soil and a sunny, sheltered place or put six corms in a 5-in. pot and grow in a sunny greenhouse or frame.

Scillas, Bluebells

Spanish Bluebell

Cuban Lily

The scillas are quite a varied group, ranging from the little Siberian Squill, *Scilla siberica*, with 4-in. sprays of deep blue flowers in February and March, to the bluebells, the English Bluebell, *Scilla nonscripta*, too well known to need description, and the Spanish Bluebell, *Scilla hispanica*, with larger, stiffer flower spikes which may be blue, pink, or white. Yet another fine species is *S. peruviana*, sometimes known as the Cuban Lily, with big heads of blue flowers on 9-in. stems in May and June.

Because the scillas and the bluebells are so varied they do not all need the same treatment, but all should be planted in autumn.

Plant the squills, including *S. siberica*, *S. bifolia*, and *S. tubergeniana* 3 in. deep in good, reasonably well-drained soil in sunny places. They are excellent for rock gardens, as edging to borders, or as a carpet beneath taller plants.

Plant English and Spanish Bluebells 4 in. deep, in any reasonably good soil and a sunny or shady place, and leave undisturbed for years. These are excellent plants to naturalize in grass or to grow in wild gardens and woodlands.

Plant *Scilla peruviana* 4 in. deep in good, well-drained soil and a warm, sheltered, sunny place.

Crocosmia masonorum is a fine summer-flowering plant for warm, sunny places. It looks much like a montbretia but the flowers are larger and set closer together so that they make an even better display

The common bluebell is an excellent bulb for planting in shady places. It often grows wild in woodlands and spreads more rapidly than the large-flowered Spanish bluebell

Snowdrops, Snowflakes

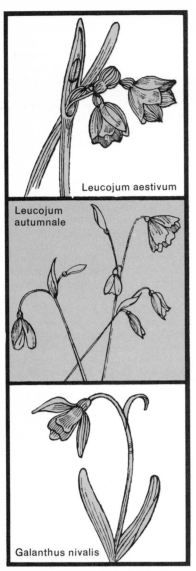

Leucojum aestivum

Leucojum autumnale

Galanthus nivalis

Snowdrops belong to the genus *Galanthus* and have small, white and green nodding flowers in winter and early spring. Snowflakes belong to the genus *Leucojum* and have more bell-shaped flowers. There are several kinds, e.g., the Spring Snowflake, *L. vernum*, with white and green flowers on 6-in. stems in early spring; the Summer Snowflake, *L. aestivum*, with similar but larger flowers on 18-in. stems in May; and the Autumn Snowflake, *L. autumnale*, with white and pink flowers on 6-in. stems in autumn.

The Common Snowdrop grows best in shade, snowflakes in shade or sun, but not in hot, dry places, and the large-flowered Mediterranean snowdrops prefer sunny places. All like good, rich, slightly moist soil.

Prepare by thorough digging and work in well-rotted manure or compost freely. Sprinkle bonemeal over the surface at 3 oz. per sq. yd.

Plant dry bulbs in September or October 4 in. deep. Or lift, divide, and replant growing plants in March (snowdrops as soon as they have finished flowering).

Leave plants undisturbed until overcrowded, then lift in summer when leaves have died down or in March as stated above. Divide bulb clusters before replanting.

Bulbs may also be naturalized in grass but this cannot be mown until the bulb foliage has died down.

Tulips

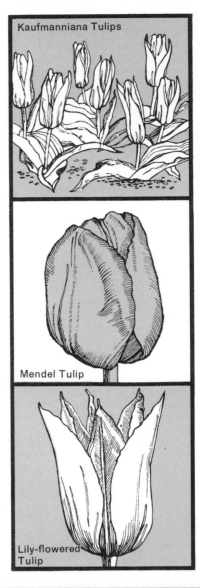

Kaufmanniana Tulips

Mendel Tulip

Lily-flowered Tulip

Tulips are classified according to their time of flowering and type of flower.

Kaufmanniana Tulips flower in March, and have widely opened flowers on short stems. They are also called Water-lily Tulips, e.g., César Franck, Heart's Delight.

Greigii Hybrid Tulips flower in April and have cup-shaped flowers on short to medium stems and chocolate-striped leaves, e.g., Oriental Splendor, Red Riding Hood.

Early Single Tulips flower in April and have cup-shaped flowers on short to medium stems, e.g., Bellona, De Wet, Pink Beauty.

Early Double Tulips flower in April and have double flowers on short to medium stems, e.g., Maréchal Niel, Murillo, Orange Nassau.

Mendel and Triumph Tulips flower in late April and have single flowers on medium stems, e.g., Elmus, Garden Party, Krelage's Triumph, Sulphur Glory.

Darwin, Darwin Hybrid, and Cottage Tulips flower in May and have single flowers on long stems, e.g., Beauty of Apeldoorn, Carrara, Golden Age, Gudoshnik, Holland's Glory, Mrs. Moon, Ossi Oswalda.

Lily-flowered Tulips flower in May and have single flowers with pointed reflexing petals on long stems, e.g., Mariëtte, Queen of Sheba, White Triumphator.

Peony-flowered Tulips flower in May and have double flowers on long stems, e.g., Mount Tacoma.

Leucojum vernum, the Spring Snowflake, looks rather like a very large snowdrop but the flowers produced in February and March are more bell shaped. It is suitable for a sunny or shady position

Darwin Hybrid Tulips providing a gay splash of color in a small paved garden. Flowering during the month of May, they are especially effective when planted in groups of a color

Bulb Hygiene

Parrot Tulip

Tulipa orphanidea

Tulipa tarda

Parrot Tulips flower in May and have very large single flowers, the petals of which are wrinkled and frilled, e.g., Blue Parrot, Fantasy.

Multi-flowered Tulips flower in May and have long branching stems carrying several flowers, e.g., Claudette, Georgette.

Viridiflora Tulips flower in May and have medium to long stems and single flowers, the petals of which are marked with green, e.g., Artist, Greenland.

Species Tulips are wild kinds, varying greatly in character, and suitable for rock gardens, e.g., *T. clusiana* (Lady Tulip), *T. orphanidea*, *T. praestans* Fusilier, *T. tarda*.

Tulips prefer a good, loamy soil and an open, sunny position. Prepare ground by thorough digging. Work in plenty of well-rotted manure or garden compost and finish with bonemeal at 3 oz. per sq. yd.

Plant bulbs at least 4 in. apart in September, October, or November with a trowel, in holes 4 in. deep and large enough to allow each bulb to sit firmly on the soil.

Lift tulips in June or July when leaves have died down and store in shallow trays in a cool, dry place until replanting time. If beds are required for summer flowers, lift tulips as soon as they have finished flowering and replant close together in any convenient place to complete growth before final lifting and storing.

Separate bulb clusters into individual bulbs before replanting, but plant undersized bulbs in a reserve bed.

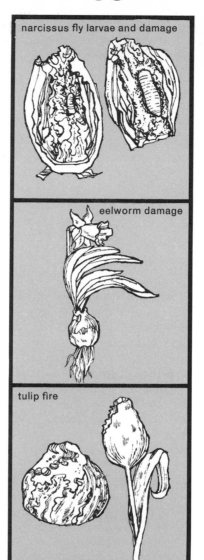

narcissus fly larvae and damage

eelworm damage

tulip fire

Apart from the ordinary pests and diseases that attack most plants, e.g., aphids, caterpillars, slugs, mice, gray mold, etc., bulbs suffer from some troubles of their own. In particular the bulbs, corms, or tubers are themselves liable to become infected with disease and should be carefully examined when lifted.

If any exhibit dark patches or spots, or appear scabby, or show any signs of decay or are wounded, dust them thoroughly with terraclor.

Tulips may be damaged by a disease known as tulip fire, which causes leaves, flowers, and stems to wither as if burned. If this disease is troublesome, spray with folpet every 10 to 14 days from March to May, except while plants are flowering.

Eelworms (a nematode) sometimes infest bulbs causing distortion of leaves and stems. Such plants should be burned and the site not used for bulbs for several years.

Tulipa tarda is a charming little species suitable for the rock garden. In April each stem will carry up to six of the distinctive star-shaped flowers. Also growing here is aubrieta

Darwin tulips, wallflowers, and forget-me-nots in a delightfully informal garden. By underplanting the tulips with other plants the rather stark stems of the tulips are concealed

Making a Rock Garden

Most rock plants are relatively small and so a considerable variety can be grown in quite a limited space. They are immensely varied in character, some being tiny shrubs, some herbaceous plants, some bulbs, corms, or tubers. Though the majority enjoy open sunny places and well-drained soils, suitable rock plants can be found for almost any situation in the garden, including those that are moist and shady. They are mostly wild plants introduced from many different lands and it is this ability to enjoy, in small compass, such a varied and interesting range of plants that accounts for much of the fascination of rock plants.

It is not essential to have a rock garden in order to grow rock plants. Many will grow just as well in ordinary beds, provided the soil is suitable and they are not overrun by larger plants. Dry walls and raised beds are also satisfactory substitutes for rock gardens and may fit more appropriately into the design of small gardens, even those of mainly formal design.

Yet another possibility is to grow rock plants in pots, pans, or other containers. Old stone troughs and sinks are excellent for this purpose provided they have adequate drainage holes through which surplus water can escape. Trough or sink gardens can make beautiful and interesting ornaments for terrace and patio gardens and if each container is restricted to plants with similar requirements, exactly the right kind of soil can be supplied and the best aspect chosen. To carry this system of individual treatment a stage further, a rock plant grown in a pot or pan can have its special soil mixture, can be placed in a frame when normally in its mountain home it would be protected by a deep carpet of snow, and can be brought into a light, airy greenhouse when it is about to flower so that its blooms are not damaged by rain.

Some rock plants prefer acid soil and can be grown most successfully in special peat beds built in shallow terraces and retained by low walls of peat blocks. A cool, partially shaded position is best and it is usually necessary to mix some coarse sand with the peat filling to improve its porosity. Provided the peat beds are built above the surrounding level, lime-hating plants can be grown even in limestone districts.

Some gardeners value rock gardens more for the beauty of the stone than for the individual qualities of the plants growing in them. There is no doubt that well-laid stone can be very attractive, but the natural type of rock garden can be a trifle incongruous in a too-sophisticated setting, cheek by jowl with trim lawns and well-kept flower beds. It is a feature for the wilder parts of the garden and one that can often be combined effectively with an informal pool or stream.

Making a Rock Garden

Buy approximately 1 ton of rock for every 10 sq. yd. of rock garden. Pieces weighing from $\frac{1}{2}$ to 1 cwt. each are best, though larger pieces are useful if help is available for placing them.

Unless the soil is naturally well drained, prepare the site by excavating to a depth of about 1 ft. and placing broken bricks or other hard rubble in the bottom as drainage. Return the soil, mixing in sand and coarse peat in the process. The finished bed may be flat, sloped, or contoured according to personal taste and the size and nature of the garden planned.

Set each stone on its broadest face and place it well into the soil so that it appears firm and as if part of a larger underground forma-tion exposed here and there to natural weathering and erosion. Place stones to form more or less level shelves or terraces, but of varying shape and size so that they do not look artificial, like a wall.

Slope the stones slightly backward into the soil and follow the same tilt throughout the construction. A brief study of natural rock outcrops on hillsides will show what is required.

Fill in behind all stones with prepared soil mixture, and leave no empty or loose pockets in which water might collect or which would permit subsidence.

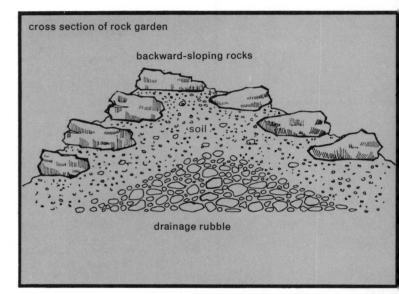

cross section of rock garden

backward-sloping rocks

soil

drainage rubble

Simple but effective rock garden construction with blocks of sandstone placed to retain shelves of relatively level soil on which the major planting is carried out

Building a Dry Wall

A dry wall is one built without mortar or cement. Such walls may be used to contain rock beds, hold up terraces and banks, or may be built as divisions or boundary walls. Any kind of stone may be used, rough hewn or faced, as well as special building blocks or bricks.

Start by excavating the foundation of the wall to a depth of at least 6 in. and ramming the bottom firmly. Set a layer of the largest available stones in this trench and spread soil over them. Place more stones on top, adding soil where necessary and ramming it in firmly between stones so that there are no loose places. Build terrace walls with a very slight backward slope for stability.

Continue to build the wall up in the same way taking care that vertical courses do not coincide. With terraces, ram soil between the wall and the bank behind as work proceeds, and set an occasional long stone back into the bank for greater security. High walls may require buttresses to be built out every 10 or 12 ft.

If boundary or division walls are to be used for plants, build them double with a core of at least 9 in. width of soil between in which plants can root.

A Raised Rock Bed

This is a method of growing rock plants which can be used without incongruity even close to a building. The bed can be of any size and shape but as a rule it is inconvenient to exceed a height of 3 ft. or a width of 6 ft. The bed is retained by dry stone walls built without mortar. Roughly dressed sandstone is an excellent material.

Begin by excavating soil and placing drainage rubble as for a rock garden. Fill up the hole with prepared soil almost to ground level and then place a course of stones around the bed, making them thoroughly firm.

Fill in with the soil mixture to just cover this first course and then set another, taking care that the vertical crevices between stones in successive courses do not coincide.

Continue building up the bed in the same way until it is completed, finishing off by half burying a few large blocks of similar stone on top and scattering stone chippings over the surface.

Plant both in the bed itself and in the surrounding walls. It is helpful to place some of the plants in position while the walls are being built.

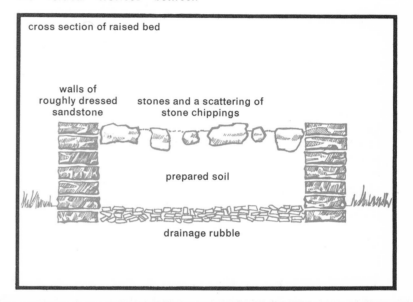

cross section of raised bed

walls of roughly dressed sandstone

stones and a scattering of stone chippings

prepared soil

drainage rubble

A well-made dry wall can be as good a place for rock plants as a conventional rock garden. Such a wall is most effective when it is used to support a bank of soil which provides ample root run for plants

Rock plants in a raised bed. This feature can often be used effectively in the more formal places as here, in the angle of a house wall, where a rock garden might appear out of place

Making a Scree

Some rock plants require a much more porous soil than that normally used for rock gardens. In nature they grow on the accumulations of rocky debris often found at the foot of steep mountains.

In gardens similar screes can be constructed either as a part of a rock garden, perhaps on the flatter part in front of the major outcrops, or as a separate feature.

Prepare a mixture for the scree bed with 4 parts of stone chippings $\frac{1}{4}$ to $\frac{3}{8}$ in. size, 2 parts loamy soil, 2 parts coarse sand, and 1 part peat. Excavate the site as for a normal rock garden but place at least a 9-in. depth of rubble in the bottom for drainage. On this place 6 to 9 in. of the prepared mixture, and set a few large, flattish stones on the surface, sinking them in for stability and a natural appearance. Scatter more of the same stone chippings all over the surface and plant solely with nonrampant rock plants.

For some ericaceous plants and gentians two or three times as much peat and less soil will give even better results. Do not use limestone for these plants.

Plants in Paving

Many small tufted or creeping plants will grow in the crevices between paving slabs provided they can root uninterruptedly into the soil below. If the paving is set in concrete it will be necessary to leave holes in the concrete to let the roots through. Paving plants can be considered in two groups, those that will stand a certain amount of wear and those that should be placed where they will not be walked on.

Prostrate plants that can be walked on are *Acaena buchananii, A. microphylla, Achillea rupestris, A. tomentosa, Arenaria balearica, A. caespitosa, A. purpurascens; Cotula squalida; Erodium chamaedryoides roseum; Geranium sanguineum; Linaria aequitriloba; Mazus reptans;* *Potentilla nitida; Raoulia australis, R. glabra; Sedum dasyphyllum, S. lydium, S. spurium, Stachys corsica, Thymus serpyllum,* and *Veronica rupestris.*

Tufted plants and others which should not be much walked on are *Antennaria dioica, Armeria maritima, Campanula cochlearifolia, C. garganica, Dianthus alpinus, Gypsophila repens, Phlox douglasii, P. subulata, Saxifraga muscoides, Sedum spathulifolium;* and *Silene acaulis.*

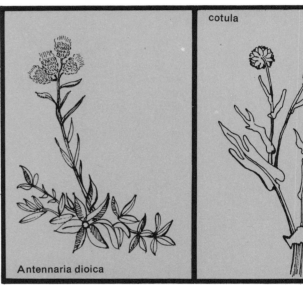

cotula

Antennaria dioica

A scree garden can be made on level or sloping ground, does not require much rock, and will provide congenial conditions for many lovely mountain plants

Many small tufted or creeping plants will grow well in the crevices between paving slabs provided they can root easily into good soil below. It may be wise to leave relatively plant-free areas for walking on

Planting Rock Plants

Most rock plants can be planted just like any other small plants, but when they are to be established in narrow crevices between large rocks or in a wall it is not easy to plant them with an ordinary trowel. Either use a very narrow-bladed trowel, such as a bulb-planting trowel, or a sharpened stick to scrape out the soil. Insert the roots carefully, pushing them well back with the fingers or a stick and then push soil in around them. Or, build the plants into position while the rock garden or wall is being made, first setting one stone in place, then spreading a little soil over it, laying the plant roots on this, covering with more soil and finally setting the next stone to hold everything firmly in place.

If rock plants are purchased in pots or other containers, remove them carefully by inverting each pot and rapping its rim smartly on some firm surface, such as a rock or a tool handle. If possible, plant without disturbing the root ball and see that this is just covered with soil.

Rock plants in pots and containers can be planted at any time of the year, even when in flower, but when lifted from the ground they are best planted in spring or immediately after flowering.

Care of Rock Plants

The greatest dangers with rock plants are that the more vigorous kinds may overrun the smaller and weaker ones or that fallen leaves may smother them. For these reasons examine them frequently, cut back or remove any plants that are spreading too far, and also collect all fallen leaves and place on the compost heap.

Remove weeds as they appear either by pulling them out or by cutting them off just below ground level. Do not use this latter method for vigorous perennial weeds such as dandelions and thistles as they will simply grow again from the severed root and make several crowns where formerly there was only one.

Some straggly rock plants, such as sunroses (helianthemum), arabis, aubrieta, and yellow alyssum, are improved by annual trimming with scissors or shears. Do this as soon as the plants finish flowering.

Most rock plants like plenty of water while they are growing, but tend to get too much water in winter. At this season protect choice plants, especially those with downy or hairy leaves, with panes of glass supported on notched sticks or bent wires 6 to 8 in. above the plants. Do not close in the sides of these rain shelters as circulation of air is essential.

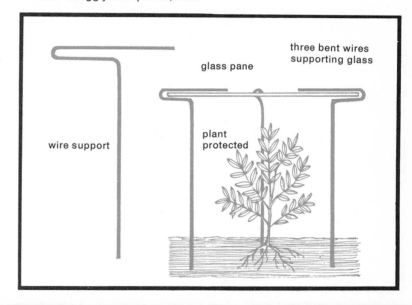

An old stone trough filled with rock plants. One advantage of this method of cultivation is that the plants can be given more individual attention than is possible in a rock garden

Achillea, Armeria

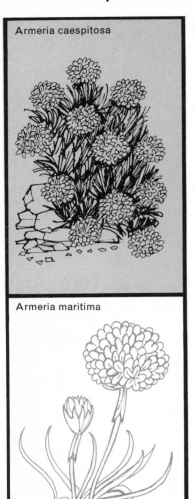
Armeria caespitosa

Armeria maritima

Achilleas are also known as yarrows. Some of them are herbaceous plants but there are also small varieties suitable for the rock garden and very easily grown in any reasonably open space and well-drained soil. Some of them spread rather rapidly, but if they grow too large they can be lifted, divided, and replanted.

Achillea ageratifolia is 9 in. high and makes a mat of silvery leaves studded with white flowers; *A. clavenae* is 6 in. high, also with silvery leaves and white flowers; *A. tomentosa* has gray green leaves and light yellow flowers and King Edward is very similar but cream in color. All varieties flower in summer.

Armerias are called thrifts or sea pinks and will grow in the poorest soils and driest places. They make close mounds of short, spiky, dark green leaves and in May and June the flowers are crowded in little ball-like heads on 4-in. stems. In *Armeria maritima*, the Common Thrift, they are pink, but Vindictive has deep carmine flowers. There is also a white variety named *A. m. alba*. *Armeria caespitosa* is a smaller plant with pale pink flowers. Bevan's Variety is a deep rose form of it, but both are more difficult to grow than the Common Thrift, requiring a very gritty soil with a reasonable water supply in late spring and summer.

Aethionemas, Androsaces

Aethionemas are little bushy plants 6 to 12 in. high with narrow blue gray leaves and heads of small pink flowers in May and June. They need plenty of light and good drainage, and they like gritty soils that contain some lime. They can be raised from seed but seedlings may vary slightly in quality, so the best varieties, such as Warley Rose with rose pink flowers and a particularly compact habit, are increased by summer cuttings.

Aethionema grandiflorum, 12 in. high, and *A. pulchellum*, 9 in., are lighter colored and sometimes shorter lived.

Androsaces make carpets or hummocks of densely downy leaves which catch the damp and can rot if not protected in winter.

They, too, like sunny, open places and good drainage. They should be divided and replanted every three or four years.

Androsace lanuginosa is the easiest to grow, a creeping plant with little pale pink, red-eyed flowers in clusters on 6-in. stems in June and July. *A. sarmentosa* makes a number of close rosettes of leaves and is more sensitive to damp. The deeper pink flowers on 4-in. stems come in May and June. *A. villosa* is still more rosetted in habit, with very downy leaves and white flowers on 3-in. stems in May and June. It requires protection in winter.

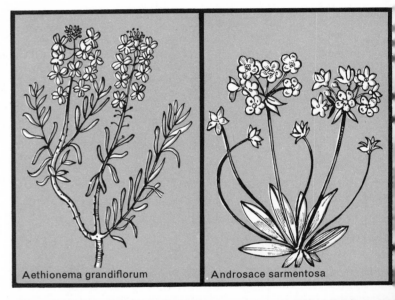
Aethionema grandiflorum

Androsace sarmentosa

Armeria maritima Vindictive, a strongly colored variety of the Common Thrift. All the thrifts will give a good account of themselves in the poorest soils and the driest places

Displaying distinctive blue gray leaves and rose pink flowers in May and June, *Aethionema* Warley Rose is a welcome plant in any rock garden especially as it is compact in growth

Antennaria and Others

All these are carpeting plants, useful in the rock garden as ground cover over small bulbs. *Antennaria dioica* has little gray, pointed leaves and pink or white flowers on 4-in. stems in April and May. It does not mind hot, dry places and is an excellent plant for walls.

Arenaria balearica makes a close carpet of tiny green leaves studded all over in June and July with tiny white flowers. Unlike many rock plants it grows best in cool, rather moist soil in a partially shaded place. It is just the plant with which to create the illusion of a little alpine meadow, and all manner of small bulbs such as crocuses and scillas can be planted under it to heighten the effect.

Arenaria caespitosa is more rounded and mosslike in growth, and there is a good golden-leaved variety named *aurea*.

Arenaria montana is more sprawling in growth, with quite large flowers freely produced in May and June. It will thrive in full sun or partial shade.

Erinus alpinus forms its carpet with tiny rosettes of leaves on which 4-in. flower stems stand in May and June. The common form has heather purple flowers, but there are several varieties: Dr. Hanelle, with carmine flowers; Mrs. Charles Boyle, pink, and *albus*, white. All will grow with very little soil and often establish themselves on walls.

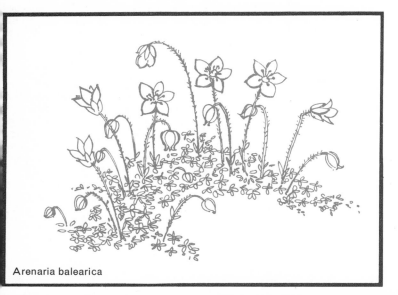

Arenaria balearica

Erinus alpinus is a useful plant for wall decoration, growing well in very little soil. The purple, carmine, or white flowers, on their slender stems, have a quiet charm and appear in May and June

Aquilegias and Others

Aquilegia glandulosa

Hepatica triloba

pulsatilla

Although from a casual inspection it might seem improbable, aquilegias, hepaticas, and pulsatillas are all related plants.

Many aquilegias, or columbines, are herbaceous plants, but *Aquilegia glandulosa* is a beautiful rock plant, easily grown in a cool place, shaded from the hottest sun in soil containing plenty of leaf mold or peat. It has light blue and white flowers on 9-in. stems in June and July, and, though not usually long lived, produces seed freely which often germinates around the plants.

Hepaticas also enjoy cool places in partial shade and leafy or peaty soil. They make slowly spreading clumps of lobed leaves and bear their blue, anemonelike flowers on 3-in. stems in February and March. *Hepatica transsilvanica* is lavender blue; *H. ballardii* is a deeper blue; and *H. triloba* a smaller plant with blue, pink, and white varieties in single- and double-flowered forms.

Pulsatillas are known as Pasque Flowers because they usually bloom at Easter. The leaves are covered in silky gray hairs and the mauve- to wine-colored flowers on silky foot-high stems are followed by fluffy white seed heads. The plants like sunny, open places and plenty of lime. They are easily raised from seed, giving attractive variations in color.

Pulsatilla vulgaris is called the Pasque Flower because it blooms at Easter. Give this plant a sunny, open position and limy soil and it will be entirely happy

Alyssum, Iberis

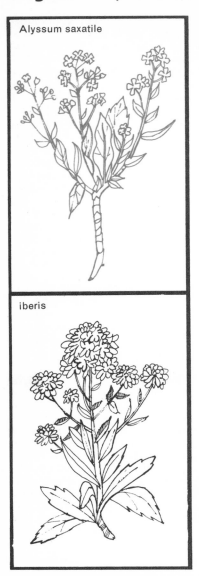

Alyssum saxatile

iberis

The alyssum to grow in rock gardens is not the annual Sweet Alyssum, but a perennial kind named *Alyssum saxatile*. It loves open places and is just the plant to grow on a sunny ledge or terrace wall. It has gray leaves and from April to June close sprays of bright yellow flowers are so freely produced that the popular name for this plant is Gold Dust. There is a lemon yellow variety called *citrinum*, and the pale yellow Dudley Neville is another attractive variety; *flore pleno* has double flowers and makes an even better display. The single-flowered varieties usually produce a lot of seed, and self-sown seedlings may appear freely, but the double-flowered variety produces no seed and is increased by spring and summer cuttings.

There are annual kinds of iberis, or candytuft, but there are also several perennial kinds suitable for rock gardens and thriving under exactly the same conditions as *Alyssum saxatile*. All can be raised from seed or from summer cuttings.

Iberis sempervirens has dark green evergreen leaves and makes a sprawling bush 9 in. high, with abundant clusters of white flowers in May and June; Little Gem is a shorter variety; and *Iberis saxatilis* is also no more than 6 in. high and produces its white flowers from February to June. *I. gibraltarica* is taller, more open, with lilac pink flowers in May.

Arabis, Aubrieta

Arabis albida
flore pleno

aubrieta

Both these plants make carpets of growth and are seen at their best planted where they can hang down a wall or shower themselves over rocks. They both flower in April and May and make admirable companions because of the similarity of their growth and the contrast of their flower colors.

Arabis albida is pure white and it has a fine double-flowered variety named *flore pleno*. There are also single-flowered pink varieties, one named *rosea*, very pale pink, and another *coccinea*, a brighter rose pink.

Aubrietas come in all shades from lavender to crimson but there are no white varieties. Representative varieties are: Bressingham Pink, clear pink double flowers; Church Knowle, gray blue; Crimson Queen, deep carmine; Dr. Mules, violet purple; Gloriosa, satin pink; Godstone, purple, and Wanda, double, red.

Single-flowered arabis and aubrieta can easily be increased by seed and self-sown seedlings often appear in the garden, but seedlings are likely to differ in flower color from their parents. Double-flowered varieties cannot be raised from seed and so they and selected varieties are increased by cuttings in the summer.

The look of established plants is improved by annual trimming with scissors or shears after flowering.

Alyssum saxatile has earned the name Gold Dust because of the brilliance of its small yellow flowers and the freedom with which they are produced. There are also double-flowered varieties which make an even greater display

Aubrietas, those gay flowers of April and May, can be easily raised from seed. Self-sown seedlings often appear in the garden, though these may well be different in color from their parents

Campanulas

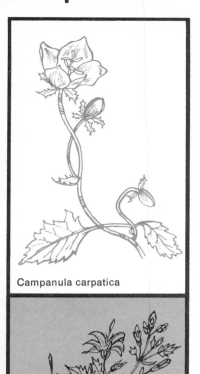

Campanula carpatica

Campanula garganica

The campanulas are known as bellflowers because most of them have bell-shaped flowers. Some kinds are large plants for herbaceous borders but there are also a great many dwarf kinds which make excellent rock plants. All thrive in open places and the more vigorous kinds will also put up with quite a lot of shade. Some spread rapidly and may need to be restricted. They can be divided in spring or after flowering.

Campanula carpatica is one of the tallest of the dwarf kinds, 9 in. high, and suitable for the front of a bed or border as well as for the rock garden. The fine blue or white flowers, appearing in July and August, are cup-shaped and face upward. *C. turbinata* is similar, but shorter.

Campanula garganica spreads almost flat and has starry blue or white flowers in June and July. W. H. Paine is a good variety, blue with a white eye.

Campanula posharskyana is a rampant grower, spreading rapidly, with long slender stems, only about 6 in. high. The flowers are pale blue and appear in June and July.

Campanula portenschlagiana is also known as *C. muralis*. It is one of the best rock plants, compact in habit with abundant bell-shaped blue flowers from June to August.

Campanula pusilla, also good, has slender stems, and from June to August dainty harebell flowers in shades of blue and also white.

Cerastium and Others

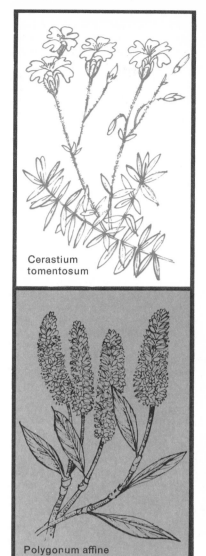

Cerastium tomentosum

Polygonum affine

These plants are of rampant growth, useful for covering banks and other open sunny places quickly, but not to be planted near choice rock plants which they may overrun. They will grow practically anywhere, are not in the least fussy about soil, and, when they get too big, can be lifted, divided, and replanted. But the underground stems of cerastium tend to get under rocks and into the crevices of walls and can be very difficult to remove once this plant is introduced.

Cerastium tomentosum is known as Snow in Summer, because it has silvery gray leaves and abundant white flowers in June. *C. biebersteinii* is very like it, but not quite so invasive.

Saponaria ocymoides will also make spreading mats of slender stems but it keeps these above ground, and so is not difficult to curb if it gets too big. The flowers, which are borne in succession from May to August, are rose pink in the common form, but carmine in the variety *splendens*.

The two best rock-garden polygonums also spread rapidly but are easily kept in control. *Polygonum affine* has close, stubby spikes 6 in. high of rose pink flowers (red in the variety Darjeeling Red) and *P. vacciniifolium* has more slender spikes of pale pink flowers. Both flower from August to October and have good autumn foliage color.

Campanula garganica is a pretty species with starlike flowers in June and July. It has a trailing habit and so is a splendid plant for a dry wall, steep slope, or the edge of a rock shelf

Saponaria ocymoides growing in association with the yellow *Linum* Gemmell's Hybrid. Both plants are very free flowering during the summer months and prefer sunny locations and well-drained soil

Dianthus

Dianthus alpinus

Dianthus deltoides

Dianthus caesius

Dianthus is the all-embracing name for pinks, carnations, and Sweet Williams. Many of them are unsuitable for the rock garden, but that still leaves a goodly number of fine rock plants for sunny places. Most, but not all, enjoy lime in the soil, though they can get on without it.

Dianthus alpinus is one of the "tinies," only 3 in. high, with deep rose flowers in May and June. It can easily be overrun by more vigorous plants, such as *Dianthus deltoides*, the Maiden Pink, a tumbling mass of thin stems and small leaves covered in July and August with carmine flowers. It is a fine plant for a ledge or as a cascade down a wall.

The Cheddar Pink, *Dianthus caesius*, looks just like a small garden pink with tufted gray green leaves and good pink flowers on 6-in. stems in June.

Dianthus neglectus makes a neat, tufted plant with quite large deep rose flowers sitting close down on it from June to August. It dislikes lime and needs a very gritty, well-drained soil.

There are also a lot of hybrid pinks with garden names that are just the right size for the rock garden. La Bourbrille, pink and crimson; Little Jock, pink; Mars, crimson, are typical, but in poorly drained soils or shade some of these may prove short-lived.

They can be readily increased by cuttings in summer, and the wild pink by seed.

Geraniums, Erodiums

These rock garden geraniums have only a slight connection with the geraniums (more correctly, pelargoniums) which are grown in greenhouses or bedded out in summer. They are perfectly hardy plants, low growing, and perennial, and are very easy to grow in quite ordinary soil, in full sun or partial shade. When they spread too far they can be lifted and divided, preferably in spring. Their popular name is cranesbill, because their seed pods look like a crane's long beak.

Geranium sanguineum has deep magenta flowers from June to August and is 9 in. high. A variety named *lancastriense* is pink, only 6 in. tall, and is a better plant. *G. subcaulescens* is more tufted, standing 9 in. high, with rosy magenta flowers from June to August.

The erodiums are closely related and are called Heron's Bill because of the similar shape of their seed pods. They thrive in exactly the same conditions as geraniums. One of the best is *Erodium chamaedrioides roseum*, which makes carpets of soft green leaves studded with pink flowers from May to October. It is also sold as *E. reichardii roseum*.

Erodium chrysanthum has gray leaves and sulfur yellow flowers on 6-in. stems in June and July. *E. macradenum* has pale violet flowers on 4-in. stems, also in June and July.

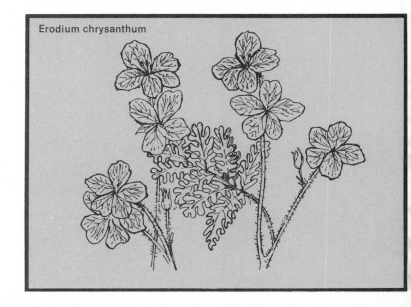

Erodium chrysanthum

Dianthus La Bourbrille, an attractive pink which grows about 3 in. tall. Given a sunny position in good soil this is one of numerous hybrids which grow well in a rock garden

The hardy herbaceous geraniums include many well suited to rock garden cultivation, one of the finest being *Geranium sanguineum lancastriense*. This is quite prostrate and flowers in summer

Gentians

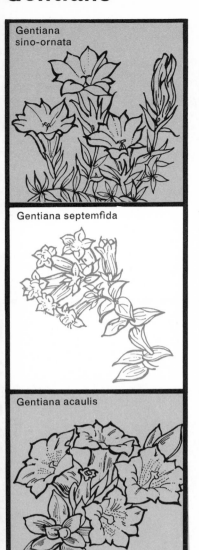

Gentiana
sino-ornata

Gentiana septemfida

Gentiana acaulis

The gentians, or *Gentiana*, vary in their ease of cultivation: some are easy, and some more difficult. All like plenty of peat or leaf mold in the soil, good winter drainage but plenty of moisture in summer. The autumn-flowering kinds, *G. sino-ornata*, *G. farreri*, *G. macaulayi*, and others, all dislike lime in the soil and need shade from the sun around midday. These have brilliant blue trumpet flowers on carpets of narrow green leaves.

The Willow Gentian, *G. asclepiadea*, will grow in shade and ordinary soil. It bears its deep blue flowers on 18-in. stems from June to August. Other easily grown summer-flowering kinds are *G. septemfida* and *G. lagodechiana*, with clusters of deep blue flowers on 6- to 9-in. stems from July to September. They succeed best in open, sunny places.

So do the spring-flowering gentians, of which the most popular two are *G. verna*, with small, intensely blue flowers on 2-in. stems, and *G. acaulis*, with large, deep blue, stemless trumpets on low mounds of leaves. *G. verna* is often short-lived, but can be fairly easily renewed from seed. *G. acaulis* likes rich soil and a sunny place, and should be fed annually with a sprinkling of bonemeal. It is sometimes shy to flower for no obvious reason.

Gypsophila and Others

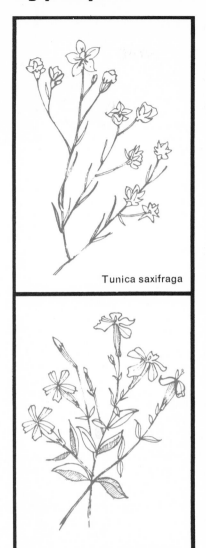

Tunica saxifraga

Silene schafta

These plants are related, and gypsophila and tunica are similar in appearance with slender, sprawling stems and little flowers in loose, graceful sprays. There are large gypsophilas suitable for borders and cutting, but *Gypsophila repens* is perfectly suited to the rock garden or may be planted on a wall down which it will cascade. It is only a few inches high, but will spread for a foot or more. There are pink and white forms which flower from May to July. *G. fratensis* is very similar and *G. cerastioides* is smaller with white flowers flushed with pink.

Tunica saxifraga, which also has tiny pink or white flowers produced during July and August, is about 9 in. high and spreading. It has two very attractive varieties with double flowers, *alba plena*, white, and Rosette, pink.

Silenes are more varied in habit but thrive in similar sunny places. *Silene alpestris* is tufted in habit and bears little white flowers on 4-in. stems in May and June. It has a double-flowered variety named *flore pleno*, which is an even better rock garden plant.

Silene maritima flore pleno is a double-flowered variety of the Bladder Campion, with slender flopping stems and white flowers which bloom from May to July. *S. schafta* also makes a widespreading plant 9 in. high, smothered in deep rose flowers in August and September.

Large, stemless, intensely blue trumpets on low mounds of leaves are the distinctive features of *Gentiana acaulis*. It thrives in rather rich soil, and should be divided and replanted every three or four years

An ideal plant for clothing a wall is *Gypsophila repens*, which varies from white to pink. Though only a few inches in height, it will spread for a foot or more and is trailing in habit

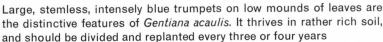

Helianthemums

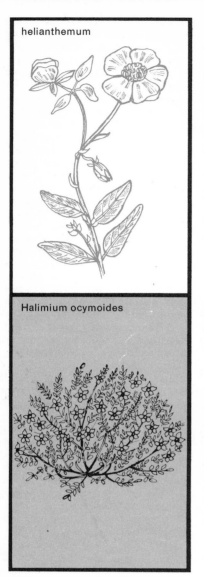

helianthemum

Halimium ocymoides

Helianthemums are known as sunroses, or rock roses, though the last name belongs to the larger cistus. They are sprawling, shrubby plants with narrow evergreen leaves and rather fragile flowers produced with great abundance in May and June. They like open, sunny places and well-drained soils and thrive particularly well on limy soils.

They can be readily raised from seed, but seedlings are likely to differ in flower color and habit, so selected varieties are best increased by summer cuttings. As plants age they tend to get straggly, a fault that can be corrected by trimming them annually with scissors or shears as soon as they have finished flowering.

Representative varieties are: Ben Afflick, orange; Ben Dearg, deep copper-orange; Ben Nevis, orange yellow; *chamaecistus*, crimson; Cerise Queen, cerise double flowers; Fireball, red double flowers; Jubilee, yellow double flowers; and *Rhodanthe carneum*, gray leaves with pink flowers. *Helianthemum lunulatum* is neater and more compact, 6 in. high, gray-leaved with yellow flowers in June and September.

Halimium ocymoides is closely allied and sometimes called *Helianthemum algarvense*. It is a little shrub, 2 ft. high, with yellow, maroon-blotched flowers in June.

Hypericums, Potentillas

Hypericums are known as St. John's-worts. Some of them are quite large shrubs but there are also numerous kinds suitable for the rock garden, all yellow flowered and all very easily grown in any reasonably well-drained soil and open place.

Hypericum coris is one of the smallest, a neat, tufted plant 6 in. high, with narrow leaves like a heather and bright yellow flowers in June. *H. polyphyllum* is about the same height but more vigorous and spreading, and there is a pale yellow variety named *sulphureum*. *H. olympicum* is more upright in habit and 1 ft. high, and it also has a pale yellow variety named *citrinum*. *H. reptans* is completely prostrate and flowers from July to September.

There are shrubby potentillas and herbaceous kinds as well as creeping plants for the rock garden. All are easily grown in well-drained soils and sunny places. *Potentilla alba* has white, strawberrylike flowers from June to October and spreads rather rapidly. *P. nitida* has silvery leaves and rose pink flowers in June and July. It does not always flower well and seems to succeed best in rather poor, gritty soils. *P. tonguei* trails about; an outstandingly good plant, it has orange flowers from June to August.

All these kinds can be divided when they get too big.

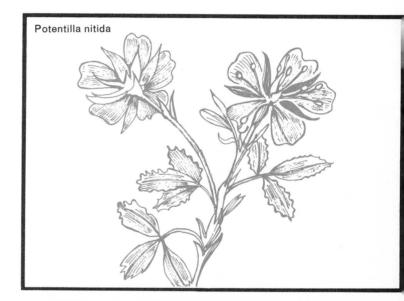

Potentilla nitida

Helianthemums, the colorful and popular sunroses, are a delight in May and June when they carry their flowers with great freedom. These shrubby plants are easily raised from seed or from summer cuttings

The free-flowering *Hypericum polyphyllum* finds a congenial home on a dry stone wall. An open position and well-drained soil are the principal needs of this and other rock-garden hypericums

Phlox, Thyme

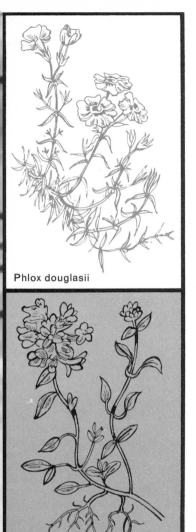

Phlox douglasii

Thymus serpyllum

In addition to the showy herbaceous phlox there are some very useful mat-forming kinds suitable for a rock garden, terrace, or walls. They are easily grown in moist soils and open places.

Phlox subulata is the most vigorous kind, making wide carpets of narrow leaves covered in flowers in May and June. Vivid and Camla are rose pink, Betty is soft pink, G. F. Wilson light blue, and Temiscaming, light crimson.

Phlox douglasii is more compact, but otherwise very similar. May Snow, also known as Snow Queen, is pure white; Effuse, also known as Boothman's Variety, is mauve; and Rose Queen is soft rose.

Phlox divaricata laphamii is a taller plant, like a miniature herbaceous phlox, with lavender blue flowers on 1-ft. stems in May and June.

Thymes are grown both for the fragrance of their leaves and for their flowers. *Thymus serpyllum* is completely prostrate. The flowers of the common form are heather pink; those of *albus* are white; *coccineus*, crimson; and *lanuginosus* has gray, hairy leaves and pink flowers. All bloom in June and July.

Thymus nitidus makes a neat bush 18 in. high, covered in mauve flowers in May; and *T. citriodorus*, a little lower, is spreading and has lemon-scented leaves. Silver Queen has silver variegated leaves, and *aureus* has yellowish green leaves. All like open sunny places and well-drained soils.

Saxifrages

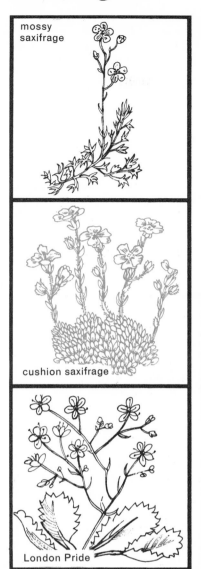

mossy saxifrage

cushion saxifrage

London Pride

There are a great many saxifrages, (saxifraga) and only the easiest to grow are included here.

The Mossy Saxifrages are so called because their deeply divided soft green leaves make low rounded mounds which at a distance look a little like moss. The flowers, carried on slender stems, come in April and May, and make a great display. These saxifrages like good, rather moist soils and half-shady places though they can be grown almost anywhere. If dried out, they go brown in the center. They can be lifted and divided when they grow too large. Representative varieties are: James Bremner, white, 9 in.; Pompadour, crimson, 6 in.; and Winston Churchill, pink, 6 in.; but there are many more.

Cushion, or Kabschia, Saxifrages make much harder, tighter cushions of leaves, often silvery gray and spiky. They flower in March and April, and must have well-drained soil and an open, sunny place. Representative varieties are: Cranbourne, lilac pink; His Majesty, white; *elizabethae*, soft yellow; *jenkinsae*, soft pink; and *burseriana*, white.

The London Prides make rosettes of green leaves and have loose sprays of small pink flowers. They will grow almost anywhere and do not mind shade. The Common London Pride, *Saxifraga umbrosa*, is 1 ft. high and flowers in June and July. *S. primuloides* Elliot's Variety is only 6 in. high and flowers in April and May.

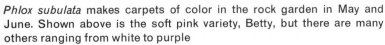

Phlox subulata makes carpets of color in the rock garden in May and June. Shown above is the soft pink variety, Betty, but there are many others ranging from white to purple

Saxifraga burseriana, one of the best Cushion, or Kabschia, Saxifrages, has large flowers on slender red stems in March and April. This is a plant for sunny places and well-drained soils

Primulas

The primrose and polyanthus are typical primulas, but not the best kinds for rock gardens. There are a great many of these and they differ so much that specialists divide them into 13 types, but for general garden purposes they may be considered in two main groups: those that like open, sunny places and good, well-drained soil, and those that like partially shaded places and moist soil.

The auricula, *Primula auricula*, is typical of the first group. It has rather leathery leaves, more or less covered in white meal, for which reason it is called Dusty Miller. The primroselike flowers are borne in clusters on 6-in. stems in May and June. There are many colors including rich purple and mixtures of green, white, and yellow.

Primula pubescens is very similar, but smaller and neater, with violet, blue, rose, milky white, or dull red flowers. *P. viscosa* is also closely allied, and also has a range of rich colors.

Primula juliae makes low mounds of neat, rounded leaves with almost stemless magenta flowers in March and April. There are a number of excellent hybrids between this and the primrose, with longer stems, larger leaves, and pink to crimson flowers. They are known collectively as *P. juliana*, and grow best in well-cultivated soil, in sun or shade.

Some kinds are called Candelabra Primulas because they carry their flowers in successive whorls up a long stem, rather like a candelabra. *Primula japonica* and *P. pulverulenta*, both with magenta crimson flowers on 18-in. stems in May and June, are typical, and easily grown in damp soil containing plenty of peat or leaf mold. They are excellent waterside plants.

The Bartley Hybrids are similar and in various shades of pink, carmine, and crimson. *P. helodoxa* is a yellow, and *P. bulleyana* deep yellow to bronze red.

Primula sikkimensis and *P. florindae* both carry their yellow flowers in big heads rather like giant cowslips. They thrive in damp places, and so does *P. rosea* with 6-in. clusters of brilliant rose flowers in April and May.

Primula denticulata is called the Drumstick Primrose because it carries its lavender, violet, rose, or white flowers in globular heads on stiff 8- to 12-in. stems like drumsticks in March and April. It will grow almost anywhere, in sun or shade, in moist or well-drained soil. *P. capitata* and *P. mooreana* with flatter heads of violet purple flowers are not quite so easy and should be given plenty of leaf mold or peat, and a partially shaded place. These conditions also suit *P. sieboldii* with soft green, crinkled leaves and loose heads of pink or white flowers on 6-in. stems in April and May.

Primula pulverulenta

Primula denticulata

Primula auricula

Primula rosea

Primula pubescens Mrs. J. H. Wilson breaks into colorful heads of flowers in May. Increase this attractive plant by division in July, or by sowing seed when ripe, but seedlings may vary in color

Moist, peaty beds of soil in rock gardens can become cheerful splashes of color in May, when planted with *Primula sieboldii*. There are numerous forms differing in flower color

Sedums, Sempervivums

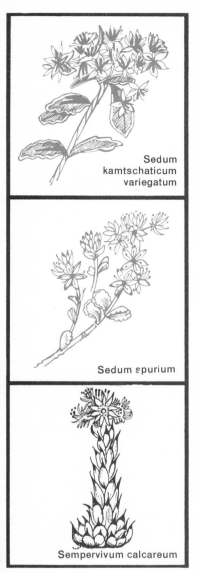

Sedum kamtschaticum variegatum

Sedum spurium

Sempervivum calcareum

Sedums, sometimes known as stonecrops, have fleshy leaves which enable them to survive periods of drought. *Sedum dasyphyllum* and *S. lydium* make close hummocks of very small leaves, gray in the former, bronze in the latter. *S. spathulifolium* makes rosettes of fat spoon-shaped leaves, dull purple in *purpureum*, gray in Cappa Blanca. *S. kamtschaticum variegatum* has golden variegated leaves and sprays of yellow flowers on 6-in. stems. *S. cauticolum* has bluish gray leaves and purplish pink flowers on 4-in. stems; *S. rupestre* has narrow gray leaves and curling heads of yellow flowers on 9-in. stems. *S. spurium* is a rampant grower with sprays of pink flowers but its variety Dragon's Blood with wine red flowers spreads less rapidly.

Closely related to the sedums is *Chiastophyllum oppositifolium*, with 6-in. drooping sprays of yellow flowers.

Sempervivums, known as house leeks, make rosettes of stiff leaves which may be small and covered with gray hairs like cobwebs in *Sempervivum arachnoideum* and *S. doellianum*, or large and shiny, green, tipped purple, in *S. calcareum* and green in *S. tectorum*. The flowers are borne in stiff sprays on short, stout stems.

All like sunny places and well-drained soil containing lime. Both sedums and sempervivums can be divided when they become too large.

Violas, Veronicas

Any violas can be planted in rock gardens, but the large-flowered bedding varieties are rather too sophisticated to look in place. Far better are the wild kinds such as the Horned Violet, *Viola cornuta*, which makes low, tumbled masses of growth covered in small, light blue flowers from April to July. A white variety is *alba*, and *purpurea* is violet purple.

Viola gracilis is neater in habit with smaller deep blue flowers. *V. g. lutea* is a yellow-flowered variety, and Grandeur is a violet purple.

Viola labradorica purpurea is an attractive violet with deep purple leaves. Like the other violas it will grow anywhere, enjoys semi-shady places with cool, slightly moist soils and can be lifted and divided when it spreads too far.

Some of the rock garden veronicas are also trailing plants that can be grown almost anywhere, but they all prefer sunny open places. *Veronica prostrata*, also known as *V. rupestris*, makes a wide carpet of green leaves covered with short spikes of blue flowers in June and July. A pink-flowered variety is *rosea*. *V. teucrium* has longer, 6-in. spikes of blue flowers, and Trehane has similar flowers contrasted with soft yellow leaves. By contrast *V. catarractae* makes a little spreading bush about 9 in. high with neat leaves and white, lilac-veined flowers from June to September.

Viola cornuta alba

The colorful *Sedum spurium* Dragon's Blood is an unusually attractive stonecrop for the late summer garden. It is sprawling in habit and needs an open sunny location where it will spread rapidly

A beautiful sprawling plant for the rock garden is *Viola gracilis*, a species which grows 4 to 6 in. tall. It flowers profusely over a long period if planted in good soil and a cool place

Annual Flowers

These are plants with a short life but a merry one. In the compass of a few months they grow, flower, and die, leaving the ground free for further cultivation, if necessary, and for other plants. They are among the cheapest flowers to grow and the quickest to give a return. They are invaluable for furnishing new gardens before more permanent plants have been put in or have become sufficiently established to require all the space. They are also excellent for filling any vacant spaces that may occur in the flower beds, and since few of them make any great demands on the soil, they can often be grown with, or close to, other plants without robbing them unduly.

There are many different kinds of annuals and innumerable varieties of some of the most popular ones, such as marigolds and petunias. They vary greatly in height and habit as well as in the color and form of their flowers. Some sprawl over the ground and make colorful flower carpets beneath taller plants. Some are bushy, some erect, and a few, such as the sweet pea, the canary creeper, the large nasturtium, and the Morning Glory, are climbers. There are also annuals, such as mignonette, stocks, and nicotiana, with sweetly scented flowers though most rely more on their color than on their fragrance to attract the insects that pollinate their flowers.

Some annuals make themselves so completely at home that once grown they continue to renew themselves year after year by self-sown seed with no help at all from the gardener. However, this is not usually a very desirable way of growing annuals, particularly the more highly developed garden varieties, which tend to deteriorate in quality rather rapidly unless grown in isolation and with careful selection to eliminate inferior forms. Seed of a few kinds can be saved and sown at home, but as a rule it is better to purchase fresh seed each year from a reliable source. This is essential in the case of those special hybrids known as F_1 or F_2 hybrids, since they have to be remade each year by crossing different parent varieties which are retained by the raiser and not sold or otherwise distributed to other producers. Often these F_1 or F_2 hybrids are superior in uniformity and vigor to ordinary varieties, but they are more costly to produce and more expensive to purchase.

Because of their relatively short life and frequent renewal from seed, annuals suffer very little from pests and diseases and are among the most trouble-free plants in the garden. They are usually favorites with children who enjoy growing them from seed and watching the seedlings develop so rapidly into flowering plants, and who so delight in their gay colors.

African Daisies

Several beautiful African daisies can readily be raised from seed for flowering during the summer months in open, sunny places and reasonably good well-drained soils. All are half-hardy annuals, seed of which should be sown in March in a greenhouse or frame in a temperature of 60° to 65°F., pricked off, and hardened off for planting outdoors in late May or early June.

African daisies cover a very wide range of colors. *Arctotis grandis* has silvery white and pale blue flowers and there are also several hybrid strains with flowers in light or rich colors including yellow, orange, red, and wine purple. Heights vary from 1 to 1½ ft.

The Swan River Daisy, or brachycome, has blue, pink, or white flowers and is 12 to 15 in. high.

The Star of the Veldt, or dimorphotheca, is also 12 to 15 in. high and includes unusual shades of beige, buff, and apricot as well as yellow and orange.

Ursinia is brilliant orange and 12 to 15 in. high. Venidium has large orange flowers with a nearly black central zone and is 2 to 3 ft. high.

Space all plants 1 ft. apart, except venidium, which needs 18 in.

This variety of dimorphotheca, Goliath, is one of many beautiful African daisies. It is very free flowering and makes a good cut flower. When growing in the garden, flowers close in the evenings

Antirrhinums

In mild climates with well-drained soils antirrhinums can sometimes be kept for several years, for they are strictly perennials. However, since the plants tend to become straggly with age, and some are likely to die, they are best if treated as half-hardy annuals and renewed each year from seed.

Sow seed in February or March in a greenhouse or frame, at a temperature of 60° to 65° F. Prick off the seedlings and give increasing ventilation, so that by early May at the latest the plants can begin to be hardened off for planting out of doors in late May or early June.

There are dwarf, intermediate, and tall varieties, each in the complete color range except blue. The dwarf varieties should be spaced 6 to 8 in. apart; the intermediate, 12 in. apart; and the tall ones about 15 in. apart.

Antirrhinums will grow in almost any soil and situation, but thrive best in reasonably good, well-drained soil and open, sunny places. In hot, dry places, some varieties are liable to suffer from rust disease (orange spots on the underside of leaves causing withering of the whole plant), but rust-resistant varieties can be obtained.

Antirrhinums are excellent for filling beds on their own, in mixed or separate colors or in patterns of contrasting colors. The low-growing varieties are also very useful as carpets beneath taller plants, or as edging plants.

China Asters

The China asters, or callistephus, must not be confused with the perennial asters which include Michaelmas daisies since, though they are related, they need quite different treatment.

The annual asters are all half-hardy annuals flowering from mid-summer until early autumn. There are many different types and varieties, some with single and some with double flowers. The doubles may have large, rather shaggy flowers (Ostrich Plume); slightly smaller, more regularly formed flowers (Comet); or still smaller, neater flowers (Pompon). Heights range from 1 to 3 ft. and there is a good color range from white, lavender, and pale pink to violet, purple, and crimson.

Sow seed very thinly in March or early April in a frame or greenhouse in a temperature of around 60°F. Prick off as soon as the seedlings are big enough, giving good ventilation, and harden off for planting out 1 ft. apart in late May or early June. Or, sow outdoors in early May where plants are to flower, and thin seedlings to 9 in. apart. Single asters are best for outdoor sowing.

Asters will grow in most places but prefer good, loamy soils and open, sunny, or only lightly shaded places.

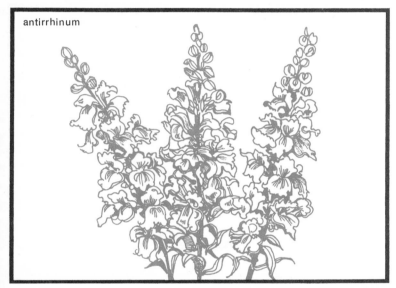

antirrhinum

callistephus

Intermediate antirrhinums planted in borders of mixed perennial and annual flowers. Many colors are available and also different heights and flower forms

Comet asters provide a riot of color during the summer and autumn months. Other types have more loosely formed or single flowers and all are available in a wide color range

Clarkia, Godetia, Mallow

clarkia

lavatera

These are among the easiest of hardy annuals to grow. They will do well either in the open in full sunlight or in partial shade and either in poor sandy soils or in good rich loams.

Clarkia carries its white, pink, salmon, or carmine single or double flowers on slender 2- to 2½-ft. spikes. Some varieties of godetia have a similar habit, but with larger flowers and spikes to 2½ ft. There are also shorter, bushier varieties known as azalea-flowered because of the slight resemblance of the flowers to those of an azalea. They may be single or double and have a similar color range to clarkia with some especially good pink and salmon pink varieties. All are ideal for beds or for the front of borders.

The two annual mallows are lavatera and malope. Both have flaring, funnel-shaped flowers, rose pink in lavatera, deep magenta red in malope, which are carried on well-branched 3-ft. tall plants.

Sow seed during March, April, or May or in early September outdoors where plants are to flower. Thin clarkia and godetia to 8 in. apart, lavatera and malope to 18 in. The taller varieties should be supported by short pea sticks (bushy hazel branches) or they may blow down in strong wind.

Cleome, Cosmos

Cleome is an attractive and rather unusual half-hardy annual known as the Spider Flower because of the spidery shape of its pink or white flowers which are carried in loose heads on 3 to 4 ft. stems in summer. Because of its height and striking appearance, it is very suitable for planting in groups toward the back of a border or in the middle of a bed.

Cosmos is a graceful half-hardy annual which has narrow ferny leaves and daisy-type flowers in late summer and early autumn. The commonest kinds have white, pink, rose, or purplish red flowers on 3 to 4 ft. stems, but there are also varieties with orange flowers on 2½ ft. stems.

Sow seed of all varieties during March in a greenhouse or frame at a temperature of 60° to 65°F. Prick off and harden off, and plant outdoors in late May or early June, 1 ft. apart.

Cosmos will grow in most places but thrive best in reasonably good soil and an open, sunny place. In shade they tend to become tall and leafy with fewer flowers.

cleome   cosmos

Godetias are very easily grown hardy annuals which produce their showy flowers over a long season. Illustrated here is Crimson Glow, a dwarf variety which can be used in borders to make brilliant displays

Cosmos bipinnatus is also known by its old name of cosmea. It is a colorful garden plant for the late summer and early autumn and the ferny foliage is highly decorative

Cornflower, Sweet Sultan

cornflower

Sweet Sultan

Both these plants are hardy annuals and are related, the Latin name of the cornflower being *Centaurea cyanus* and of the Sweet Sultan, *Centaurea moschata*. Both are useful cut flowers as well as being good garden plants.

Cornflowers are commonly blue though there are also white- and pink-colored varieties. They are so tall (3 ft. or more) that they need the support of pea sticks or something similar to hold them up. However, there are dwarf kinds (9 to 12 in.) which need no staking and can be used as edging plants.

Sweet Sultans are about 18 in. high and are similar to cornflowers in shape. The color range, however, also includes yellow, mauve, and purple but not pure blue.

Sow seed in March or April outdoors where plants are to flower. Thin seedlings to 9 in. apart but 12 in. apart for tall cornflowers.

Cornflowers will grow almost anywhere, though they prefer well-drained soils and open, sunny places.

Sweet Sultans like rather good, well-cultivated and well-drained soil, and a warm, sunny, sheltered position. They are not as easy as cornflowers to grow successfully.

Daisy Flowers

The annual chrysanthemum, coreopsis, and gaillardia all have perennial relations with which they must not be confused as they need quite different treatment.

Annual chrysanthemums are 18 to 24 in. high and have variously colored flowers which are like large single or double daisies. There may be several colors in one flower in concentric rings or the flowers may be entirely lemon or yellow.

The annual coreopsis is often known as calliopsis. Its daisy-type flowers have big petals and small central discs and are yellow, usually splashed at the base with crimson or maroon. They are carried in sprays on slender 2 to 3 ft. stems.

The annual gaillardia has very showy flowers which are deeply frilled. They are either yellow and red or all red and grow to about 18 in. high.

Sow seeds of annual chrysanthemum and annual coreopsis outdoors in March or April where plants are to flower and thin seedlings to 9 in. apart. Sow annual gaillardia during March or early April in a greenhouse or frame, prick off, and harden off for planting outdoors in late May or early June, 9 in. apart. All like reasonably good soils and open, sunny places.

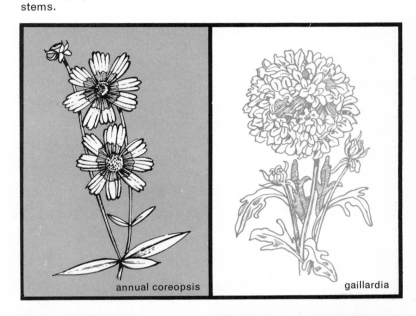
annual coreopsis

gaillardia

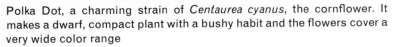
Polka Dot, a charming strain of *Centaurea cyanus*, the cornflower. It makes a dwarf, compact plant with a bushy habit and the flowers cover a very wide color range

Chrysanthemum segetum, one of the annual chrysanthemums, is showy in the garden and useful also as a cut flower. Commonly called the Corn Marigold, it grows to about 18 in.

Edging Plants

Alyssum, ageratum, candytuft, and lobelia are four of the most popular edging and carpeting plants since they are quite short and soon cover the area of a dinner plate or more.

The annual alyssum is also known as Sweet Alyssum because of its honey fragrance. It must not be confused with the yellow *Alyssum saxatile*, a perennial requiring quite different treatment. The Sweet Alyssum has white or purplish flowers and is 6 to 8 in. high.

Ageratum has fluffy little heads of soft blue or lilac flowers and is from 4 to 9 in. high.

Candytuft has white, lavender, rose, and carmine flowers and is from 9 to 15 in. high.

Lobelia varies in color from light to deep blue and white to purple. There is also a trailing kind, *Lobelia tenuior*, which is especially suitable for hanging baskets and window boxes.

Alyssum and candytuft are hardy annuals. Sow during March, April, May, or early September outdoors, where they are to flower, and thin seedlings to 6 in. apart.

Ageratum and lobelia are half-hardy annuals. Sow in March or early April in a greenhouse or frame, in a temperature of around 60°F.; prick off and harden off for planting out in late May or early June, 6 to 8 in. apart.

All will grow well almost anywhere, but prefer reasonably good soils and open, sunny places.

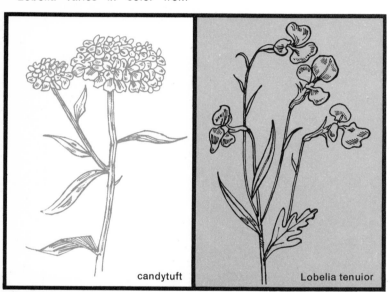
candytuft   Lobelia tenuior

Dwarf varieties of ageratum are ideal annuals to use for the groundwork of bedding schemes, for edging, or for furnishing window boxes. Taller varieties are also available up to 18 in. in height

Annual Grasses

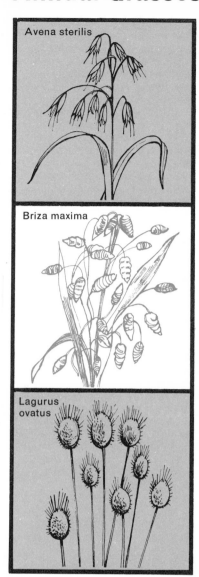
Avena sterilis

Briza maxima

Lagurus ovatus

Agrostis nebulosa is a 1-ft. high hardy annual known as Cloud Grass with sprays of small flowers.

Avena sterilis is a 3-ft. high hardy annual known as the Animated Oat because the flowers move as the humidity varies.

Briza maxima and *B. minor* are known respectively as the Large and Small Quaking Grasses, because their nodding, heart-shaped flowers are hardly ever still. They are hardy annuals 12 to 18 in. high.

Coix lachryma-jobi is called Job's Tears because of its pearly white flower clusters. It is a 2-ft. perennial usually grown as a hardy annual.

Eragrostis tenella, also known as *E. elegans*, is a 2-ft. hardy annual with sprays of tiny flowers.

Hordeum jubatum, called Squirrel-tail Grass because its flowers hang in close, tail-like trails, is a 1-ft. hardy annual.

Lagurus ovatus, known as Hare's-tail Grass, has rounded fluffy flower heads and is a 1-ft. tall hardy annual. Cut in dry weather for winter decoration.

Panicum violaceum has silky green and purple flower plumes and is a 3-ft. hardy annual.

Pennisetum villosum (*P. longistylum*), has feathery flower spikes on 2-ft. stems. It is grown as a half-hardy annual.

Zea mays is the maize of commerce. Ornamental varieties are about 4 ft. tall and grown as half-hardy annuals, or seed may be sown out of doors in early May where the plants are to grow.

Briza maxima, the Large Quaking Grass, is a handsome annual grass with nodding, heart-shaped flowers which are hardly ever still. It reaches a height of 12 to 18 in.

Larkspurs

annual larkspur

There are both annual and perennial larkspurs, all of which are delphiniums, but in gardens the name delphinium is usually reserved for the perennial kinds, and the annual varieties, derived from *Delphinium ajacis*, are known simply as annual larkspur. The two groups need quite different treatment.

Annual larkspurs carry their flowers in slender 2- to 3-ft. spikes. They have a good color range from white, pale blue, lavender, and pink to scarlet and violet.

Sow seed during March, April, or in early September outdoors, where plants are to flower, and thin seedlings to about 12 in. apart. Support the flower stems as they appear by pushing short pea sticks into the soil around them.

Larkspurs like well-cultivated soil and an open, sunny position. For a September sowing the position chosen must be well drained. Plants from this sowing should begin to flower in May.

Annual larkspur is a good cut flower and is also excellent for large beds or for making groups among lower-growing plants or at the back of borders.

Larkspur is a favorite annual for bedding and cutting. This strain, Giant Imperial, produces double flowers on slender spikes 4 ft. high. Other shorter varieties are available

Marigolds

The Pot Marigold, or calendula, is a hardy annual with yellow or orange flowers which in good garden varieties are always double, though self-sown seedlings may revert to single flowers. They will grow in almost any soil and situation but prefer it to be open and sunny. Sow during March, April, May, or September outdoors and thin seedlings to 9 in. apart.

French and African Marigolds are half-hardy annuals derived from various tagetes. Typically the French Marigolds are shorter and have smaller orange and chestnut red flowers, the African Marigolds are taller and have large, almost globular yellow or orange flowers. However, they have been much interbred so that the distinction between the two types is becoming blurred. All are fine plants for beds and borders, and like well-cultivated soils and open, sunny places. Sow during March or early April in a greenhouse or frame, in a temperature of about 60°F. Prick off seedlings and harden off for planting outdoors in late May or early June; dwarf varieties, which reach a height of 6 to 12 in., 9 in. apart; tall varieties 12 in. apart.

The Dwarf Marigold, *Tagetes signata*, makes a dome-shaped plant about 9 in. high, covered in small, single yellow or orange flowers. It is a half-hardy annual, likes the same conditions as the French and African Marigolds, and is excellent for edging beds and borders. Space 6 to 8 in. apart.

Pot Marigold

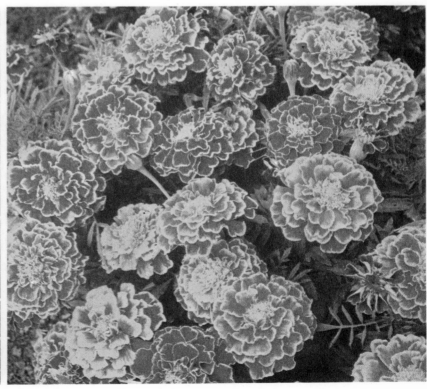

Excellent annuals for beds and borders, the French and African Marigolds continue to flower well into the autumn. Fiesta is a typical example of the French type with bicolor flowers

Mesembryanthemum, etc.

These are creeping, half-hardy annuals with fleshy leaves which enable them to grow in very hot, sunny places.

The annual mesembryanthemum, *Dorotheanthus bellidiformis* (syn. *Mesembryanthemum criniflorum*), is also called the Livingstone Daisy because it comes from Africa and has daisylike flowers, though it is not a true daisy. There is a wide range of brilliant colors. There are also perennial mesembryanthemums which need different treatment.

Portulacas also have very showy flowers in a wide range of brilliant colors and they may be either single and cup shaped or double and ball-like.

Sow seed during February or March in a greenhouse or frame, at a temperature of 65°F., prick off seedlings and harden off for planting outdoors in late May or early June. Space mesembryanthemums 9 in. apart, portulacas 6 in. apart in a warm, sunny place and well-drained soil.

Mignonette thrives best of all in limy soils, though it will grow in any reasonably good, well-drained soil and open, sunny position. Sow during March, April, or early May outdoors, where the plants are to flower, and thin seedlings to about 6 in. apart. The heads of green and dull red flowers on foot-high stems are not very showy, but make a useful contrast to more brilliant flowers, and are very fragrant.

Nasturtium, Morning Glory

The nasturtiums are varieties of tropaeolum which are treated as if they were hardy annuals, even though they are killed by frost. However, they grow so rapidly that if sown outdoors in April or May, they will escape all but exceptionally late frosts and yet be in flower from about midsummer. There are dwarf and trailing or climbing varieties, the first suitable for beds, borders, and edging, the second for covering trelliswork, fences, sheds, etc. Colors are in various shades of yellow and red. All flower most freely in rather poor soils and warm; sunny places. Sow seeds separately 1 in. deep and 6 to 8 in. apart where plants are to flower.

Morning Glory (ipomoea) is a twining plant with blue funnel-shaped flowers, easily grown as a half-hardy annual. Sow during March or early April in a frame or greenhouse, temperature 60° to 65°F., two seeds in each 3-in. pot and harden off for planting outdoors in late May or early June against warm, sunny walls or fences. Place strings or wires for the plants to twine around.

The annual convolvulus is closely related and has similar but smaller blue, purple, pink, or cherry red flowers, but the sprawling plants are only about 1 ft. high and are suitable for beds, borders, and edging. Sow seeds during March or April in good well-drained soil and a sunny place and thin seedlings to 9 in. apart.

mesembryanthemum

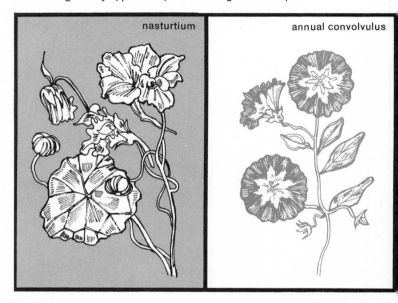
nasturtium

annual convolvulus

Portulaca is a showy annual for a sunny bank, rock garden, or the top of a dry wall. It offers a wide range of brilliant colors, on both single- and double-flowered forms, the latter shown above

Morning Glory is a vigorous twining plant which is grown as a half-hardy annual though it is truly perennial but not winter hardy. It will flower throughout the summer in a warm, sunny place

Nemesia, Nicotiana

nemesia

nicotiana

Nemesia makes a neat half-hardy annual 8 to 12 in. high with flowers in a wide range of colors, including white, yellow, orange, red, lavender, and blue. It likes rather rich, well-cultivated soil and open, sunny places, though it can be grown almost anywhere. It is excellent as an edging, for filling small beds, or for growing in groups among other plants.

Sow seed during March or early April in a greenhouse or frame, in a temperature of about 60°F., prick off seedlings and harden off for planting outdoors in late May or early June. Space plants 6 in. apart.

The garden nicotiana is a relative of the tobacco plant and is also known as sweet-scented, or jasmine, tobacco because of its sweet scent which is most noticeable in the evening. Flowers of some varieties do not open until evening, but daylight-opening varieties are available and are to be preferred. Plants are 3 to 4 ft. high and have white, lime green, rose, or carmine flowers. They like good, rich soil and will thrive in partial shade as well as in the open.

Sow seeds during March or early April in a greenhouse or frame, temperature 60° to 65°F., prick off seedlings and harden off for planting outdoors 1 ft. apart in late May or early June.

Nigella, Scabious

Love-in-a-Mist, or nigella, is a very elegant hardy annual about 18 in. high, with fine, ferny leaves and blue, rose, purple, or white flowers a little like cornflowers but nestling among their leaves. It will grow in any reasonably good soil and open position. Sow seeds during March, April, or early September outdoors, where plants are to flower, and thin seedlings to 9 in. apart.

The annual, or Sweet, Scabious must not be confused with the Caucasian Scabious, which is a hardy perennial requiring different treatment. The annual scabious, despite its name, is not a true annual, but a perennial too tender to overwinter outdoors in most areas, and so readily raised from seed that it is always treated as an annual. The pincushion-shaped, fragrant flowers are in various colors from white, pink, and lavender to crimson and purple. It grows about 3 ft. high.

Sow seed during March in a frame or greenhouse, temperature about 60°F., prick off seedlings and harden off for planting out 1 ft. apart in May or early June. Push some short, bushy twigs into the ground around the plants for support.

Or, sow during April or early May outdoors, where the plants are to flower, and thin seedlings to 9 in. apart.

The annual scabious likes good, well-drained soil and an open sunny position.

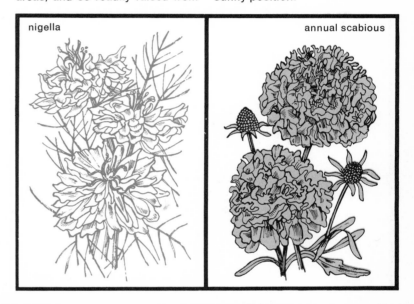

nigella

annual scabious

A delightful planting of mixed petunias and nicotianas which, together with fuchsias, brighten a shady corner and hide a dark wall. White nicotianas are usually the most fragrant

An accommodating hardy annual with a charming name is Love-in-a-Mist, or nigella. It is well loved by flower arrangers who use the curious inflated seed heads in dried arrangements

Petunias

These immensely showy, half-hardy annuals succeed best in rather light, well-drained soils and warm, sunny places, though they can be grown almost anywhere. There are a great many varieties, some with medium-sized, single flowers, some with larger, single flowers, and some with big double flowers. All are available in a wide range of shades of blue, purple, red, and pink together with white and pale yellow. The single-flowered kinds are excellent plants for filling beds and borders or for associating with other plants, also for growing in window boxes, tubs, etc. The double-flowered varieties are less satisfactory in beds, but make good pot, tub, or window-box plants.

Sow seed in February or March in a greenhouse or frame, temperature 65°F., prick off seedlings and harden off for planting outdoors in late May or early June. Space plants about 9 in. apart or, if grown throughout in pots, have one plant in each 5 in. pot in potting mix or one of the peat potting mixtures.

Petunias do not grow so well in cool, wet districts, though rain-resistant varieties are available and should be used in such places.

petunia

Excellent for bedding, window boxes, and hanging baskets, petunias have a long flowering period and cover an incredible range of beautiful colors. They enjoy warm, sunny places

Phlox, Pinks, Carnations

The annual phlox are very different in appearance from the perennial phlox though individually the flat, round flowers in a variety of rich and brilliant colors are similar. The plants are sprawling and good for carpeting in sunny places.

Sow seed during March or early April in a greenhouse or frame, temperature 65°F. Prick off and harden off for planting outdoors in late May or early June, 9 in. apart. Keep trailing stems pegged to the soil to prevent them being blown about and broken.

There are a great many annual pinks and carnations, many rather similar in appearance to the perennial pinks and carnations, but requiring quite different treatment. Particularly recommended are the

Indian Pinks (*Dianthus heddewigii*), 6 to 12 in. high, with single or double-fringed flowers in many shades of pink, carmine, and crimson with white, and the Chabaud Carnations, 18 in. high, with large, double flowers in a variety of colors, which are excellent for cutting.

Sow seed during March or early April in a greenhouse or frame, temperature around 60°F., prick off and plant out in May or early June, 9 in. apart. Alternatively, sow annual pinks in April or early May outdoors, where they are to flower, and thin seedlings to 6 in.

annual phlox

Indian Pink

An enchanting strain of the annual phlox is Twinkle, Dwarf Star Mixed. Growing no more than 8 in. high, it has dainty starlike flowers which are carried in great profusion well above the foliage

Poppies

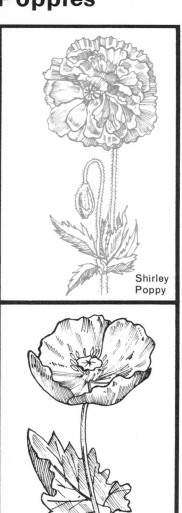

Shirley Poppy

Carnation Poppy

The annual poppies must not be confused with the Oriental Poppy (*Papaver orientale*) which is a perennial and needs quite different treatment.

There are three main groups of annual poppies. The Shirley Poppies (*Papaver rhoeas*) are 18 to 24 in. high, slender, green leaved, with mainly pink and white, rose or red flowers. The decorative Carnation Poppies (*Papaver somniferum*) are 2 to 3 ft. high, stouter stemmed with blue gray leaves and larger flowers in a wide range of colors. The Californian Poppies (*Eschscholzia californica*) are more sprawling in habit, about a foot high, with flowers mainly cream, yellow, apricot, orange, or coppery red.

All the annual poppies are available in single- and double-flowered varieties. They all like warm, sunny places and well-drained soils, but will grow practically anywhere.

All are hardy annuals. Sow seed during March, April, May, or September outdoors where the plants are to flower. Thin seedlings to 9 in. apart (12 in. is probably better for Carnation Poppies). Do not retain self-sown seedlings, which are liable to produce flowers that are of inferior quality.

Sweet Peas

Sweet peas are hardy climbing annuals which can be sown out of doors in March or April where they are to flower in summer. Sow the seeds 1 in. deep and 2 to 3 in. apart in a sunny, open place in good, well-cultivated soil. Sow in double rows 1 ft. apart with at least 4 ft. between each pair of rows, or in circles or groups. Place pea sticks (hazel branches are best) or netting to support the plants to a height of at least 5 ft., then allow the sweet peas to grow naturally. Pick the flowers regularly.

Finer flowers with better stems for cutting are obtained by growing on a single stem. For this method sow in late September or early October three or four seeds in 3-in. pots in peat-based seed compost, and germinate them in a frame. Early in January pinch out the tip of each seedling and, keeping the best shoot on each plant, in March remove all the others.

Harden off the seedlings in late March or early April for planting out in ground that has been well manured. They should be planted 9 in. apart in a double row 1 ft. apart with 5 ft. between each pair of rows. Each plant should be supported by an 8-ft. cane lashed to horizontal wires strained between posts. Remove all side-shoots and tendrils, thus restricting each plant to a single stem. Feed the plants occasionally with a compound fertilizer and keep them well watered in dry weather.

A red form of *Eschscholzia californica*, the Californian Poppy. This hardy annual will succeed in any soil but prefers a sunny position and will survive in places too hot and dry for many other plants

Sweet peas are strongly recommended as flowers for cutting, for the more often they are picked, the more flowers they will produce. This variety is Lavender Lace

Salvias

Scarlet Salvia

The annual salvias are sages but they must not be confused with culinary sage, which is a small shrubby plant requiring quite different treatment.

The two most popular annual salvias are *Salvia splendens* (the Scarlet Salvia) and *Salvia horminum*. The first is actually a perennial but is almost invariably grown as a half-hardy annual, the second is a hardy annual.

The Scarlet Salvia makes a well-branched plant 12 to 18 in. high, with long slender spikes of scarlet flowers. It is a fine plant for filling beds or borders or for making bold splashes of color with other plants. It likes good, well-cultivated soil and warm, sunny places. Sow during January or February in a greenhouse, temperature 65°F., prick off seedlings and later pot singly in 3-in. pots. Harden off for planting outdoors in late May or June. Pink and purple varieties are available.

Salvia horminum grows 18 in. high and has long, violet purple or rosy purple spikes. It thrives in any reasonably good soil and open position. Sow during March, April, or early May outdoors, where plants are to flower, and thin seedlings to 9 in. apart.

Stocks

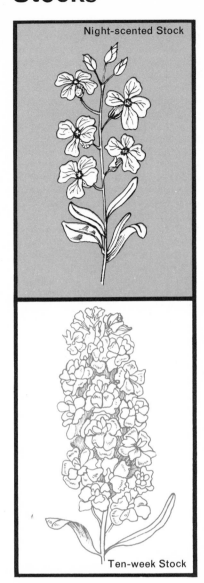
Night-scented Stock

Ten-week Stock

There are several different types of stock and all have scented flowers. The Ten-week Stocks are the most popular, 1 to 2½ ft. high with a good percentage of double flowers and a color range from white, cream, mauve, and pink to crimson and purple.

Even earlier are the Trysomic Seven-week Stocks, earliest ever developed, which will grow satisfactorily where other stocks will not do well. Delightfully perfumed, mostly in doubles.

Night-scented Stock is a small plant 9 to 12 in. high with insignificant flowers which are shut by day and which are intensely fragrant at night.

Virginian Stock is also a small plant with many-colored small flowers, rather like confetti.

Sow seed of night-scented and Virginian stock thinly during March, April, or May outdoors where the plants are to flower in sun or partial shade and ordinary soil. Do not thin seedlings.

Salvia splendens, a tender perennial treated as a half-hardy annual. It is an excellent bedding plant. This popular early variety, Blaze of Fire, grows 1 ft. tall and has a compact habit

One of the best known annuals is Virginian stock. It is very hardy and easy to grow with small flowers on 6-in. stems and is popular with children since it quickly produces a colorful display

Sunflowers, Coneflowers

There are both annual and perennial sunflowers and coneflowers, some annual kinds looking much like the perennial kinds, though they need quite different treatment. All have big, showy, daisy-type flowers, single or double, mainly yellow or orange though in some varieties splashed or ringed with crimson or maroon. The coneflowers are sometimes called Gloriosa Daisies and are mainly derived from *Rudbeckia hirta*. There are numerous varieties differing in color and in height from 1 to 3 ft.

The annual sunflowers are all derived from *Helianthus annuus* and range in height from 3 to 7 ft. All grow almost anywhere, but thrive best in reasonably good, well-drained soil and an open, sunny place.

Sow the coneflowers during February or March in a greenhouse or frame, prick off and harden off for planting outdoors in May about 18 in. apart. Or sow outdoors in July and plant out in September in a sunny, sheltered, and particularly well-drained place.

Sow annual sunflowers during March and April outdoors where they are to flower, spacing them 6 in. apart and thin seedlings to at least 18 in. apart.

coneflower

sunflower

Verbena, Zinnia

verbena

zinnia

Verbenas are really perennial plants, but they are too tender to survive the winter in most areas and are so readily raised from seed that they are usually treated as half-hardy annuals. They are trailing plants with clusters of flowers in many shades of blue, pink, and red.

Sow during February or March in a greenhouse or frame, temperature 65°F. Prick off and harden off for planting outdoors in late May or early June, 9 in. apart, in good, well-cultivated soil and an open, preferably sunny position. Shoots may be pegged to the ground to cover it completely with a carpet of growth.

Zinnias are erect-growing plants with large, single, or double daisy-type flowers in a variety of colors, including yellow, orange, pink, salmon, scarlet, and purple, some varieties having quilled petals like those of a chrysanthemum. Heights range from 1½ to 3 ft.

Sow in March or April in a well-ventilated greenhouse, in a temperature of 60°F. Prick off and harden off for planting out, 1 ft. apart, in late May or early June in good rich soil and an open, sunny place. Or sow in early May outdoors where they are to flower, and thin the seedlings to 1 ft. apart.

The familiar sunflower, *Helianthus annuus*, is a great favorite for bold effect. It is a hardy annual preferring an open, sunny place and well-drained soil

Zinnias are half-hardy annuals which often succeed best when sown in May wherever they are to flower. They do not then suffer the check of being transplanted

A Selection of Biennials

Many biennials flower in May and June, thus usefully filling an awkward gap that can occur between the spring and summer flowers. Like annuals, they are temporary plants which should be pulled up and burned or put on the compost heap when they have finished flowering. Also, as with annuals, though it is easy enough to save seed of most kinds it is usually impossible to prevent cross-fertilization of different varieties, as a result of which home-saved seed produces only a mongrel population. The distinction between annuals, biennials, and herbaceous perennials is not always clear-cut since sometimes varieties of one group can be treated as if they belonged to one of the other groups; e.g., hollyhocks can be grown as annuals, biennials, or short-lived perennials. However, to be sure of a regular succession of biennials it is necessary to sow seed every year at the correct season.

Since biennials must, as a rule, spend one winter out of doors, they run more risks and require a little more thought than annuals. Excessive wet often causes more losses than cold, though it is a combination of the two that can do the greatest damage. Good soil drainage is very helpful to most biennials and it also pays to get them well established before the winter. A common routine is to plant biennials in the beds used for annuals or other temporary summer flowers such as dahlias and geraniums (pelargoniums). Because some of these may go on flowering well into October, there is a temptation to delay the planting of biennials until late October or even November. In cold districts or on poorly drained soils this is asking for trouble. Far better results are obtained by letting the biennials follow those summer flowers that finish, and so can be cleared away, relatively early, leaving the later flowers to be followed by such spring-flowering bulbs as tulips and hyacinths which do not suffer from being planted in late October.

Similar forethought will prevent another difficulty that can occur with biennials—what to put in their place when they finish flowering in July. This need present no problem if some annuals are sown late, the young plants being grown on in seed trays or small pots until they are required to fill up the gaps left by the biennials. Outdoor chrysanthemums are also excellent for the same purpose, since they can be grown, if desired, in a reserve bed and then be moved to the ground in which the biennials have been flowering, even if by that date the chrysanthemums themselves are already coming into bloom. It is by such devices as these that resourceful gardeners will maintain a constant supply of flowers where others with less forethought have only a spasmodic display.

What Is a Biennial?

Biennials are plants which must be renewed annually from seed, since they die after they have flowered and set seed. In this they resemble annuals, but unlike them biennials take over a year to complete their cycle of growth. Seed sown one year will produce plants which will flower the next year, ripen their seed, and die before the second winter.

Some plants that are not truly biennials are usually grown as such in gardens because this is the way to see them at their best. For example, wallflowers will live for years in poor, well-drained soil, but they get straggly with age. Their flowers are of better quality in good, rich soil in which their softer growth is likely to die during the course of the second winter.

It is also true that some plants which are really biennials can be treated as annuals, that is, induced to flower the first year, if the seed is sown very early in a greenhouse and the seedlings are later planted out.

But the general rule with biennials is to sow seed in a frame or out of doors in May or June, transplant the seedlings to a reserve bed in July, spacing them a few inches apart each way, and finally plant them in September or October where they will flower the following spring or summer.

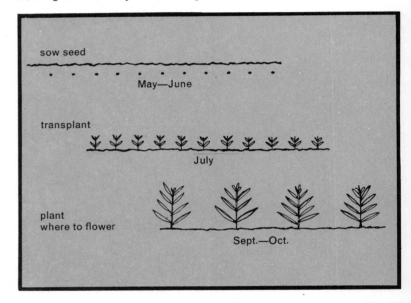

sow seed

May—June

transplant

July

plant where to flower

Sept.—Oct.

The large, bell-shaped flowers of the Canterbury Bell (*Campanula medium*) are produced in June and July on 2½-ft. stems. Seed should be sown in May or June, to flower the following summer

English Daisies, Forget-me-nots

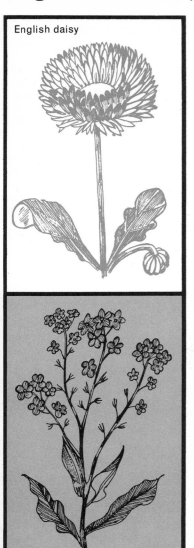

English daisy

forget-me-not

The showy white, pink, or red double-flowered daisies so popular for a spring display are giant varieties of *Bellis perennis,* the familiar daisy of lawns and meadows. These fine double-flowered varieties are excellent for interplanting in beds of tulips, hyacinths, and other spring bulbs.

Sow seed in May or June in a frame or out of doors, transplant seedlings 3 or 4 in. apart in a sunny place and well-cultivated soil and transfer plants in September or October to where they are to flower, spacing them 6 to 8 in. apart. They can be lifted, split up, and replanted after flowering, but it is more satisfactory to raise anew from seed each year.

Forget-me-nots, or myosotis, are the favorite blue-flowered plants for interplanting in spring beds of tulips. They also make good beds on their own and may be grown under shrubs and in woodlands as they do not mind shade. In addition to blue there is also a pink-flowered variety.

Sow seed in June or early July out of doors in well-broken soil. Transplant the seedlings 3 in. apart in rows 6 to 8 in. apart in a cool, partially shaded place, keep well watered and transfer to flowering beds in October or November, spacing the plants 6 to 9 in. apart.

After flowering, pull up the plants and scatter some over a prepared seedbed on which they will shed their seeds and give a new crop of seedlings.

Foxgloves, Hollyhocks

hollyhock

Foxgloves, or digitalis, carry their tubular flowers in tapering 4- to 6-ft. spikes in July and August. In the ordinary varieties the flowers droop and are all on one side of each spike, but in the Excelsior varieties they are held outward all round the spike. Both types are available in a range of colors from white, cream, and pink to rose red. All grow well in any reasonably well-drained soil in the open or in shade.

Hollyhocks carry their large flowers in stout spikes 6 to 8 ft. high. The flowers may be single, like little plates, or double like rosettes, in a range of colors from white, cream, and pink to salmon and crimson. They flower in July and August and like well-drained soils and sunny places. In some places they suffer severely from a disease which produces rusty pustules on the leaves and where this is troublesome plants should be sprayed frequently from May to August with Bordeaux mixture. Rust-resistant varieties are available.

Sow seed of foxgloves and hollyhocks out of doors in May or June; transplant seedlings 6 in. apart in rows 9 in. apart in well-cultivated soil and transfer plants to their flowering positions in September or October, spacing foxgloves 1 ft. apart and hollyhocks 2 ft. apart.

Varieties are also available which can be sown in a greenhouse in February or March to flower the same year.

The popular English daisies, available in red, pink, or white are decorative on their own or they can be used as groundwork beneath the taller spring-flowering bulbs

Excelsior Hybrids are especially attractive foxgloves with flowers held outward all round the stems. Foxgloves of all kinds are equally at home in sunshine or shade

Pansies, Violas

There is very little difference between pansies and violas, but in general violas are a little more tufted and less straggly in habit of growth and the flowers of pansies are almost always of two or more colors, one prominently blotched on the other. Nowadays it is customary to treat both as biennials, but the small-flowered violas are much easier to keep from one year to another. Both are available in a wide range of colors and seed can be purchased to give mixed or separate colors. Both flower in spring and summer and some varieties of viola are available which flower from late winter.

Sow seeds in May or June in a frame or greenhouse or a sheltered place out of doors in soil with which plenty of peat or leaf mold has been mixed. Prick off the seedlings 2 in. apart in boxes or beds of finely broken soil, keep them well watered and plant them in September or October 6 to 9 in. apart where they are to flower.

Alternatively, sow seed in a greenhouse with a temperature of 60°F. in February or March, prick off the seedlings into boxes and plant them out in May to flower the same year. Seedlings raised in this way are on sale each spring.

Pansies and violas like fairly rich, well-cultivated soil and will grow in sunny or shady places. The flowering season is extended by removing dead flowers.

Primroses, Polyanthuses

The main difference between primroses and polyanthuses is that whereas the former carry only one flower on each slender stem, polyanthuses have stouter stems each bearing a cluster of flowers. Primroses are more graceful but polyanthuses make a more solid display. Both are available in a great range of colors from white, cream, pale pink, and lavender to deep orange, crimson, and deep blue and all flower from March to May. Seed can be purchased to give separate or mixed colors.

Sow seed in a frame or greenhouse in March or April or out of doors in May or June using soil in which plenty of peat or leaf mold has been mixed. Prick off frame- or greenhouse-raised seedlings 1½ in. apart in shallow boxes filled with potting mix and plant out of doors when the seedlings are filling the boxes.

Grow longer in a partially shaded place in good, well-cultivated soil with which plenty of leaf mold or peat and some rotted manure or garden refuse has been mixed. Transfer the plants to their flowering beds in September or October, spacing them about 9 in. apart. After flowering, the plants can be lifted, divided, and replanted, but the best results are obtained by raising from seed each year.

Primroses and polyanthuses will grow in sunny or shady places.

Pansies are available in a great range of colors and sizes but most have the cheerful "faces" with central streaks or blotches seen in this early-flowering variety

Many delightful colors are available in the polyanthus. Shown here is a selection of the Pacific strain which is notable for the large size of its individual flowers carried on very fine trusses

Sweet William and Others

Canterbury Bell

Canterbury Bells are varieties of *Campanula medium*. They carry their large, bell-shaped flowers in broad spikes 2½ ft. high in June and July. The cup-and-saucer varieties have an extra ring of flat petals behind each bell, and the double varieties have several bells one inside the other. All are available in white, pink, rose, mauve, and blue varieties.

Sweet Williams are varieties of *Dianthus barbatus* and they carry their brightly colored flowers in large, flattish heads in June and July. There are many varieties, in heights ranging from 6 in. to 2 ft. in separate or mixed colors. The auricula-eyed varieties all have a conspicuous white eye to the colored flower.

Brompton Stocks resemble other stocks but are taller, more branching, and flower from March to May. The color range is from white, lavender, and pink to crimson and violet.

All these plants like sunny places and well-drained soil and Brompton Stocks are sometimes difficult to overwinter out of doors in heavy soil or in cold gardens. Sow seeds of Sweet Williams in May or June, or of Brompton Stocks in July, in a frame or outside in well-prepared soil. Transplant seedlings 6 in. apart in good soil and an open, sunny position, and transfer to flowering beds in September or October. Brompton Stocks may also be grown in an unheated greenhouse.

Wallflowers

cheiranthus

Wallflowers are among the most richly scented of spring flowers, and are available in a fine range of colors. Dwarf varieties are about 1 ft. high and normal varieties 18 in. high.

The Siberian Wallflower, *Cheiranthus allionii*, has vivid orange flowers on foot-high plants and continues to flower into June, but the flowers are not scented.

Sow seeds in April or early May out of doors in drills ½ in. deep. Transplant the seedlings when about 3 in. high to a reserve bed of well-cultivated soil in an open, sunny position, planting them 6 in. apart. After two weeks pinch off the top of each plant to encourage branching from low down. Keep down weeds all summer.

In September or as early as possible in October, transplant to where they are to flower, spacing the plants about 1 ft. apart. They can be grown with the colors mixed, in beds or blocks all of the same color, or patterns of different colors can be arranged.

After flowering, remove the plants and either put them on the compost heap or burn them.

The Sweet Williams are welcome border plants for early summer color. They are available in separate and mixed colors in heights from 6 in. to 2 ft. but all are derived from *Dianthus barbatus*

Wallflowers and forget-me-nots combined with tulips bring all the gaiety of spring to this attractive garden. The first two are grown as biennials for best results, although both are really perennials

Garden Pools

Water can be used in many ways in the garden. It provides a medium in which plants of a special kind, the aquatics, can be grown. It can also be stocked with fish which bring life and movement to the garden. Plants and fish combine well, as the latter benefit from the protection which floating and submerged leaves provide. But if the fish are to be enjoyed to the full, planting must not be too dense or they will be screened almost completely from view. One advantage of having both fish and plants in a pool is that they will assist in keeping the water fresh. However, if crystal-clear water is required it will be best to have no living things in it and to rely on chemicals to prevent growth of weeds and scum.

The smooth surface of water provides a texture quite different from anything else in the garden and also acts as a mirror, capturing the changing color of the sky and reflecting the plants, ornaments, or buildings placed sufficiently close to it. Fountains and cascades bring both movement and the pleasant sounds that falling or rushing water can create. But it is only still water that reflects clearly, so if the mirror effect is uppermost in the garden maker's mind, fountains and cascades must either be banned altogether or be kept sufficiently far away to prevent disturbance of that part of the water which is to provide reflections.

Almost any moving-water effects are possible, even in quite a small garden, by the use of an electrically operated pump which can be submerged in the pool to circulate water from it through fountains or pipes. If plants are to be grown in the water or it is to be stocked with fish this is far better than using water from an outside source, such as the water main, since this will constantly change the temperature of the pool, as well as robbing it of valuable nutrients and possibly introducing chemicals harmful to the life in the pool.

Fountains can be of many different types, single jet, multiple jet, or simply bubbling up a few inches above the surface of the water. It is even possible to obtain fountains which produce changing patterns by a simple mechanism operated by the pressure of the water passing through the fountain.

If water is used in formal parts of the garden, the shape of basin or pool should contribute to the design. By contrast an informal pool should appear as natural as possible, with plants, turf, or rocks concealing any concrete, glass fiber, or plastic sheeting used in its construction.

One other possible use of water is as a fine spray over statues, ornaments, or stones to keep parts or the whole moist, thus producing a gleaming in place of a dull surface.

Siting and Planning

Water gardens in which water lilies are to be grown should be located in a reasonably open place where they at least get the afternoon sun which is so necessary to open the flowers effectively. Fish, on the other hand, benefit from some shade, and the green, scummy growth which sometimes obscures water is less likely to prove troublesome in pools that are not fully exposed to the sun.

A happy compromise is to provide some shelter to the north and east, but to leave pools fully open to the south and west. However, if the purpose of the water is purely ornamental and there is no intention to stock it with plants or fish the location is immaterial.

Water gardens may be formal or informal. The first-mentioned may take the form of circular, rectangular, or other symmetrical shapes, usually clearly defined by flagged or otherwise paved edges; alternatively, they may be bowls or basins of water raised above the level of the soil. They may contain fountains or be fed by dripping wells or other architectural features.

Informal pools will usually, though not invariably, be of irregular outline with grass or soil to water level. They may be features on their own or form part of a rock garden. They may be combined with streams, cascades, or other natural-looking features.

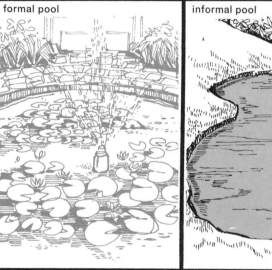

formal pool   informal pool

This small informal pool makes a delightful feature. Water brings a completely new element into the garden and allows for the introduction of many water-loving plants

Construction

Informal pools can sometimes be made by damming a stream and allowing it to flood the surrounding land, but more usually they are excavated and lined with some impervious material, such as glass fiber, plastic, or rubber sheets, or concrete.

Glass fiber pools can be bought ready-made in a variety of shapes and sizes. All that is then necessary is to excavate a hole large enough to accommodate the pool, set the mold in place, and fill in with soil around it so that it is firmly supported. Such pools are very durable, and when well installed and properly planted their artificial nature can be concealed so well that they appear natural.

Special plastic or rubber sheets can be purchased as pool liners. They must be welded together by the manufacturer to provide a single sheet that will completely line the bottom and sides of the pool and just overlap the edges where it can be held down by soil and/or rockery or paving stones. All large stones and other hard, sharp objects should be removed from the bottom of the excavation. A layer of sand is an advantage in providing a smooth bed for the sheet.

Fountains and Cascades

Moving water adds greatly to the attractiveness of many water gardens. If electricity is available, fountains, cascades, and the rest are best operated by small electrically operated pumps. The pump may either be installed close to the pool, the best method if a large volume of water is to be used, or it may be actually submerged for which purpose special units are available in which all the electrical parts are completely watertight. By either system, the water is constantly circulated from the pool and returned to it so that the only loss is by evaporation, requiring a minimum of topping up. This is also better for fish and plants than frequent renewal by water from the mains which is usually chemically treated and may be at a different temperature.

Fountains are available in many patterns either on their own or combined with ornaments or statues. Cascades can be lined with concrete or with plastic or rubber sheets like the pools themselves. Glass-fiber cascades can be obtained in sections, but it is rather hard to screen the artificiality of these. The best results are often obtained by forming cascades of large rocks embedded in concrete, but with no concrete actually showing.

Constructing an informal pool. The shape has been well marked out and is being excavated. Note the polyethylene liner which will be used to cover the bottom and sides of the pool completely

This illustrates well the construction of a pool, with a cascade, using glass-fiber sections. This is a comparatively easy method but it is often difficult to mask the artificiality of the glass fiber

Planting and Stocking

From mid-April to the end of May is the best period for planting in water, but the surrounding beds can be planted earlier or even in summer if plants are obtained in containers.

The easiest and cleanest way to grow aquatics is in special plastic baskets which can be purchased for the purpose. Each plant is given a basket to itself and is planted in good garden soil with which bone-meal has been mixed at 2 oz. per 2 gal. bucket of soil. Fill the baskets to the brim and plant so that the crowns are just level with the surface of the soil. Then stand the baskets in the pool where they are to grow. Most water lilies thrive in about 1 ft. depth of water, but most marginal plants prefer only an inch or so of water over the roots. Pools may be made with a shelf around the edge for these shallow water plants or, alternatively, the baskets can be stood on bricks to bring them to any required level.

If fish are to be kept in the pool there should be some oxygenating plants to keep the water sweet and provide shelter. These are free-floating plants and they can simply be dropped into the water without any soil, or a small stone can be tied to the bottom of each to sink it where it is required.

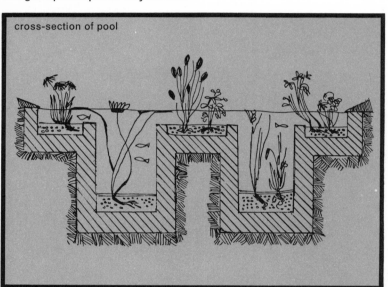

cross-section of pool

Floating Leaves

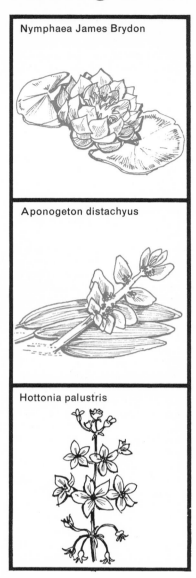

Nymphaea James Brydon

Aponogeton distachyus

Hottonia palustris

There are numerous varieties of water lily, or nymphaea, all flowering in summer and differing in vigor as well as in the size and color of their flowers. All have floating leaves and display their flowers just above these. Most suitable for pools of medium size with from 1- to 2-ft. depth of water are the varieties of *Nymphaea marliacea*, with pink, crimson, or yellow flowers, varieties of *N. laydekeri* with pink or crimson flowers, and such varieties as Escarboucle, crimson; James Brydon, red; Rose Arey, scented; and Mrs. Richmond, pink. For very small pools with only 5 to 8 in. of water, varieties of *N. pygmaea* and *N. tetragona* may be used.

Aponogeton distachyus is known as the Water Hawthorn and has little spikes of sweetly scented white flowers from late spring to early autumn. It thrives in water up to 18 in. deep. *Menyanthes trifoliata* is known as the Bog Bean. It has three-part leaves and clusters of white or pale pink flowers. It likes 4- to 6-in. depth of water.

Nymphoides peltatum has clusters of bright yellow flowers with fringed petals. It likes water up to 18 in. deep.

Elodea, hottonia (Water Violet), myriophyllum, and utricularia are oxygenating plants.

Planting a water lily in a special plastic basket designed for aquatics. Good garden soil to which bonemeal has been added is used and a coarse hessian liner helps to retain this mixture

The water lily Mrs. Richmond. The immense flowers of this variety color to deep rose as they age. It is a handsome subject for pools with 1- to 2-ft. depth of water

Marginal Plants

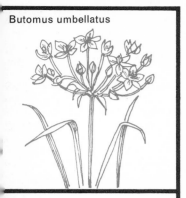
Butomus umbellatus

Caltha palustris

Sagittaria japonica

Alisma (Water Plantain) has 2-ft. sprays of small pink flowers in summer. It likes 2 or 3 in. of water over its roots. Butomus (Flowering Rush) has heads of pink flowers on stout 3-ft. stems in late summer. It likes 3 to 4 in. of water.

Calla palustris (Bog Arum) has little yellow and green arum lily flowers in early summer. It can be planted outside the pool or in up to 2 in. of water. *Caltha palustris* (Kingcup, or Marsh Marigold) has large buttercuplike flowers in spring. A double-flowered variety is named *flore pleno*. Treat like calla.

Iris laevigata and *I. kaempferi* have large, showy white, violet, or purple flowers in May and June. The first likes an inch or so of water, the second prefers to be just outside the pool.

Lysichitum (Skunk Cabbage) has large yellow or white flowers like arum lilies in spring. Treat like calla. *Mimulus luteus* (Musk) has yellow- or red-blotched flowers in summer. Treat like calla.

Pontederia has spikes of light blue flowers in summer and likes 2 to 3 in. of water. Sagittaria (arrowhead) has stiff sprays of white flowers in summer. There is a double-flowered variety and both like 3 to 4 in. of water. *Scirpus tabernaemontani zebrinus* has quill-like leaves banded yellow and white. It likes 2 to 4 in. of water.

Typha (reed mace) has cigar-like flowers in late summer. The best garden kinds are *Typha angustifolia* and *T. minima*. Both like 3 to 4 in. of water.

Keeping Water Clean

It is only possible to have crystal-clear water in pools that have no living things in them. Wherever plants are grown and fish breed and feed there will be some discoloration of the water and some growth of weed which must be removed if it gets too thick.

Much weed can be removed with a garden rake or a sieve drawn through the water or by fixing a piece of wire mesh over the tines of a garden fork. Green scum and blanket weed, a dense growth like green cotton wool, are most likely to be troublesome in hot summer weather in pools that are fully exposed to the sun.

Chemical treatment with copper sulfate, or other weed killers, is not recommended in stocked pools because of the danger of killing plants and fish.

Pools should be emptied, cleaned, and refilled every second or third year. Fish can be placed in buckets of water and plants stood on one side for a few hours while the pool is scrubbed and flushed with clean water. Do not use chemicals or detergents during the cleaning process.

An attractive feature of this well-kept pool is the Water Hawthorn with its little spikes of sweetly scented flowers. Well-balanced planting and correct stocking with fish can help to keep the water clean. Suitable for U.S. Zone 10

A fine display of well-contrasted marginal plants around a charming natural pool in late spring. The double-flowered kingcup, *Caltha palustris flore pleno*, is prominent in the foreground

Patios and Plants in Containers

Planning

A patio is virtually an outdoor room, a part of the garden which can be frequently used as a place in which to sit, eat, and meet one's friends. For these reasons it must be private and sheltered, and it must be well paved so that it can be used with comfort and without danger of bringing dirt into the house, even after heavy rain.

The natural place for a patio is adjacent to the house; indeed the original Spanish patio was always an inner courtyard surrounded by the house. But the term has been given a wider meaning, and is now used to describe any small, formal, and to some degree enclosed, garden.

The actual size, shape, and design of the patio is a matter for individual taste and may be determined to a considerable degree by the site itself. In very small, town gardens it may be best to treat the whole area as a patio, but in larger or country gardens it is more probable that the patio will be a small part of the whole, possibly looking out on to the rest of the garden, though it may be entirely separated from it.

Whatever the size and character of the patio, firm lines and a strong sense of design are desirable.

Fashions have a habit of going full circle, though they may take a long time to do so. That is precisely what has happened in gardening. In medieval times all gardens were small and enclosed, mainly because the world outside was a dangerous place and private property had to be well protected by walls. As the power of central authority and the wealth of the nation increased, gardens grew in size, discarded their walls and hedges, and eventually developed into landscapes encompassing the surrounding countryside, or such parts of it as seemed desirable. Now, in the twentieth century, gardens are again small, though for very different reasons. It is the immense value of land in and near great cities and centers of industry that has progressively reduced the size of building lots, until now the house often occupies more ground than the garden. The effective planning of such tiny spaces presents special problems to which two quite different approaches have been made. In the United States and Canada, open-planned gardens have been seen as the major solution. Walls, hedges, fences, and even simple rails or chains to mark the boundary between one lot and another, have been swept away and all the gardens in a street or block have been planned as one. This can produce a remarkable impression of spaciousness but it does tend to destroy privacy and prevent an individual approach to plants and planning.

In Britain open planning has only proved moderately acceptable. Instead, there has been a return to the medieval conception of the garden as an extension of the house; a courtyard or outdoor room in which leisure can be spent and friends entertained. Early in this century such concepts were already being used to break up large gardens. Gertrude Jekyll, who at this period influenced garden styles greatly, often divided gardens into several compartments. At Hidcote, near Chipping Campden in Gloucestershire, Major Lawrence Johnston made a garden which is virtually a whole succession of outdoor rooms differing in size and treatment. This garden is now the property of the National Trust, as is Sissinghurst Castle, another fine compartmented garden made by Victoria Sackville-West and her husband, Sir Harold Nicolson, and both provide many object lessons for those who wish to design small gardens in this modern and intimate style. Even without any soil at all plants can be grown successfully in containers of peat compost and by such means balconies and rooftops can be filled with color and fragrance. The advantage of peat compost here is that it is much lighter than soil and so places less strain on rafters or balcony supports.

An attractive patio garden is an asset to any house, as it can be used as an outdoor room. Flowering plants give a touch of color, and shrubs give privacy and protection from wind

Paths and Terraces

Though grass need not be excluded from a patio it should not form the main paths or sitting places, which should be well paved so that they remain clean and usable. Rectangular paving slabs are ideal since they accord with the formal style of a patio, are comparatively easy to lay, and can be obtained with a good, non-slippery surface. Bricks look nice but become dangerously slippery in wet weather. Crazy paving is rather too rustic in appearance for most patios and is difficult to lay well. Gravel is apt to pick up on the feet and asphalt has a poor appearance. Concrete is probably the best substitute for paving slabs. It can be tinted to give it a better appearance, and scored with the point of a mason's trowel to simulate the joints between paving slabs.

If paving slabs are used they should be bedded in concrete so that they are completely secure and cannot ride up and cause accidents. If creeping plants are to be grown between the slabs, leave planting spaces for these when the slabs are laid. They must be able to root down freely into the soil below.

Patterns in paving can be created by using specially shaped paving slabs designed for pattern making, or by making panels of pebbles set in concrete. It is even possible to use pebbles of different colors to produce designs.

Walls and Screens

Patios require shelter to give protection from winds and hot sunshine, and also to give privacy. This can be provided with wooden or metal screens of various kinds, by building walls of brick, stone, or special walling blocks, or by evergreen plants.

Probably the cheapest form of screening available is woven wooden panels. Various patterns of closeboard fence are a little more expensive, while some of the most attractive effects in wood can be obtained with either close or open horizontal boarding.

If more money is available, wrought-iron may be considered either as a complete screen or in panels inserted in walls.

Equally attractive effects can be obtained with concrete screen blocks available in a variety of patterns. The openwork blocks can be clothed with clematis, honeysuckle, jasmine, ornamental vines, or a thornless rose, such as Zéphirine Drouhin. These will grow through the blocks and find their own support.

Part of the patio may be covered with beams in the manner of a pergola and wisteria or laburnum may be trained so that the flower trails hang down inside.

If evergreens are used choose kinds that will grow fast so that they give the required protection rapidly, and yet can be kept at whatever dimensions are necessary. Leyland Cypress has precisely these qualities.

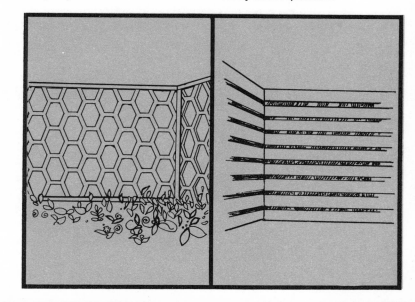

A wide range of paving materials are now available from garden centers and paving specialists. Here, concrete paving slabs in varying colors have been used to make an abstract design

Wooden beams and plastic sheeting are used to protect this patio and make it a really sheltered place both for sitting in and for cultivation of plants that enjoy some protection

Water

Water can be a great asset in a patio since it introduces a new texture and the possibility of using sound as an additional attraction. It also means that one can enjoy a further range of plants, the beauty of reflections, and the movement and color of fish.

As a rule the patio pool will be formal in design; perhaps a simple rectangle or a circle, either placed in a central position or set against a wall, with a dripping fountain trickling into it. The pool need not be deep: six inches of water is sufficient for miniature water lilies, such as *Nymphaea pygmaea* and its varieties, and twelve inches will grow almost anything. Plants are best grown in pots or plastic baskets which will restrict their growth to some extent and make it easy to lift, divide, and replant them when they grow too large. Very pleasing effects can be obtained by covering the bottom of the pool wholly or partially with large pebbles.

Fountains can be operated by small electric pumps and can be of many different types from single jets to multiple sprays, or a gentle water jet may simply be used to disturb the surface or bubble up through a bed of pebbles.

Hardy ferns grown in pots or a soil bed can make an attractive screen for the pool.

Planting

It is quite possible to make an attractive patio with very few plants, or it can be more or less filled with plants if desired. Often, comparatively tender plants will thrive in sheltered patios.

Unless evergreen shrubs are used to screen the patio it will be wise to include one or two in the planting so that it still looks attractive in winter. Some of the low-spreading junipers may be used or flowering evergreens with an interesting shape of leaf, such as mahonias and yuccas. Camellias, the smaller rhododendrons, and evergreen azaleas, lavenders, and rosemaries are also excellent, and among deciduous shrubs, Japanese maples and hydrangeas.

Herbaceous plants with good foliage look attractive for months. *Acanthus mollis*, astilbes, dicentra, heucheras, hostas, irises, incarvilleas, rodgersias, and *Tiarella cordifolia* are a few that may be used with excellent effect.

Creeping plants in the crevices between flagstones or encroaching on paths from the edges of beds should be really prostrate, such as acaenas, arenarias, *Mazus pumilio*, and *Mentha requienii*.

To maintain color, bulbs and bedding plants in season are invaluable. Some fragrant varieties should be included, such as heliotropes, nicotianas, and stocks, and also plants with a long-flowering season, such as antirrhinums, *Begonia semperflorens*, fuchsias, pelargoniums, and petunias.

A simple pool with a fountain makes an interesting feature in this paved garden. The pebbles which line the pool form a further attraction and give a clean finish appropriate to the whole design

Green foliage plants have a refreshingly cool appearance and make a pleasant change from vivid flowering plants. Included here are *Rodgersia aesculifolia*, epimediums, rheums, and ornamental grasses

Plant Containers

Pots, vases, tubs, troughs, and other containers can be most useful in patios, both because they can themselves be ornamental and also because they can be filled with permanent or bedding plants to further the display. If room is available elsewhere in the garden, it may even be possible to have a reserve of containers which can be moved on to the patio when the plants growing in them are capable of making their greatest effect.

The choice in ornamental containers is very wide, ranging from simple wooden tubs to elaborate reproductions in plaster or glass fiber of antique lead or stone vases and troughs. Excellent modern designs in concrete or asbestos cement are also available, and lovely pottery vases and jars, some of the best being imported from Provence.

Containers may either stand on the ground or be raised on pedestals or walls. Whichever method is chosen, they should stand on a hard surface with a free outlet for surplus water and no likelihood that worms will enter from below.

Hanging baskets can also be used with excellent effect in patios. They should be suspended from beams or from brackets.

Care of Container Plants

Plants grown in window boxes, hanging baskets, vases, tubs, troughs, and other containers are almost completely dependent on the gardener for water and food. The rainfall they receive will certainly not be adequate for their needs, since much of it will drain away or be evaporated. Dryness and starvation are the two commonest causes of failure with container-grown plants of any kind.

In hot weather, such plants are likely to need daily watering and even in dull, showery weather they may need watering two or three times a week. When watering, apply direct from the spout of the can or through a very coarse rose and give enough to soak right through the soil and begin to trickle out at the bottom.

If good fresh potting soil is used, plants should not need feeding for the first six weeks of their container life. After this time, feed once every two weeks with seaweed extract fertilizer or a liquid fertilizer, used as directed by the manufacturers.

The only pests that are likely to be troublesome are aphids. Occasional syringing with a good insecticide will get rid of these.

Faded flowers should be removed as they appear, not only for the sake of tidiness, but also because this helps to prolong the flowering life of the plants.

Containers are often as decorative as the plants themselves. They should be chosen so that they enhance the plants, provide good growing conditions, and fit in with the style of the garden

A delightful planting of summer flowers used to decorate a back yard. Standard fuchsias and hanging baskets of pelargoniums give an added dimension to the scene

163

Hanging Baskets

Hanging baskets are usually made of wire or plastic, are bowl shaped and from 12 to 18 in. in diameter. They are filled with growing plants and suspended by chains from greenhouse rafters, or in verandahs, loggias, garden rooms, porticos, or other places where they will add to the decorative display. Though it is possible to use hanging baskets at any time of the year, they are most useful in summer and the usual practice is to make them up in May or early June and to empty them in October.

Almost any of the plants commonly used for summer bedding may be used for hanging baskets, but pelargoniums, fuchsias, dwarf nasturtiums, lobelias, and petun-ias are particularly suitable. *Campanula isophylla*, Zone 7, a slightly tender, trailing, perennial bell-flower with blue or white flowers is also very useful and so are the various ornamental forms of asparagus, ivy, tradescantia, and zebrina.

There are also pendulous varieties of begonia which are ideal for hanging baskets in greenhouses, loggias, and other similar protected places.

Before filling hanging baskets, they should be lined with a thick layer of moss to prevent the compost from being washed out. The plants are then placed in position with a peat-based potting mix around their roots.

An upright growing plant such as a zonal pelargonium or a fuchsia may be placed in the center of each basket with a few trailing or spreading plants around to fill it comfortably. The basket must not be overfilled at the start as the plants will grow considerably during the summer and will become overcrowded.

Fill each basket almost to the rim with potting mix, then water thoroughly, and hang up to drain. It is an advantage if baskets can be kept in a greenhouse for a week or ten days after they have been made up, so that the plants may become a little established before they are taken to colder and more exposed places.

As the plants grow, peg some of the trailing varieties to the outside of the baskets with pieces of bent wire so that they are more or less completely covered.

Hanging baskets should be watered daily in warm weather, as they tend to dry out rapidly.

A fine example of *Fuchsia* Swingtime, growing in a hanging basket. Often these baskets are more effective if they are planted with just one particular variety. Suitable for U.S. Zone 10

A hanging basket giving added interest to a plain brick wall. Among the plants are several types of pelargoniums, including some grown for their colored leaves, lobelias and fuchsias. Pelargoniums and fuchsias are suitable for Zone 10

Vases, Tubs, Troughs

Vases, tubs, and troughs of many kinds can be used both as ornaments in the garden, and to be filled with flowers in season to add still further to the display. Vases and troughs may be of stone, pottery, concrete, metal, or plastic. Lead was once largely used, beaten or cast in elaborate designs, but this is too expensive a material to be used much nowadays. Instead, excellent reproductions of old lead vases and troughs in glass fiber or plastic can be purchased, and have the merit of being both light and durable. Wooden troughs are also available, and tubs are normally made of wood, often being barrels sawed in half, and provided with extra metal bands for strength.

Whatever kind of container is used, if plants are to be grown in it, it should be provided with drainage holes to allow surplus water to escape. If these holes are at the bottom of the sides, the containers may stand directly on the ground, but if the holes are in the bottom itself, it will be better to raise the container on slates or tiles, so that there is a space through which water can escape freely.

Wooden containers of all kinds, including window boxes, must be either charred inside or treated with a wood preservative, such as copper naphthenate, which is harmless to plants. Creosote should not be used as a preservative, as this gives off fumes which are toxic to plants.

Containers should be filled with a peat-based potting mix before planting takes place. If it is possible, this mix should be changed once a year, but if not, feed the mix when plants are renewed with fertilizer at the rate of 4 oz. per bushel of soil.

Any of the plants that are used for spring and summer bedding may be used for ornamental containers. Pelargoniums (geraniums), fuchsias, petunias, lobelias, gazanias, and mesembryanthemums are particularly suitable for summer displays and wallflowers, polyanthuses, tulips, and hyacinths for spring.

In addition, there are other plants which make good permanent oc-cupants for containers, including the African Lily or agapanthus, hydrangeas, camellias, many of the smaller kinds of rhododendrons and evergreen azaleas, clipped bay and box, both green and variegated, and the slower-growing varieties of cypress, juniper, and thuja. African Lilies are not completely hardy, so they should be moved to a greenhouse or shelter in winter, if possible in the containers in which they are growing.

Fuchsias, pelargoniums, lobelias, and various foliage plants in an old lead trough. These troughs are fairly hard to come by, but glass fiber copies are readily available. Pelargoniums and fuchsias are suitable for Zone 10

These stone troughs blend well with the surrounding paving and wall, making an ideal background for the gay flowers. Similar troughs can be obtained made from concrete suitably prepared and colored

Window Boxes

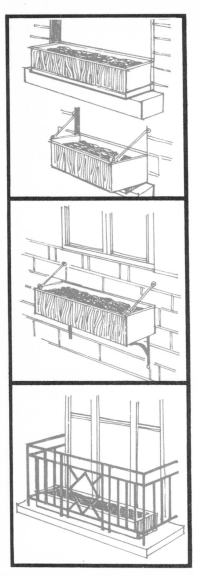

Even in town houses without gardens it is still possible to grow plants by using window boxes. If the windows are of the sash type the boxes should stand on the window ledges, raised an inch or so on blocks so that surplus water can escape, but secured with bolts, metal straps, or bars so that they cannot be dislodged accidentally. For casement windows, boxes must be fixed a few inches below the ledge so that the windows can be opened over the tops of the plants. This may be done with metal straps fastened to the ledge or the boxes may be supported on brackets firmly fixed to the wall.

Window boxes may be made of wood, plastic, or metal. They should not normally be less than 8 in. wide and 6 in. deep and must be well supplied with drainage holes to allow surplus water to escape.

One of the lightweight peat mixes may be used to fill the boxes. If possible, it should be renewed each year, but if not, fertilizer should be added to the soil at the rate of 4 oz. per bushel of soil before new plants are put into it.

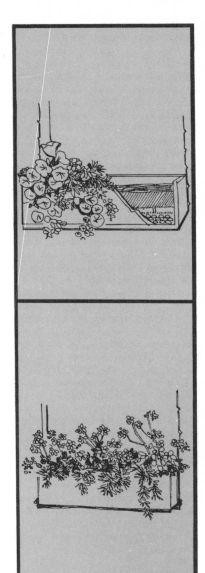

Almost any of the kinds of plants that are used for spring and summer bedding, including annuals and bulbs, may also be used for window boxes, but the shorter varieties are to be preferred.

For spring, dwarf wallflowers, primroses, polyanthuses, violas, pansies, and double daisies are particularly suitable; also crocuses, tulips up to 1 ft. high, and hyacinths.

For a summer display, violas and pansies may also be used with Sweet Alyssum, dwarf begonias, lobelias, dwarf French and African Marigolds, petunias (the double-flowered varieties particularly), Tom Thumb nasturtiums, and verbenas. *Lobelia tenuior* and *Campanula isophylla* in blue and white varieties are useful trailing plants to hang over the edges of boxes, and ivy-leaved pelargoniums can be used in the same way. Zonal pelargoniums and short or weeping fuchsias, such as Tom Thumb and Alice Hoffman, Molesworth and Cascade, may also be used.

Even in winter, window boxes can be made attractive with a variegated variety of periwinkle (*Vinca minor*), dwarf conifers, *Hebe pageana*, and other small evergreen shrubs.

An attractive wooden window box filled with fuchsias, begonias, pelargoniums, and ivy-leaved geraniums. In the autumn, these summer-flowering plants can be replaced by spring-flowering bulbs

In this gay window box, the trailing stems of Creeping Jenny, *Lysimachia nummularia*, unite the flowers with the branches of *Cotoneaster horizontalis* spreading up the wall below

Plants can be removed from window boxes or added to them as required so that a constant succession of interest is maintained. One of the advantages of using a peat-based potting mix is that these changes can be made more easily than with a soil-based mix since it does not become so consolidated.

When moving the plants, always lift them carefully with a hand fork and plant equally carefully with a trowel. During this operation, avoid breaking or disturbing the roots of neighboring plants unnecessarily. Immediately after planting, water well and subsequently inspect the boxes daily, watering thoroughly as soon as the soil begins to dry.

From June to August feed every week with a seaweed-based fertilizer or any other suitable liquid fertilizer used in a very diluted state. Stake where necessary.

Pick off all faded flowers regularly and also remove discolored or dying leaves. In hot weather, syringe the plants daily with water, increasing this to two or three times a day if it is really hot. Plants enjoy a moist atmosphere as this prevents them from wilting, and the moisture also helps to keep some pests away.

When planting a combination of bulbs and plants, place an inch or so of mix or peat in the bottom of the box, space out the bulbs on this, add a little more mix, then put the plants in position and fill in with mix.

Furniture

Chairs or benches of some kind will almost certainly be required for a patio, and also possibly tables and a barbecue. All should be chosen and placed with as much care as ornaments, since they can serve an ornamental as well as a utilitarian role.

There is no shortage of good design in furniture from which to choose, and a variety of materials is also available. For the traditional style of patio, wrought-iron furniture may be preferred. It can be obtained with a natural finish, painted or nylon coated, the latter giving the greatest durability.

Modern furniture may be constructed of one of the African hardwoods, such as sapele or teak, or be of lightweight metal. Or, folding or stackable furniture may be used, but this seldom adds much to the appearance of a patio.

Soft furnishings should be of nylon or some other waterproof and readily washable material. Colors should be considered not only in relation to the house and the permanent features of the patio but also in relation to the flowers which are to be grown.

Gardening without a garden. All the plants contributing to this medley of color are growing in containers of some kind including window boxes, tubs, and flowerpots

These metal-work chairs are ideal for a patio or roof garden, for not only are they able to withstand sun and rain, but they are also attractive to look at. An annual coat of paint will keep them looking new

Bedding Plants

Bedding out means putting plants in the garden for a limited period only, while they are able to contribute most to the display, and then replacing them with other plants. Spring bedding plants are those that make this display from March to May; summer bedding plants those that continue from June to September. There are also some plants that make their peak display in May and June and so provide a useful link between spring and summer. In public parks and large gardens, winter bedding with evergreen plants is also occasionally practiced, but this is seldom attempted in small gardens.

To maintain a constant display from spring to autumn necessitates several changes and a considerable reserve of plants. Most amateur gardeners are satisfied with a simpler program consisting of two main changes, one made in late May or early June, when the summer plants are put out, and the other in September or October, when the spring bedding is planted. Bedding out may be used in any way in conjunction with any other type of planting. However, traditionally it is done in clearly defined patterns which may be simple or complex according to taste. Beds, as well as the patterns created by the plants in them, are usually in regular, geometric shapes and so this kind of planting is specially suitable for formal gardens.

Carpeting plants are those that are naturally low growing or can be kept so by pinching, clipping, or pegging to the soil. Taller plants may be used above these to produce a second or even a third tier of flowers, but this can involve considerable expense. Less costly is to use dot plants, that is, taller plants well spaced out among the lower-growing varieties. Standard plants, like little formal trees 3 or 4 ft. high, may be used in the same way but may take several years to form since they must be carefully trained and pruned to get the desired effect and this takes time. Because most summer bedding plants are not fully hardy these prepared standards must be overwintered in a frostproof greenhouse or suitably light yet sheltered place.

Beds may be simple or elaborate according to taste and the patterns may be given permanent form by being edged with small shrubs, such as box, lavender, rosemary, or rue, kept close trimmed. A special form of box, known as edging box, is used for this purpose and is sold by the yard of edging. The best rue for edging is Jackman's Blue, and the best lavender, a dwarf variety such as Hidcote. All may need to be clipped three or four times each summer to keep them sufficiently neat. One advantage of this kind of edging is that it looks attractive at all seasons even when there are no flowers or colored leaves to fill in the patterns.

Begonias

Begonia semperflorens

tuberous-rooted begonia

Begonias are perennials, but *Begonia semperflorens*, a fibrous-rooted type, is always grown as a half-hardy annual, and is much used in summer bedding because of its neat habit and continuous flowering. Plants are from 4 to 8 in. high, have slightly fleshy leaves which may be green or bronze and clusters of white, pink, or red flowers. Organdy, with green leaves, and Galaxy, with bronze leaves, are good varieties to give a mixture of colors, but separate colors can also be obtained.

Sow seed in late January or February in a temperature of 60°F., prick off seedlings and grow longer in boxes or pots until late May or June when the threat of frost has passed and it is safe to plant out of doors. The plants like good, well-cultivated soil and plenty of water.

The large-flowered tuberous-rooted begonias can also be raised from seed in the same way as fibrous-rooted types, or tubers can be obtained and started into growth in the spring in a greenhouse.

These large-flowered kinds are not so adaptable for bedding as *Begonia semperflorens* but look attractive in beds on their own.

Begonia multiflora is intermediate in habit between the tuberous-rooted begonias and *B. semperflorens*. It can be raised from seed or grown from tubers and is a useful alternative for bedding. The plants reach a height of about 10 in.

The scarlet in this summer display is provided by *Begonia* Indian Maid with the deep blue of lobelia as a surrounding screen and the silver of *Centaurea gymnocarpa* as dot plants for contrast

Dahlias

coltness hybrids

Dahlias of all kinds can be used for summer bedding, but the most useful and adaptable are the bedding varieties, such as the single-flowered Coltness Hybrids and various other strains of Dwarf Hybrids, 1½ to 2 ft. high, with semi-double or double flowers in mixed colors. These types are readily raised from seed.

Sow in a greenhouse, at a temperature of 60° to 65°F. in February or March, and prick off as soon as possible at least 2 in. apart as the plants grow rapidly. Or they may be potted singly in 3-in. pots in a peat-based mix. Keep the plants well watered and harden off for planting out in late May or early June. Space the plants 1½ ft. apart in good, well-cultivated soil and an open sunny place.

There are also a number of dwarf dahlias which can be grown from tubers, and are propagated by cuttings in the spring. These cuttings will produce flowers that are identical in color and shape to the parent, and are ideal for use in bedding schemes where color patterns are required. The tubers that are produced during the growing season can be lifted in the autumn, stored, and used again the following year.

dwarf hybrids

Balsams, Heliotropes

impatiens

The balsams, or impatiens, are commonly grown as pot plants, but dwarf varieties of *Impatiens sultanii*, such as Imp, available in white, rose, carmine, scarlet, orange, purple, and in mixtures of these colors, and growing to a height of 9 in., make excellent summer bedding plants.

Sow seed in a greenhouse, at a temperature of 70°F. and do not shade the seed pans. Prick off and harden off for planting out of doors in late May or June in a sunny or partially shaded place. Space the plants 9 to 12 in. apart.

Heliotropes are also popular pot plants which are excellent for summer bedding. Marine is an excellent variety with violet purple flowers, compact, well branched, and 15 in. high. It can be grown from seed, or plants can be raised from cuttings in spring or August.

Sow seed in February or early March in a greenhouse, at a temperature of 65°F., prick off the seedlings and later pot them singly in 3-in. pots. Harden them off gradually for planting out in late May or early June, in good, well-cultivated soil and a sunny position. Space dwarf plants 1 ft. apart, standards 2 to 3 ft. apart. Plants can be lifted in late September or early October, potted singly, and kept in a greenhouse with a minimum temperature of 45°F. for another year or to give spring cuttings.

heliotrope

Bedding dahlias are easily raised from seed. They produce a very rewarding crop of flowers, continuing to do so until the plants are cut back by frost. This is a typical Coltness Hybrid

Impatiens sultanii Orange Baby is one of the many varieties of dwarf balsam which are now available. The popular name of these plants is Busy Lizzie. Zone 10 for all-year outdoors

Fuchsias

Many varieties of fuchsia make excellent summer bedding plants. They can be grown as bushes or trained as standards, and can be raised from cuttings, or plants can be purchased in May or early June ready for planting out.

Bush fuchsias are best planted on their own in beds or blocks of one variety but standard fuchsias may be associated with almost any other summer bedding plants. They look particularly attractive over a groundwork of *Begonia semperflorens* or antirrhinums.

Space bush plants 1½ ft. apart and standards at least 3 ft. apart. Give them a good, well-cultivated soil and water the plants freely in dry weather. Stake standard fuchsias straightaway with 1 in. by 1 in. stakes as the heads become very heavy and are easily snapped off by wind.

In October, lift the plants carefully and either pot them separately or pack them close together in boxes with some old potting soil or peat around the roots. Bring them into a reasonably frostproof greenhouse (they are nearly hardy and will survive a degree or two of frost) or place them in a light shed for the winter. Water very sparingly until March, then shake out the soil, prune off any damaged roots, repot in a size smaller pot and water more freely as growth restarts.

Geraniums

zonal-leaved pelargonium

ivy-leaved pelargonium

The geraniums used for summer bedding are correctly named pelargoniums. There are two main types: zonal-leaved with round, slightly downy leaves and strong stems, and ivy-leaved with smooth, angular leaves and weak stems.

All pelargoniums like warm, sunny places and well-drained soil though they will grow almost anywhere. They can be raised from cuttings, or plants can be purchased in May or June.

Plant zonal pelargoniums 12 to 15 in. apart, ivy-leaved pelargoniums 18 in. apart. Either peg the stems of the ivy-leaved varieties to the soil, spreading them out so that eventually they completely cover it, or tie them to short canes to make columns. The plants can be lifted in September or October and brought into a greenhouse with a minimum temperature of 45°F. for the winter.

Ornamental leaved varieties are: Chelsea Gem, green and silver; Crystal Palace Gem, green and gold; Mrs. Henry Cox, green, yellow, and red.

Standard fuchsias make particularly attractive plants with their large heads of dangling flowers. A plant such as the one shown here would take two or three years to develop from a cutting. Zone 10

Zonal pelargoniums (geraniums) are always popular bedding plants. Here they are mixed with stocks and the silvery foliage of *Senecio cineraria* and set off beautifully by the well-kept grass verge. Zone 10

Silver and Gray

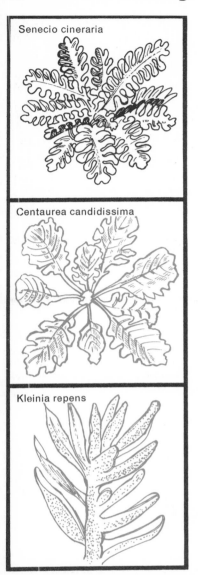

Senecio cineraria

Centaurea candidissima

Kleinia repens

Plants with silver or gray leaves are useful in summer bedding schemes as a foil to the colors of the flowers. They are often used as dot plants.

One of the most popular is *Senecio cineraria*, also known as *Cineraria maritima*, a bushy, fairly hardy perennial with deeply divided silvery white leaves. It can be grown from seed sown in a warm greenhouse in February—March, or by cuttings inserted in a frame or greenhouse in August—September and protected until the spring. *Senecio leucostachys, Centaurea gymnocarpa*, and *C. rutifolia* (*C. candidissima*) are similar in appearance and are grown in the same way.

Calocephalus brownii, also known as *Leucophyta brownii*, is even more silvery, with wiry stems and narrow leaves. It can be grown as a small column, about a foot in height, and used as a dot plant, or the growing tips can be pinched off frequently, thus making it into a dwarf, spreading plant suitable for carpet bedding.

Kleinia repens, also known as *Senecio repens*, is a creeping plant only an inch or so high, with blue gray leaves. It is useful for outlining the finer details of carpet bedding or for forming letters or figures in floral clocks, etc., in public parks. It is grown from cuttings taken in spring or summer and rooted in a warm greenhouse.

Colored Leaves

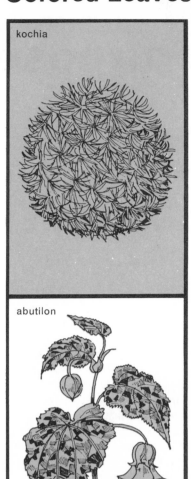

kochia

abutilon

Colored foliage can be as useful as silver and gray foliage in diversifying the effects in summer bedding displays. Kochia is an annual known as Summer Cypress, because it makes a 2-ft. column of fine leaves and looks like a miniature conifer; these are green at first, turning to purplish red in late summer. Sow seed in a warm greenhouse in March and harden off seedlings for planting out in late May or early June as dot plants.

Abutilon thompsonii is a shrubby plant with light green leaves heavily mottled with yellow, and with orange, drooping, trumpet-shaped flowers. It will quickly grow to a height of 3 ft. and can be used as a background or a centerpiece. The plants can be bought in May or June or raised from summer cuttings which are kept in a frostproof greenhouse in winter.

Chrysanthemum parthenium aureum (*Pyrethrum parthenifolium aureum*) is known as Golden Feather because it has bright yellow feathery leaves. It is grown like kochia from seed and planted out 6 in. apart to form a carpeting or groundwork plant 4 to 6 in. tall.

Alternantheras and iresines are used for carpet bedding in a similar manner, but are pinched or clipped to keep them short and compact. Varieties are available with leaves in various combinations of green, yellow, cerise, and crimson. Plants can be purchased in late May or June, or raised from cuttings in a warm greenhouse in spring.

Gray foliage plants, such as *Centaurea gymnocarpa*, add further interest to a border, both in color and in texture, and help to set off other plants. Also shown are geraniums in the background and heliotropes

The bright red leaves of *Iresine herbstii brilliantissima* are as colorful as flowers. *Fuchsia* Golden Treasure beyond has golden foliage, and *Ruta graveolens*, in the foreground, has feathery blue gray leaves. Iresine and fuchsia Zone 10

Plants for Special Purposes

A Child's Garden

The first essentials for a child's garden are that the plants must be easy to grow and give a reasonably quick result.

Many annuals and bulbs fulfill both requirements and bulbs have the additional merit that good ones are almost certain to flower the first year. Narcissus (daffodils), crocus, chionodoxa, muscari (Grape Hyacinths), and *Scilla siberica* are likely to continue for years with minimal attention. Hyacinths and tulips, though highly reliable the first season, are less certain in subsequent years.

Among the most suitable hardy annuals which can be sown where they are to flower are: Sweet Alyssum, calendula, clarkia, coreopsis, eschscholzia, godetia, gypsophila, lavatera, malope, mignonette, nasturtium, nigella, and annual poppies. A few plants of antirrhinums, double daisies, pansies, and petunias put in when they are just coming into flower are valuable, and perennials such as dicentra (Bleeding Heart), polygonatum (Solomon's Seal), and lupines are liked for their flower shapes. So is the miniature rose Cécile Brunner.

Many children enjoy growing radishes and lettuces and even sweet-scented herbs such as sage and thyme.

Beds for children should be not more than 3 ft. wide with access from both sides, and mown grass is the ideal surrounding.

lupine

Plants for a child's garden must be easy to grow and give quick results. *Scilla siberica*, primulas, and muscari are ideal for this purpose since they will look very attractive for many years with minimal attention

However difficult a soil or situation may be it is usually possible to find some plants that will grow in it. But this is only one way of dealing with this problem. Another is to improve the condition that is causing the difficulty and so widen the selection of plants that can be used successfully. Lime soils are limiting because they are often deficient in iron and manganese which suffer chemical changes that render them insoluble and therefore unavailable as plant food. Special preparations of these chemicals, known as iron chelate compounds, can be used to make good the deficiencies, and the soil can be made less alkaline by giving it heavy dressings of acid peat or leaf mold.

Heavy clay soils are difficult because they retain too much water, are poorly aerated, and tend to become sour. Generous liming will improve their texture and correct sourness, but it can make it difficult to grow lime-hating plants such as rhododendrons, pieris, and many heathers. Peat, well-rotted garden compost, stable manure, and coarse sand will all help to improve the texture of clay soils.

Plants growing in seaside gardens are often battered by gales which may bring salt spray as an added hazard. Here the remedy is to provide a substantial windbreak on the seaward side. There is nothing better for this than *Cupressus macrocarpa*, which grows rapidly and is evergreen. The yellow-leaved variety is even more salt resistant than the green. *Pinus radiata* is a fast-growing pine that does well by the sea and makes a tall and substantial windbreak. While such plants are growing, temporary shelter can be provided with wattle hurdles or interwoven fencing.

In very hot sunny places improvement can be effected by planting trees to give some shade, but since in such places dryness is often as damaging as the intensity of the sunlight, the trees must be planted sufficiently far away not to fill the flower beds with their roots. Some kinds, such as the cypresses, do not make very extensive root systems, and some, such as oak, push their roots downward rather than outward, and these are to be preferred as shade givers in such places. Water sprinklers permanently installed can also transform the planting possibilities in a hot, dry garden. Sprinklers that give a fine, rainlike spray are the most satisfactory, as the water then has time to soak in.

Plants that spread densely over the surface of the soil are often recommended as ground cover to smother weeds and so save labor. This works well provided the soil is well cleared of weeds first and any perennial weeds that appear later are removed promptly. But if weeds are allowed to become established under the ground cover it can be a major operation to get rid of them.

Limestone Soils

Limestone soils are normally alkaline, and being usually porous and quick draining they are slow to accumulate humus. The plants listed are those which are known to do well on limestone, but many others will grow well if kept moist. Humus is best added in the form of peat.

Good hardy perennials for limestone soils are achillea, aster (Michaelmas daisies); campanulas, centaurea (perennial cornflowers), centranthus (valerian), *Chrysanthemum maximum* (Shasta Daisies), coreopsis; delphiniums, dianthus (pinks, Sweet Williams, and carnations), doronicum; eremurus; gaillardias, hardy geraniums, geums, gypsophila; helenium, helianthus (sun-

flowers), helleborus; iris; *Papaver orientale* (Oriental Poppy), phlox, pyrethrum; rudbeckia; *Salvia superba, Scabiosa caucasica*, sedum, sidalcea, solidago; thalictrum, and verbascum.

Good rock plants are aethionema, alyssum, arabis, armeria, aubrieta, campanula, dianthus, erodium, gypsophila, helianthemum (sunrose), hypericum, iberis (candytuft), linum, phlox, potentilla, sedum, and thymus (thyme).

Good annuals and bedding plants are antirrhinum, aster, candytuft, coreopsis, dianthus, gypsophila, lavatera, linum, mignonette, nasturtium, pansies, poppies, rudbeckias, scabious, violas, and wallflowers.

Good shrubs for limestone soils are berberis, buddleia, bupleurum, buxus (box); caryopteris, cistus (rockrose), chaenomeles (cydonia or Japanese Quince), colutea, *Cornus alba* and varieties, cotoneaster (all varieties), *Cotinus coggygria* (Smoke Tree), cytisus (broom); deutzia, escallonia; forsythia, fuchsia; genista (broom); hypericum, hebe (shrubby veronicas); lavandula (lavender), ligustrum (privet); philadelphus (mock orange), *Potentilla fruticosa;* rhus (sumac), rosmarinus (rosemary); sambucus (elderberry), santolina, *Senecio laxifolius*, spartium (Spanish Broom), syringa (lilac); viburnum, vinca (periwinkle), and weigela.

Good trees are carpinus (horn-

beam), crataegus (thorns), fagus (beech), ilex (holly), laburnum, malus (apple), prunus (almond, cherry, peach, and plum), sorbus (Mountain Ash or Rowan, Whitebeam), and taxus (yew).

Good climbers are clematis of all kinds, honeysuckles, pyracantha, and ornamental vines.

Conifers that do well on limestone soils are cedrus (cedar), cupressus, chamaecyparis and cupressocyparis (cypresses), gingko (Maidenhair Tree), juniperus (juniper), larix (larch), metasequoia, *Pinus sylvestris* (Scots Pine), taxus (yew), and thuja.

Good bulbs are alliums, crocus, erythronium, iris, narcissus (daffodils), and tulips.

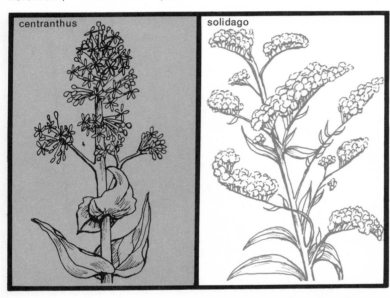

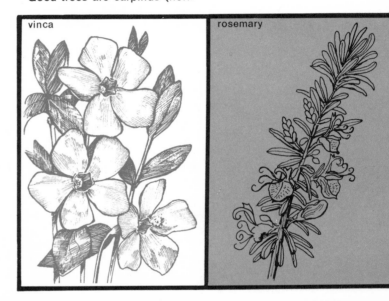

Perennial asters and goldenrod are two very useful herbaceous plants for a limy soil. They will flower well together in the September border and are best divided and replanted fairly frequently

Among the conifers which will thrive in a limy soil is *Thuja occidentalis* here shown in its slow-growing variety *ellwangeriana*. Also shown is *Campanula carpatica*, in blue and white varieties

Shady Places

digitalis

Shade or low light intensity varies from the shadow thrown by fences or buildings where the plant receives little or no direct sunlight but is open to the sky and normal rainfall, to deep shade under trees where the plant also has to compete with the tree roots for water and food. In such conditions it is well worth feeding and watering it.

Good hardy perennials for shady places are acanthus, aconitum, *Anemone japonica*, aquilegia, *Artemisia lactiflora*, *Aruncus sylvester*, astilbe, astrantia; bergenia, *Brunnera macrophylla*; campanula, convallaria (lily of the valley); dicentra, digitalis (foxglove); *Helleborus niger* (Christmas Rose), *H. orientalis* (Lenten Rose), hemerocallis, hosta; lysimachia; mertensia; phlox, polygonatum (Solomon's Seal), primroses, polyanthus, pulmonaria; thalictrum, tiarella, *Tradescantia virginiana*, trollius, and violas.

Good rock plants are arenaria, campanula, epimedium, *Gentiana asclepiadea*, haberlea, meconopsis, omphalodes, *Primula denticulata*, *P. juliae*, *P. juliana*, ramonda, sanguinaria, *Saxifraga umbrosa* (London Pride), mossy saxifrages, and rock violas.

Bulbs and tubers for shady places are *Anemone apennina*, A. *blanda*, *A. nemorosa*, colchicums, hardy cyclamen, eranthis (Winter Aconite), erythronium (Dog's-tooth Violet), *Fritillaria meleagris*, lilies, narcissus, scilla, and snowdrops.

Good shrubs for shady places are azaleas, aucuba; bamboos, *Berberis darwinii*, *B. stenophylla*, buxus (box); camellias; *Danae racemosa* (Alexandrian Laurel); enkianthus, *Euonymus japonicus*, *E. fortunei (E. radicans)*; forsythia; gaultheria; hydrangea, hypericum; ilex (hollies); kerria; ligustrum (privet); pernettya, *Prunus laurocerasus* (Cherry Laurel), *P. lusitanica* (Portugal Laurel), pyracantha; *Ribes sanguineum* (Flowering Currant), *Ruscus aculeatus* (Butcher's Broom); sarcococca, skimmia, symphoricarpos (Snowberry); *Viburnum tinus* (Laurustinus), and vinca (periwinkle).

Climbers for shade are chaenomeles (cydonia or Japanese Quince), clematis, *Forsythia suspensa*, hedera varieties (ivies), *Hydrangea petiolaris*, *Jasminum nudiflorum*, *Kerria japonica flore pleno*, lonicera (honeysuckles), pyracantha, and *Schizophragma hydrangeoides*.

Annuals and bedding plants to grow in shade are annual asters, begonias, *Bellis monstrosa* (double daisy), *Calceolaria integrifolia*, impatiens, *Matthiola bicornis* (Night-scented Stock), *Mimulus tigrinus* (musk), myosotis (forget-me-not), nicotiana, pansies, *Saponaria vaccaria*, and violas.

symphoricarpos

A charming collection of naturalized bulbs under the shade of trees. Narcissus, erythroniums, muscari, and scillas combine to provide this delightful spring scene

There are many beautiful species and varieties of clematis like this one which is named Lasurstern and has very large flowers

Ground Cover

Some plants will cover the ground with such a dense growth that weed seeds have little chance to germinate. Such plants are known as ground-cover plants. Provided the soil has been cleared of perennial weeds before the ground cover is planted, subsequent maintenance will be reduced to a minimum. It is important that the plants chosen are reasonably sturdy but not so vigorous that they become almost as great a nuisance as the weeds they are replacing.

Some ground-cover plants make such a low carpet of growth that bulbs can be planted to grow through them. Others are too vigorous for this but are quite suitable as ground cover beneath shrubs and trees.

Good plants for ground-cover purposes are *Acaena buchananii, A. microphylla, Arenaria balearica, A. caespitosa, A. purpurascens; Cotula squalida; Erodium chamaedryoides roseum; Linaria aequitriloba; Mazus reptans; Raoulia australis, R. glabra; Sagina glabra* and its golden-leaved variety, *Saxifraga muscoides, Sedum dasyphyllum, S. lydium; Thymus serpyllum,* some of the veronicas such as *Veronica rupestris* and *Waldsteinia sibirica.*

Plants of moderate vigor suitable for growing with shrubs are *Ajuga reptans, Alchemilla mollis, Arisarum proboscideum, Arundinaria pumila, Asperula odorata,* astrantia; bergenia; *Calluna vulgaris* (heather), *Cornus canadensis, Cotoneaster dammeri; Doronicum cordatum;* epimediums, low-growing ericas such as *Erica carnea, E. darleyensis,* and *E. vagans, Euonymus fortunei radicans, Euphorbia cyparissias; Fragaria indica; Gaultheria procumbens;* small varieties of *Hedera helix* (ivy) such as *cristata,* Jubilee, and *tricolor, Heucherella tiarelloides, Hosta lancifolia, H. undulata; Lamium galeobdolon, L. maculatum; Myosotis dissitiflora,* (forget-me-not); *Omphalodes verna; Pachysandra terminalis,*

Polygonum affine, Prunella grandiflora, pulmonarias; *Sarcococca humilis,* mossy saxifrages, *Sedum spurium; Tellima grandiflora, Tiarella cordifolia, Tolmiea menziesii; Viola labradorica;* and *Vinca minor* (periwinkle).

Vigorous ground-cover plants, best planted on their own, are *Cerastium tomentosum, Gaultheria shallon, Hedera helix* (ivy, common kind and vigorous varieties), also *Hedera colchica dentata variegata, Hypericum calycinum, Polygonum campanulatum,* Rose Max Graff, *Stachys lanata;* and *Vinca major* (periwinkle).

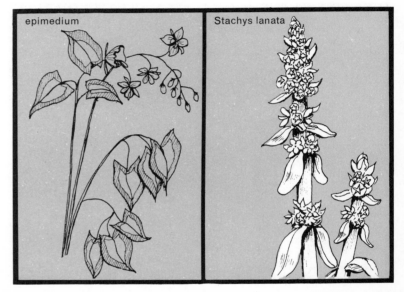

There are several species of veronica which will make delightful ground-cover plants and provide a carpet of blue to set off other plants such as the variously colored primroses seen here

The attractive leaf coloring of *Lamium galeobdolon variegatum* contrasts well with the red brickwork. Known by the common name of Variegated Yellow Archangel, it is a rapidly spreading ground-cover plant

Hot, Dry Places

Hot, dry soils mean those which, because of their aspect and rapidity of drainage, become arid for weeks or months in summer. They are excellent for bulbous plants such as tulips or nerines, which benefit from a good baking. Gray-leaved, many fleshy-leaved plants (succulents), and some with spiny leaves are adapted to survive periods of drought, and mulching after rain or watering will help to conserve moisture. Plant at the beginning of a rainy period, such as autumn, rather than spring.

Good hardy perennials for hot, dry places are achillea, anaphalis, anchusa, anthemis; catananche, centaurea, centranthus, coreopsis; dianthus, echinops, erigeron, eryngium, gaillardia, galega, geum, gypsophila; linum, lupinus; nepeta; oenothera; *Papaver orientale*, potentilla; schizostylis, sedum, and verbascum.

Good rock plants are alyssum, arabis, armeria, aubrieta, cerastium, dianthus, erodium, *Geranium sanguineum*, gypsophila, helianthemum, linum, othonnopsis, oxalis, *Polygonum affine*, sedums, sempervivums, and zauschneria.

Good annuals and bedding plants are Sweet Alyssum, anagallis, antirrhinum, clarkia, coreopsis, dianthus, dimorphotheca, eschscholzia, gaillardia, gazania, godetia, gypsophila, lavatera, linum, lupine, malope, mentzelia, mesembryanthemums, nasturtiums, poppies, portulaca, ursinia, and venidium.

Good shrubs for hot, dry places are abelia, *Acacia hispidissima*, atriplex; buddleia; caryopteris, ceratostigma, cistus, colutea, cytisus (broom); genista (broom); halimium, hedysarum, *Hibiscus syriacus*, *Hypericum calycinum*; indigofera; lavandula (lavender), *Lupinus arboreus* (Tree Lupine); *Olearia scilloniensis*; perovskia, phlomis, phormium, piptanthus, *Potentilla fruticosa*; romneya, rosmarinus (rosemary); santolina, *Senecio laxifolius*, spartium; *Teucrium fruticans*; *Ulex europaeus plenus* (double-flowered gorse), and yucca.

Climbers for hot, dry places are *Campsis grandiflora*, C. Madame Galen, *Ceanothus impressus*, C. *rigidus*, C. *thyrsiflorus*, *Cotoneaster horizontalis*; hedera varieties (ivies); *Magnolia grandiflora*; *Passiflora caerulea* (passionflower), *Polygonum baldschuanicum* (Russian Vine); *Solanum crispum*, S. *jasminoides*, and ornamental vines (including ampelopsis, parthenocissus, and vitis).

Bulbs suitable for hot, dry places are agapanthus, alstroemeria, allium, *Amaryllis belladonna*; babiana, brodiaea (triteleia); camassias, *Crinum powellii*, Crocosmia masonorum, Curtonus paniculata (*Antholyza paniculata*); ixias, ixiolirion; lapeirousia; montbretias, *Nerine bowdenii*; sparaxis, *Sprekelia formosissima*; tigridia, tulips, and zephyranthes.

Nasturtiums can be sown out of doors from mid-April to mid-May and they will present a blaze of color all summer until the first frosts of autumn. They prefer poor, dry soil and a sunny position

Passiflora caerulea is a fairly hardy passionflower, a vigorous quick-growing climber that can be grown successfully in favored gardens against a sunny sheltered wall

Seaside Gardens

In seaside gardens temperatures tend to be less extreme, so that many less hardy plants will survive most winters. But seaside gardens are frequently exposed to salt, gale-force winds, and blown sand, and a windbreak is usually needed for the more tender plants.

Trees and shrubs which form an outer windbreak resistant to salt spray are *Atriplex halimus, Euonymus japonicus,* griselinia, *Hippophae rhamnoides* (Sea Buckthorn), *Lycium chinense, Olearia albida, O. haastii, O. oleifolia, O. traversii,* and tamarix.

In the milder parts of the Pacific West may be added *Cupressus macrocarpa, Olearia macrodonta, Pinus radiata,* pittosporum, and *Senecio rotundifolius.*

Good shrubs to plant within such a sheltered belt are abelia, arbutus; berberis, buddleia; callistemon (bottle brush) in mild districts, calluna, camellia, caryopteris, ceanothus, ceratostigma, choisya, cistus, clerodendrum, colutea, *Convolvulus cneorum, Corokia cotoneaster, Coronilla glauca,* cotoneaster, cytisus; daphne; erica, escallonia; fatsia, fuchsia; genista, hebe, *Hibiscus syriacus,* hydrangea, hypericum; lavender, leptospermum, *Lupinus arboreas* (Tree Lupine); mahonia, myrtus; perovskia, phlomis, phormium, potentilla; romneya, rosmarinus, ruta (rue); *Salvia grahamii;* teucrium, tricuspidaria (mild districts only); *Viburnum tinus;* weigela, and yucca.

Good trees for mild districts are *Acacia dealbata* (Mimosa), *Cordyline australis* (New Zealand Cabbage Palm), embothrium, hoheria, paulownia, and *Trachycarpus fortunei* (hardy palm). Laburnums do well by the sea and are completely hardy.

Good hardy perennials are achillea, agapanthus, anthemis, armeria, *Aster pappei;* catananche, crambe, *Cynara scolymus* (Globe Artichoke); dianthus (pinks, carnations, and Sweet Williams), dierama, dimorphotheca; echinops, eryngium, euphorbia; kniphofia; limonium (statice), lupine, lychnis; sedum, stachys, and zantedeschia (Arum Lily) for mild districts only.

Good bulbs and tubers to grow are *Amaryllis belladonna,* babiana, brodiaea (triteleia), cannas, crinum, dahlias, gladiolus, hyacinths, iris, montbretia, muscari (Grape Hyacinth), narcissus (daffodils), nerine, scillas (bluebells and squills), and tulips.

Good annuals and bedding plants are Sweet Alyssum, anagallis, arctotis, annual asters; *Begonia semperflorens;* calendula, clarkia, convolvulus; dianthus (annual pinks and carnations), dimorphotheca; eschscholzia; gazania, godetia; lavatera, limonium (annual statice), *Linum grandiflorum;* malope mesembryanthemum; nemesia; annual poppies, petunias; stocks; tagetes (marigolds); ursinias; venidium, wallflowers, and zinnias.

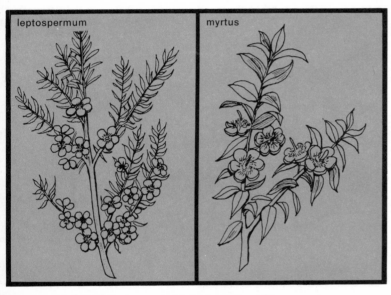

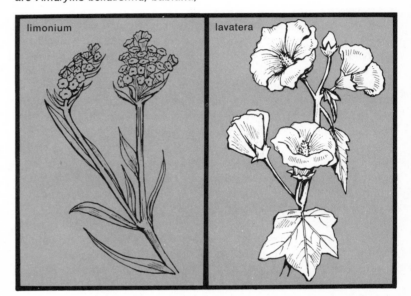

Seaside gardens face a special problem with salt-laden winds. *Fuchsia magellanica riccartonii,* which flowers all summer, is one of the plants which does well in such conditions

All the brooms make good seaside shrubs. This one, *Cytisus praecox,* is covered in flowers during April and here it has been planted with aubrieta and *Alyssum saxatile* which also do well by the sea

Flowers for Cutting

Hardy Annuals

preparing seed drills

sowing seed

covering seed

The following annuals can be grown from seed sown out of doors in spring where the plants are to flower. All like moderately rich, well-cultivated soil and an open, sunny position. Sow the seeds thinly in straight drills ½ in. deep and 1 ft. apart, thin out the seedlings to about 6 in., and discard after flowering.

Calendula (Pot Marigold): orange or yellow daisy flowers. Best in double-flowered varieties such as Pacific Beauty, Kablouna and Dwarf Sunny Boy.

Chrysanthemum: there are several annual kinds, some with single, some double flowers. Tricolor, with rings of different colors, is particularly useful for cutting.

Cornflower: the tall varieties, in blue and pink, are best for cutting but need support when growing.

Gypsophila: the annual gypsophila has larger flowers than the perennial kind but not such big sprays. There are white and pink varieties.

Helianthus Excelsior hybrids: 5 ft., browns and dark reds.

Larkspur: slender spikes of white, blue, pink, or scarlet flowers.

Mignonette: valued for its fragrance, it likes a limy soil.

Nigella (Love-in-a-Mist): rather like a cornflower, but with feathery foliage.

Sweet Sultan: another cornflowerlike plant with a good range of colors.

Any flower can be cut but not all flowers are equally good for the purpose. Many do not last well in water and some have unsuitable stems or an unpleasant smell. Equally, not all flowers that are good for cutting are satisfactory for garden display. Some continue to flower for months but never make much of a show at any one time and some have flowers that quickly look shabby if left uncut. All these points must be considered when choosing flowers for the garden that will be suitable for cutting.

It must be decided, too, whether cut flowers are to be taken from the ordinary flower borders or whether special beds are to be set aside for them in a concealed part of the garden. The latter course is preferable if space permits since the plants can be given the special attention they may need and the flowers cut without denuding the ornamental garden. But in small gardens there may be no room for special beds and then flowers must be selected for cutting by thinning carefully rather than by stripping plants completely.

Most flowers last best if they have been cut from plants that have grown vigorously and fast. Good feeding and adequate watering will help to produce the soft, succulent stems which take up water readily. Rose bushes that are to be used for cutting need to be pruned rather more severely than those grown for garden display only. This will reduce the number of flowers but increase the length of flower stems. When the roses are cut a fair length of stem should be taken, each cut being made just above a well-developed leaf, since where the leaf joins the stem there will be a growth bud which may produce another stem and more bloom. Similar hard pruning often helps shrubs used for cutting by improving the length of stems, making them stouter and more succulent, and also increasing the size of the flowers.

However well grown they may be there are some flowers that take up water badly. It always helps to carry a bucket of water round while cutting flowers and place them directly in this before air has entered the base of the stem and perhaps caused an air lock. If this cannot be done it will pay to cut off a little from the bottom of each stem when it can be put into water and perhaps to slit the stem vertically. It is also wise to change the water in vases daily. Foliage is also of great value to flower arrangers and provision should be made for this in sufficient variety and quantity at all times of the year. With bulbs it is never wise to take too many of their leaves since the bulbs are then starved and may not produce flowers the following year. The removal of the flower is, on the whole, beneficial since it prevents any possibility of seed production which always puts a considerable strain upon a plant.

Chrysanthemum spectabile Cecilia, an attractive annual chrysanthemum which produces its flowers very freely over a lengthy period. The single blooms may reach 4 in. in diameter

Half-hardy Annuals

Half-hardy annuals are best sown in February or March in a moderately heated greenhouse or frame. Prick seedlings off into boxes of peat-based potting mixes or soil and harden off for planting outside in late May.

Arctoris: single daisy-type flowers in a good range of colors, including silvery blues and wine reds.

Antirrhinums (snapdragons): the tall varieties are particularly good for cutting.

Asters: there is great variety in the character of the flowers—some are single, some ball-like, some shaggy.

Carnations: the annual carnations are readily raised from seed and have a good color range. Some varieties have an attractive scent.

Cosmos: elegant single daisy flowers in white, pink, crimson, and orange with ferny foliage.

Marigolds: the tall, double-flowered African F_1 hybrid varieties are best for cutting.

Molucellas (Bells of Ireland): green flower spikes. They require a temperature of 65° to 70°F. for germination.

Rudbeckia: bold yellow, orange, or mahogany red daisy flowers, single and double.

Ten-week Stocks: Hansen's 100% Double Column Stocks are best for cutting.

Zinnia: the tall, double-flowered varieties are fine cut flowers, both flat-petaled and quill-petaled varieties.

Biennials

Biennials are plants that must be sown one year to flower the next, after which they are discarded. Most can be sown out of doors in May or June and planted in September where they are to flower.

Canterbury Bells: the tall, single-flowered and cup-and-saucer varieties are best for cutting. They flower in June and July.

Honesty (lunaria): this is grown primarily for the oval, parchment-like seed heads which last all the winter, but the purple flower sprays are also decorative and there is an attractive variety with variegated leaves.

Iceland Poppies: these are the most useful for cutting because of their good color range, including yellow, orange, apricot, salmon, pink, rose, and red. As soon as cut the stems should be stood for half a minute in 1 in. of boiling water to prevent air entering and so enable them to take up water.

Sweet Williams: fine, flat heads of flowers in pink, scarlet, crimson, and white. The auricula-eyed varieties have a white eye.

Wallflowers: tall varieties are best for cutting.

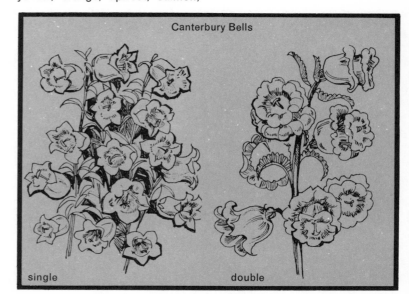

Molucella laevis, Bells of Ireland, is an unusual-looking plant often used for flower arrangements. The small white flowers are usually removed as it is the bell-shaped calyces that are most decorative

Sweet Williams (*Dianthus barbatus*) are always popular garden flowers, and are also suitable for cutting. They are easily raised from seeds sown in May or June

Flowering Perennials

A great many hardy herbaceous perennials can be used for cutting and the following are only a few of the most useful.

Achillea, The Pearl: small, double white flowers freely borne in sprays most of the summer.

Alstroemeria, Ligtu Hybrids: elegant heads of pink or salmon flowers in July—August. Grow in a warm, sheltered place where the plants can remain undisturbed.

Chrysanthemum maximum (Shasta Daisy): large, white daisies on long stems in July and August.

Doronicum, Harpur Crewe: large yellow daisies in May.

Gypsophila, Bristol Fairy: large sprays of small, double white flowers in July and August which look excellent with sweet peas. Do not disturb the plants.

Gaillardias: large yellow, bronze red or red and yellow daisies from June to September.

Heucheras: sprays of small pink or red flowers from June to August.

Peonies: single, semi-double, and double varieties are all excellent. Leave them undisturbed.

Pyrethrums: large single or double daisy-type flowers, white, pink, or red in June. They need well-drained soil.

Scabiosa caucasica: lavender or white flowers from July to October. They like lime.

Solomon's Seal (polygonatum): useful for foliage as well as for its pendant green and white flowers appearing in May. It likes shade.

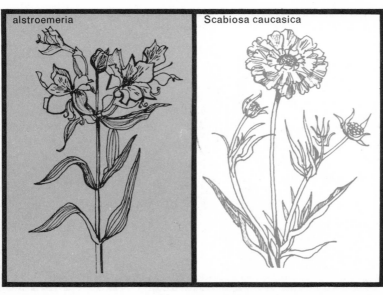

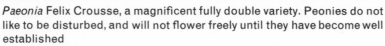

Paeonia Felix Crousse, a magnificent fully double variety. Peonies do not like to be disturbed, and will not flower freely until they have become well established

Foliage Perennials

Good foliage can be cut from many hardy herbaceous perennials, but the following plants have particularly distinctive leaves.

Acanthus (bear's breeches): large, divided, deep green leaves, broad lobed in *A. mollis*, narrow lobed in *A. spinosissimus*.

Arum pictum: arrow-shaped leaves, dark green, veined white.

Bocconia (Plume Poppy): large, rounded, gray green leaves sometimes shaded with bronze.

Cynara: more familiar as the cardoon and globe artichoke of the vegetable garden. Long, deeply divided, silvery gray leaves. It may need protection with straw and dry salt hay in winter.

Hostas: there are several kinds, all with fine leaves broadly lance shaped in some, heart shaped in others; shining green, blue gray, or green and cream according to the variety. They do well in shade.

Rodgersia: there are several species, all with large, deeply divided or fingerlike leaves, green or bronze. All like rich, damp soil.

Sedum (stonecrop): *Sedum spectabile variegata* has cream and light green leaves, *S. maximum atropurpureum* purple leaves.

Thalictrum: several kinds have leaves like the maidenhair fern. *T. glaucum* and *T. dipterocarpum* are especially attractive, the latter with sprays of small amethystlike flowers in July—August.

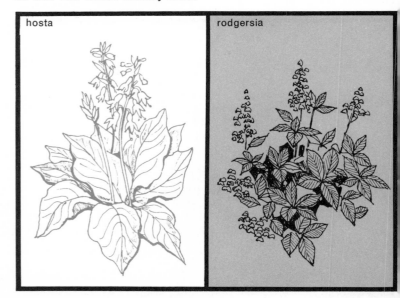

Rodgersia pinnata is a handsome foliage plant for damp, peaty places. Delicate sprays of flowers are produced in the summer and provide an added attraction

Flowering Shrubs

Flowers can be cut from most flowering shrubs but the following varieties are especially recommended for cutting. Keep these shrubs well fed and watered so that they make strong growth which is able to take up water readily. Slit the bottoms of the stems after cutting or crush them to help them take in water.

Flowering in March, forsythia can be cut in bud and allowed to open indoors. Lynwood is a fine variety.

Spiraea arguta, sometimes known as Bridal Wreath because of its abundant, small white flowers, and *S. thunbergii* also flower at about the same time.

Chaenomeles, another March-flowering shrub, may be grown against a wall or as a bush. There are red, pink, and white varieties.

Camellias flower from February to May. The varieties of *C. williamsii*, including the double-flowered Donation, are particularly good for cutting.

Deutzia elegantissima has long sprays of mauve purple flowers in April—May.

Choisya ternata (Mexican Orange Blossom) has good, shining, evergreen foliage and the fragrant white flowers appear in May. Suitable for U.S. Zone 7.

Lilacs of all kinds also come out in May. If they are to be used for cutting they must be hard pruned.

Philadelphus (mock orange) flowers in June. Many varieties are highly fragrant.

Foliage Shrubs

The following shrubs are worth growing specifically for the value of their foliage for cutting.

Acer japonicum aureum: a Japanese maple, rather slow growing, with soft, yellow leaves which last quite well in water.

Chamaecyparis and cupressus: various kinds of cypress, particularly the gray and the golden-leaved varieties, all of which are evergreen.

Cryptomeria japonica elegans: an evergreen with feathery leaves which turn russet red in autumn.

Cytisus scoparius: the Common Broom, valuable for the highly stylized effects that can be obtained with its whippy, evergreen branches.

Danae racemosa: the Alexandrian Laurel, with narrow green leaves, will thrive in dense shade.

Elaeagnus pungens aureo-variegata: shining evergreen leaves splashed with gold.

Eucalyptus: fast growing and handsome; usually with blue gray leaves, they should be pruned fairly hard each March for the best foliage. *E. gunnii* is one of the hardiest varieties.

Euonymus fortunei Silver Queen: shining evergreen leaves bordered with silver.

Hollies: all kinds, but especially the variegated ones.

Pittosporum tenuifolium: slender black twigs with waved pale green evergreen leaves. Silver Queen has silvery green leaves.

Camellia williamsii

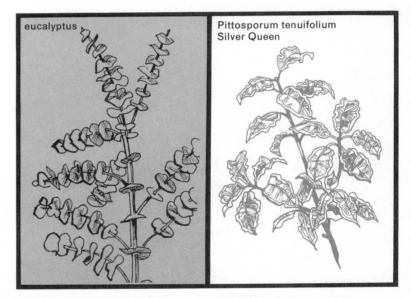

eucalyptus

Pittosporum tenuifolium
Silver Queen

A fine example of Japanese Quince (chaenomeles) growing on the wall of a house. The angular, branched stems look well in a Japanese-style decoration and the large fragrant fruits are also decorative

A foliage border containing shrubs with pleasing leaf color and shapes can provide much material. This attractive grouping includes *Cornus alba spaethii*, variegated sage, Golden Marjoram, and hosta

Spring-flowering Bulbs

Daffodils of all kinds are excellent as cut flowers. They are easily grown in the garden in sun or shade and in any reasonably good soil. By making a careful selection it is possible to have flowers from February to May.

The earliest to bloom are cluster-flowered varieties. These are followed rapidly by cyclamineus daffodils such as February Gold and Peeping Tom. Then come hundreds of varieties of many types and the last to flower is the Old Pheasant Eye daffodil, *Narcissus poeticus recurvus*, in May.

Tulips do not last as cut flowers as well as daffodils and are not usually quite so permanent or so ready to increase, but the tall ones, particularly the darwin, cottage, lily-flowered, and viridiflora tulips, are all beautiful flowers for cutting, blooming in late April or May. The early-flowering tulips are mostly rather short stemmed, but the mendel and triumph varieties, flowering in April, have excellent stems for cutting.

Tulips prefer open, sunny places and when grown for cutting should be lifted each July and be re-planted in October 4 in. apart in rows 1 ft. apart. They need well-cultivated, well-drained soil which should be dressed with bonemeal at 4 oz. per sq. yd. before planting.

Lilies of the Valley

Lilies of the valley, excellent for cutting in May, can be produced from a permanent bed in the open. Plant single roots, known as crowns, in October or March 4 in. apart in well-cultivated soil and a partially shaded place, just only covering the crowns. If the soil is of clay or sand, work in plenty of leaf mold or peat before planting. Keep the bed clear of weeds and water freely in dry weather.

Beds can remain undisturbed for years until a falling off in the quality and number of the flowers indicates that the roots are over-crowded and starved. Lift the roots in October, split up into single crowns, and start again.

For winter and early spring blooms, lilies of the valley must be grown in a greenhouse. For earliest flowering, purchase specially retarded crowns in early autumn, potting 8 or 10 in each 5- or 6-in. pot in a peat-based potting mix. Keep in a dark place in a temperature of 65° to 70°F. and water freely. After 7 to 10 days bring the pots into the light, reducing the temperature a little, and the flowers will be produced in about one month.

For later flowering use ordinary crowns potted in the same way, keeping them in an unheated frame for five or six weeks, then bringing them into a greenhouse at 55° to 65°F.

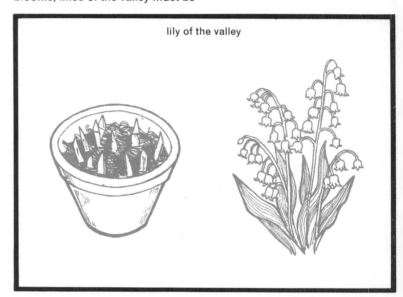

lily of the valley

Spring-flowering bulbs are always a welcome sight in the garden for they foretell of better weather to come. Shown here is *Narcissus* Beryl, a cyclamineus type with the characteristic reflexed perianth

The fragrant scent of the lily of the valley (convallaria) makes it a delight to grow. It prefers a shady spot if grown out of doors, but for early flowers it can be grown under glass

Summer-flowering Bulbs

Nerine bowdenii

The most useful summer-flowering bulbs for cutting, apart from gladiolus, are the Dutch, Spanish, and English Irises. All three are very similar in appearance and differ mainly in their time of flowering. The Dutch are the first to open in June, the Spanish following a week or so later, and the English in July. The widest selection of colors is in the Dutch group.

Plant irises in September 3 or 4 in. deep and 4 in. apart in rows 1 ft. apart in well-cultivated soil and an open, sunny position. Lift, divide, and replant the bulbs every third or fourth year.

For earlier flowers plant the bulbs in pots or boxes in peat-based potting mix, keep them in a frame for 6 or 8 weeks and then bring them into a light greenhouse, with a temperature of 50° to 60°F. Even earlier flowers can be obtained by growing *Iris tingitana* and Wedgwood (a hybrid variety) in the same way.

Other summer-flowering bulbs useful for cutting are montbretias, particularly the large-flowered Earlham Hybrids; *Crocosmia masonorum*, and in sheltered places *Nerine bowdenii* and *Amaryllis belladonna*. All like sunny places and well-drained soil. The Earlham Hybrid montbretias are best lifted and placed in a frame each October.

Gladiolus

planting gladiolus corms

staking

tying

Gladiolus are slightly tender, but since the corms of the popular summer-flowering kinds can be stored dry in winter, this is no disadvantage. However, the early-flowering, or nanus, varieties must be planted in October and, except in very mild districts, must be grown in a frostproof greenhouse in pots, boxes, or beds of fairly rich, porous soil.

Plant summer-flowering gladiolus in succession from mid-March to mid-May, 3 to 4 in. deep and 6 in. apart in good, well-cultivated soil in an open, sunny position. Water freely in dry weather and feed in June and July with a sprinkling of a good compound fertilizer. Place a 3-ft. cane to support each flower spike of tall varieties and tie twice, once low down and again just below the bottom flower bud. Cut the flower stems as soon as the bottom flower buds begin to show petal color, but leave some leaves to feed the corm.

Lift the plants about six weeks later, cutting off all top growth 1 in. above the corm. Remove the old, withered corm from the base of the plant and store the new corms in a dry, frostproof place until the following spring. Tiny corms (cormels) clustered round the large corms may also be kept and planted in spring $\frac{1}{2}$ in. apart to grow on to flowering size in a year or so.

Dutch Irises flower in June, producing their interestingly shaped blooms on long stems. If the flowers are cut, the leaves should be left to return food to the bulb for the following year's crop. Suitable for U.S. Zone 7

The distinctive spikes of summer-flowering gladiolus are always popular for cutting. For this reason they are often planted in a separate part of the garden so that the main flower display is not spoiled

Sparaxis, Ixia

These are natives of South Africa and are accustomed to a warmer climate than our own. They can be grown successfully outdoors in milder areas and in some sheltered gardens elsewhere, but in cold climates they are better grown as pot plants in an unheated or slightly heated greenhouse.

The flowers of sparaxis are very gay, usually in two contrasting colors such as red, purple, or maroon with white or yellow, and for this reason it is known as the Harlequin Flower. The flowers come in spring in sprays on 9-in. stems.

The flowers of ixia are also in many colors from white, yellow, and pink to orange, scarlet, and magenta, and are produced in May and June on wiry, arching 18-in. stems.

Plant both sparaxis and ixia in early autumn 3 in. deep and 4 to 6 in. apart in light, well-drained soil and a sunny, sheltered position. They succeed well in rock gardens, raised rock beds, and terraced walls. Leave undisturbed until overcrowded.

Or place five or six bulbs in a well-drained 5-in. pot filled with potting mix and water moderately at first and fairly freely in spring, but allow to dry off in July. Keep in a greenhouse or frame in winter, but stand outdoors in summer.

ixias

Roses for Cutting

All well-grown roses can be cut and used for decoration in the house but some are better for this purpose than others. Old-fashioned roses look lovely but do not usually last as well as the more closely formed hybrid tea varieties. Cut all roses just as the buds start to open. This is particularly important with semi-double and single varieties.

Cut roses in the early morning and not in the middle of the day when the sun will have been shining on them for several hours. Immediately place cut roses in water deep enough to come to within an inch or so of the flowers and leave them in the water in a cool place for at least an hour before arranging them. Change the water daily and cut a little from the bottom of each stem when doing so.

Hybrid tea roses which are particularly suitable for cutting include Fragrant Cloud, Peace, Perfecta, Sterling Silver, Oklahoma, Chrysler Imperial, Mister Lincoln, and Americana.

Among the floribundas suitable for cutting are: Evelyn Fison, Iceberg, Spartan, Fashion, and Europeana.

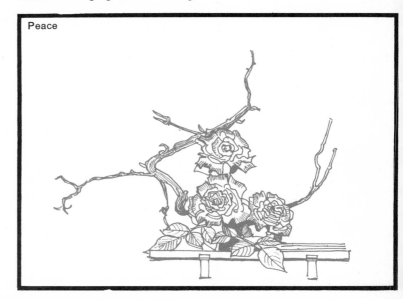

Peace

Ixias, or African Corn Lilies, are natives of South Africa, and should be grown in a warm, sheltered position. They produce their gaily colored flowers on slender but wiry stems. Suitable for U.S. Zone 7

The attractively marked blooms of Perfecta make excellent, long-lasting cut flowers and they are well complemented by the foliage which is tinted purple

Border Carnations

border carnation

planting a rooted layer

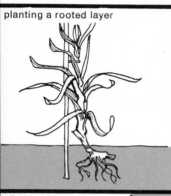

Border carnations are hardy and may be grown out of doors all the year, though they are often grown in pots and kept in a cool greenhouse during the winter, sometimes until they have flowered in summer, after which they may be stored out of doors or transferred to a frame.

Border carnations like a sunny, open position and fairly rich, well-dug soil containing plenty of lime. Plant or pot them in spring or early autumn and, if they are to be placed in beds, space them at least 18 in. apart each way. Tie the flowering stems to 2-ft. canes and reduce the flower buds to one per stem, retaining the topmost bud. Water them freely in dry weather and feed each March with a compound fertilizer, repeating at half rate in early June.

In July, layer nonflowering stems to produce young plants. Choosing healthy stems only, make a slanting incision through a joint where it can easily be brought to ground level, scrape away a little soil, peg the layer into a depression with a piece of wire bent like a hairpin, and cover it with a mixture of good soil and sand. Keep it well watered, and by September the layer should be well rooted. Then sever the young plants from the parents and a week later lift and either plant or pot them as before. Old plants are usually best discarded after two or three years.

Everlastings

The name "everlasting" is given to flowers with a papery texture which can be easily dried and used for winter decoration.

Cut the flowers just before they are fully open, tie them in small bunches, and suspend them head downward in a dry, airy place but not in direct sunshine. When dried, the stems of many kinds may need strengthening with florists' wire.

Acroclinium (Helipterum roseum) is a hardy annual to be sown out of doors from March to May where it is to flower. The double, daisylike flowers vary from white to rose. Rhodanthe (*H. manglesii*) has small pink or white flowers on slender 12 in. stems.

Helichrysum bracteatum monstrosum has larger flowers in a wider range of colors. A hardy annual, it can be sown outside but does better if raised in a greenhouse or frame and planted out later.

Give similar treatment to *Statice sinuata (Limonium sinuatum)* which has blue, pink, or yellow flowers. *Statice latifolia (Limonium latifolium)*, with larger sprays of smaller lavender flowers, is a perennial. Plant in a sunny place in good, well-drained soil and leave alone.

Honesty (*Lunaria biennis*) is a biennial grown for its parchment-like fruits. Sow in May or June for cutting the next year and discard the plants after cutting.

Physalis is a perennial grown for its inflated orange fruits. Plant in good, well-drained soil.

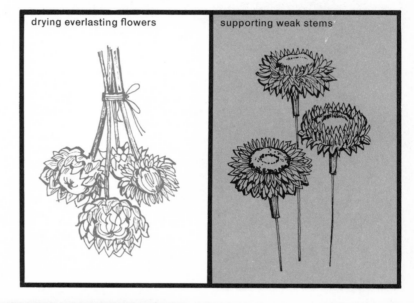
drying everlasting flowers   supporting weak stems

A selection of border carnations, showing the clearly defined colorings. These plants are hardy, but may be protected to improve the quality of the flowers

Helichrysum bracteatum monstrosum, one of the best of the everlasting flowers, ranges in color from white, yellow, and orange to red. It is a half-hardy annual

Dahlias

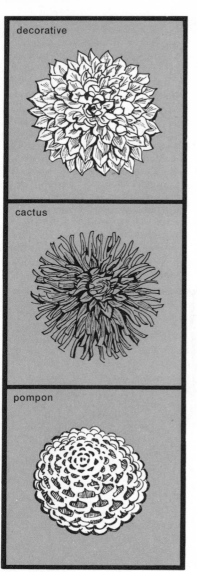

decorative

cactus

pompon

Many kinds of dahlia make admirable cut flowers, of which the best are those with small or medium-sized double flowers carried on long stems. Many of the so-called water-lily dahlias are excellent, as they have not too many petals, take up water well, and look delightful in floral arrangements. Small decorative, small cactus, and the pompons are also very good types.

For cutting it is essential to thin the plants well, so that they are not overloaded with flowers at any time. Each stem should be restricted to one flower, the terminal one, with all side buds and side-shoots removed at an early stage, and the plants must be watered and fed well.

Cut dahlias when they are about three-quarters open, with some of the center of the flower still closed. Choose good long stems and cut just above a pair of leaves, since new flower stems will then grow from the axils to continue the crop. Stand dahlia stems in water as soon as they are cut. Carry a bucket around the garden for this purpose.

Chrysanthemums

Chrysanthemums are usually grown from cuttings which are taken from plants cut right down after flowering and kept through the winter in pots or packed close together in boxes. These old plants, kept specifically to provide cuttings, are called "stools." Cuttings are taken from them any time between January and April or even May.

The best cuttings are prepared from shoots growing through the soil directly from the roots of the stools. Cut them off just below soil level when about 3 in. high, sever each cleanly with a razor blade just below a leaf joint, remove one or two of the lower leaves, and dip the base of each cutting in hormone rooting powder. Insert the cuttings in a soilless seed or potting mix in pots, boxes, or in a bed, whichever is most convenient. The essential thing is that they must be kept moist and in still air at a temperature of 50° to 60°F. For early cuttings (January to March) a propagator or propagating frame inside the greenhouse is convenient.

After insertion, water the cuttings well, place them in the propagator or frame if available, and shade them for three weeks from strong sunshine. Continue to water sufficiently to keep the soil or peat moist but not sodden. Cuttings should root in 3 to 5 weeks, which will be evident when they start to grow.

Dahlias, especially those with small- to medium-sized flowers, such as this Border Prince, are excellent for cutting as well as making a splendid show in the garden

Goya, an early-flowering chrysanthemum belonging to the reflexed decorative group. It has flowers of medium size which reveal their best qualities when restricted to one per stem

Violets

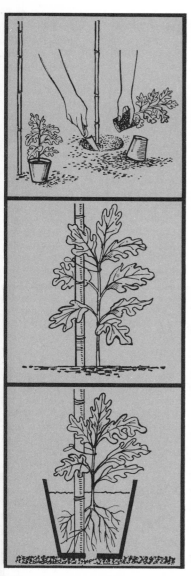

Provided they have been properly hardened off in a frame or sheltered place out of doors, early-flowering chrysanthemums can be planted out between late April and mid-May.

Select an open, sunny place for them and prepare the soil by thorough digging or forking. Work in manure or well-decayed garden refuse at 1 cwt. to 10 sq. yd. and give a dusting of a well-balanced compound fertilizer before breaking down the surface of the soil to a crumbly condition.

Plant at least 15 in. apart and, if planting in rows, leave a 30-in. alleyway between each pair of rows. Drive a 4-ft. cane into the soil to support each plant and tie it to this at once. Water well.

Stopping means pinching out the growing tip of a plant or shoot to make it branch. The time of stopping has some effect on the time of flowering and plants that are stopped twice tend to produce flowers with fewer petals than those that are stopped only once.

Left to their own devices chrysanthemums will produce flowers in clusters or sprays. To obtain larger flowers, one per stem, they must be disbudded. Watch for the tiny flower bud appearing at the top of each stem some time between July and October, according to variety, and carefully remove any other flower buds or shoots around or below it.

Spray the plants occasionally with an insecticide to kill aphids.

single

double

Both Parma violets, with double flowers, and single violets may be grown, but the latter are hardier, freer flowering and, if the right varieties are chosen, have longer stems. Princess of Wales is one of the best.

Violets can be grown out of doors all the year in rich, well-cultivated soil in a position shaded from the hottest sunshine. Excellent spring flowers can be obtained in this way, but for winter flowers it is necessary to grow plants in frames from September onward.

Raise new stock annually by removing rooted offsets from old plants in March or early April. Plant single varieties 1 ft. apart in rows 18 in. apart, double varieties 6 in. apart in rows 1 ft. apart. Water freely in dry weather and spray occasionally with malathion or derris to kill red spider mites. Remove all runners thrown out from the main plants and feed with a good compound fertilizer in June and July.

Lift the plants with as much soil as possible in September and replant them side by side in a frame, watering them in well. Ventilate freely at first but sparingly from November onward and keep the soil moist but not sodden. Pick the flowers regularly.

Spray chrysanthemums are becoming increasingly popular due to the fact that they require less attention than disbudded types. This attractive variety, Pinnochio, has reflexed petals

Violets flowering in a shady spot are a delightful sight in spring. They may be allowed to grow naturally in a woody area, or can be cultivated in frames specially for picking early

Winter Flowers

The following plants can be grown out of doors without protection and are excellent for cutting.

Garrya elliptica: an evergreen shrub with long, gray green catkins, of which the male form is the more effective. It will flower extra early if trained against a sunny wall. Suitable for U.S. Zone 8.

Hamamelis mollis: the witch hazel, with fragrant yellow flowers. A variety named *pallida* is sulfur yellow.

Helleborus niger: the Christmas Rose. It will grow in sun or shade, and if the plants are covered with cloches or frame lights the white flowers will be cleaner and appear earlier.

Iris stylosa: the Algerian Iris. It grows best in fairly poor soil in a warm, rather dry position such as near the foot of a south-facing wall, and should be left undisturbed. Cut while in bud.

Mahonia japonica: a handsome evergreen shrub with sprays of pale yellow flowers scented like lily of the valley appearing from February to April.

Prunus subhirtella autumnalis: an ornamental cherry with small, pale pink flowers produced freely from November to March whenever the weather is mild. It opens well indoors.

Viburnum fragrans: small clusters of white and pink flowers, very fragrant. *V. bodnantense* is similar but is a deeper pink and the branching habit is more angular. Both open well indoors.

Berries, Fruits

All berries and fruits can be used in flower arrangements but the following shrubs and small trees are specially recommended.

Berberis jamesiana: long arching branches carrying pendulous clusters of coral red berries.

Callicarpa: several kinds, with clusters of small violet berries. They need a warm, sunny position.

Crataegus prunifolia: a thorn with quite large scarlet fruits which last well into the winter.

Cotoneaster: most varieties, but particularly *C. wardii* and *C. watereri* with their arching stems.

Cydonia oblonga: the Common Quince with golden yellow, scented fruits the size of small pears.

Decaisnea fargesii: vigorous deciduous shrub with hanging blue gray fruits, cylindrical in shape.

Euonymus europaeus: the Spindle Tree, a vigorous deciduous shrub with rose-colored fruits splitting to reveal orange seeds.

Malus: any of the crab apples, such as Siberian Crab, Dartmouth, Golden Hornet, and John Downie.

Pernettya mucronata: an evergreen with white, pink, lilac, or purple berries.

Pyracantha (fire thorn): all varieties. The leaves are evergreen, and the berries scarlet, orange, or yellow.

Sorbus aucuparia: the Mountain Ash, or Rowan, with scarlet fruits.

Symphoricarpos racemosus: the Snowberry with round, white, berries.

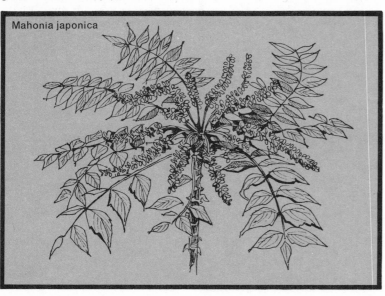

Mahonia japonica

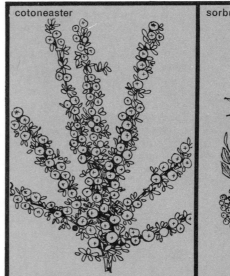

cotoneaster

sorbus

Garrya elliptica, with its decorative male catkins which are produced during the winter. It is particularly effective when trained against a sunny wall but will make a bush in the open. Suitable for U.S. Zone 8

The hawthorns are all very hardy small trees growing well in town gardens. This is one of the most decorative, *Crataegus prunifolia*, with large, persistent berries and shiny leaves which follow in autumn

Index

Index

Page references in italics
refer to illustrations